Macroeconometric Models for Portfolio Management

by
Jeremy Kwok
University of Westminster

Series in Economics
VERNON PRESS

www.vernonpress.com

In the Americas:	*In the rest of the world:*
Vernon Press	Vernon Press
1000 N West Street, Suite 1200,	C/Sancti Espiritu 17,
Wilmington, Delaware 19801	Malaga, 29006
United States	Spain

Series in Economics

Library of Congress Control Number: 2020950199

ISBN: 978-1-64889-301-8

Also available: 978-1-62273-884-7 [Hardback]; 978-1-64889-268-4 [PDF, E-Book]

Cover design by Vernon Press using elements designed by upklyak / Freepik.

Table of Contents

Preface

Macroeconometric models have become the fundamental tool in the academia and central bank community. It is now almost impossible to have a rigorous understanding of the global economies without such tools. The widespread use of macro models, particularly DSGE and increasingly GVAR models in the policymaking community, shows the usefulness of these models for analyzing and simulating economic experiments. Given the cheap data access and numerous software available for the users, the importance of macro models will only increase.

One area that is under-researched by the macroeconometric community is portfolio management. Often we can find numerous academic papers on macro models but are not related to portfolio management. In practice, the financial industry has a long track record of applying macroeconomic analysis for portfolio management but rarely refers to the academic literature of macroeconometrics. However, this trend is now changing as more systematic fund managers are employing quantitative models to forecast and trade their portfolio positions. The rise of algorithmic and systematic trading has driven the explosion of research in high-frequency econometrics, quantitative finance and machine learning as practitioners are keen to discover a more efficient, automatic way to model the economy and forecast the actions while staying profitable.

This book offers a detailed explanation of the various types of macro models and shows their applications by demonstrating with empirical tests. For each model, it begins with the construction, calibration/estimation and simulation. The book is intended for readers who have training in economics but have not yet been exposed to the research in macroeconometric models. Practitioners who work in the industry would also find it very handy as a guide to all major macro models and how they can be applied to portfolio management.

The first part of this book introduces the basics of financial-economic theories and how they are related to portfolio management. The second part looks at all major models that are found in macroeconometrics, such as DSGE, GVAR and FAVAR. It also contains chapters on volatility models such as GARCH. Numerous software packages are available either for free or at a low cost for the reader to apply these models.

The last part is focused on bringing the models to a portfolio management context. The most important purpose of this part is to demonstrate how macro model forecasts can be applied and translated into actual trading positions in light of the risk and reward preference by the investor. A backtesting workbook is also included, and the reader will be able to backtest trading strategies with inputs from the forecasts. It allows the reader to enter either a long or short position based on the forecast. The reader can also fine-tune criteria such as expected risk and trading size. Returns will be calculated automatically to show whether the forecast and the trading strategy worked. The workbook can be downloaded from the book's homepage on Vernon Press.

It is my hope for this book to be a bridge between academia and industry. I'll be very grateful if the reader is encouraged to further pursue the subject matter.

Jeremy Kwok, London, 2021

List of acronyms

2SLS	Two-Stage least squares
3SLS	Three-stage least squares
ACF	autocorrelation function
ADF	Augmented Dickey-Fuller test
AIC	Akaike information criterion
APT	Arbitrage Pricing Theory
APW	APW statistic
AR	Autoregressive
ARCH	Autoregressive conditional heteroskedasticity
ARIMA	Autoregressive integrated moving average
BOE	Bank of England
BVAR	Bayesian VAR
CAPM	Capital Asset Pricing Model
CC	Cowles Commission
CUSUM	Maximal OLS cumulative sum statistic
DGP	Data generating process
DOF	Degree of freedom
DSGE	Dynamic stochastic general equilibrium model
ECB	European Central Bank
EMH	Efficient Market Hypothesis
ETF	Exchange-traded fund
FAVAR	Factor-augmented VAR
FED	Federal Reserve System -central banking system of the US
FOC	First-order conditions
FTSE	Financial Times Stock Exchange. The most prominent index being the FTSE100 for the UK market
G7	Group of Seven
GARCH	Generalised ARCH

GDP	Gross domestic product
GIRF	Generalised impulse response function
GLS	Generalised least squares
GMM	Generalised Methods of Moments
GVAR	Global VAR
IMF	International Monetary Fund
IRF	Impulse response function
IV	Instrumental variables estimation
JBT	Jarque-Bera test
LM	Lagrange Multiplier Test
MA	Moving Average
ML	Maximum Likelihood
MW	MW statistic
OMX	OMX Nordic - shares from the four stock markets in the Nordic countries
NF	No forecast
NYMEX	New York Mercantile Exchange
OFEVD	Orthogonalised forecast error variance decomposition
OIRF	Orthogonalised impulse response function
OLG	Overlapping-generations model
OLS	Ordinary least squares
OPEC	Organization of the Petroleum Exporting Countries
P&L	Profit and loss
PCA	Principal component analysis
PC	Principal components
QE	Quantitative Easing
QLR	Quandt statistic
RBC	Real Business Cycle
RMSE	Root mean squared error
S&P500	Market index that measures the performance of 500 large companies listed on US exchanges
SBC	Schwarz Bayesian criterion

SEM	Simultaneous equations model (Cowles Commission approach)
SMA	Simple moving average
SVAR	Structural VAR
TFP	Total factor Productivity
VAR	Vector autoregression
VaR	Value at Risk
VARX	VAR with exogenous variables
VECM	Vector error correction model
VECMX	VECM with exogenous variables
VR	Variance Ratio test
WTI	Crude oil West Texas intermediate

List of Figures and Tables

Figures

Tables

Part I:
Overall Framework
and Financial Theories

Chapter 1

Introduction

1.1 Crystal balls

Imagine that you now have a crystal ball in front of you and it shows you the future. Just like the ones in fortune-telling, it tells you the future. It shows you exactly what will happen in the markets. What, then, does this knowledge of the future bring to you now? Most importantly, how are you going to act since you have glimpsed the future from this omniscient, prescient object? Does it imply that you will now become all-powerful and live happily forever?

Unfortunately, the short answer is no.

The long answer is it depends but it is complicated. Specifically, it depends on the crystal ball you have and, secondly, how you are going to act on it. The crystal ball—be it an oracle from insiders or a mathematical model which takes all the available information into account—will burp out forecasts that may or may not be accurate with a margin of error. Not only the output from the crystal ball can be inaccurate, but it can also be inappropriate, not suitable for actions. Even if the forecast is actionable, the logical question will then be: what are you going to do and how, exactly? Despite all these problems, the reader is tempted to ask: why bother forecasting? The answer is simple. The need to gain insight into the future will always be with us. It is a fundamental human urge to all things we do. This is an action that we cannot avoid and should be dealt with precisely. The crystal ball is certainly attractive, but the silver bullet isn't. Therefore the answer to this question is half crystal ball and half application of the crystal ball. To solve the problem of the crystal ball itself, this book seeks help from macroeconometrics. For the application of the crystal ball, it looks for the science and art of portfolio management.

The purpose of macroeconometrics is to model the national or global economies, thus enabling the modeller to create forecasts and simulations to predict what will happen in the future. This field has always been very attractive to not only academia but also central bankers and policymakers. This is evidenced by the wide adoption of the models in central bank research bodies such as the European Central Bank, the Fed, and the Bank of England. As a result, applications developed are mostly for monetary, fiscal and growth policy analysis. The publication of research related to macroeconometric models has been ever-increasing recently due to the available tools for computing these models. This allows the user to build complex models quite easily. As such, the application of this field is also of important interest not only to academia but also in the private sector due to its accessibility. Like other academic disciplines, macroeconometrics also have different schools of thought with widely different approaches. In light of the failure of previous macro models, many solutions have been put forth. In general, there are two broad camps of models that are either data-driven or theory-driven, while some are in between. One of the most promising approaches that are data-driven but also allowed for theory is the method of Global Vector Autoregressive (GVAR) models. The GVAR approach is closely related to the VAR modelling approach but provides a relatively simple yet effective way of modelling interactions in a complex high-dimensional system such as the global economy, where it can contain many variables for each country. Other existing large models, such as the simultaneous equations model (SEMs) and Dynamic stochastic general equilibrium models (DSGEs), are the main working models in academia and industry. It is easy to see the values these models bring to decision-making in the context of portfolio management. Having a correctly estimated model is similar to holding a crystal ball informing the future. While there is no shortage of research for applications in the public sector, such as national government and central banks, there is little research on how to integrate these models for portfolio management in the industry.

Portfolio management is the economic science for determining an investment policy (such as buying equity for a long period, e.g., 20 years), forecasting returns (such as variables like GDP growth, inflation and their effect on equity or commodity prices), asset allocation (determining the portion of assets to allocate for the portfolio) and risk management for a portfolio of investments. This art is practised by fund managers, bankers and even ordinary retail investors. A fitting and accurate model for forecasting can generate enormous wealth for its users, and, therefore, it is easy to see that the models being used by private fund management companies are proprietary and are never publicized. In light of this knowledge gap, this book aims to fill the void by proposing a framework and application integrating macroeconometric models for managing a portfolio while considering its role in forecasting, asset allocation and risk management. An excel file with examples is also available to allow readers to use it immediately.

1.2 Overall framework

By the end of this book, the reader will be able to have an in-depth understanding of macroeconometric models and how to apply them to their portfolios. This book is presenting a new framework for economists and investors. However, it is not just a theoretical presentation. Readers will learn how to estimate the models and apply the forecasts into their portfolio with a backtested strategy. Specifically, the ensuing chapters in this book attempt to answer these questions:

1)   Which forecast models to use and how to estimate?
2)   Once estimated, how to validate whether the models work?
3)   How to forecast from the models?
4)   How to use forecasts as part of portfolio management?

5) How to backtest a trading strategy, given the forecasts?
6) How to translate the forecasts into trading positions given the risk and reward criteria?

Figure 1.1: Overall framework

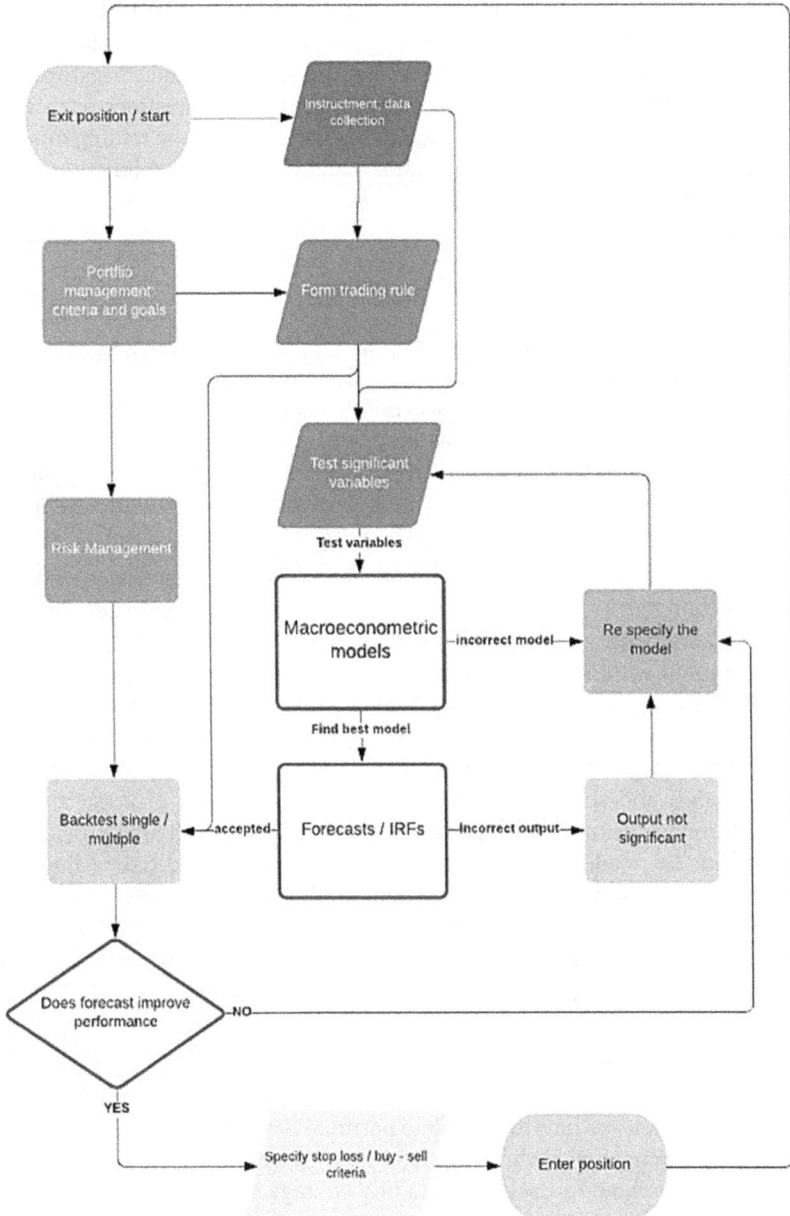

An overall framework in figure 1.1 shows the flow of different components in this book. The framework connects the macroeconometric models to a backtesting workbook. The book follows this framework which shows the reader how to understand and apply the macroeconometric models (Part II, chapter 4-7), calibrate/estimate (chapter 8.9), produces forecasts and assesses their merits (chapter 9). Having produced the forecasts, part III of the book looks at the beginning, where the investor outlines an investment policy with criteria and goals (10). Trading rules that are fitted are then backtested in chapter 11. The last chapters (13, 14 and 15) then show the reader how this can be done with the excel workbook provided. After assessing the trading rule and forecast in light of the risk and rewards outlined in the portfolio criteria, the reader will be able to test and confirm which model is the best that allows maximum returns.

1.3 Road map

The book is divided into three parts. The first part introduces the overall framework and how classic financial theories are related to predictability and portfolio management. There are six chapters in part II. The CAPM model and EMH theory are the focus here as they are too influential to ignore by any modellers. The portfolio management chapters in Part III relate to chapters 1 and 2 by asking the readers' beliefs and how much they rely on the CAPM and EMH theory.

The chapters in part II first take the reader to the historical development of macroeconometrics before embarking on a journey to the major types of macroeconometric models. Chapter 4 provides an extensive account of the development within the field from the beginning of econometrics up to the recent research in DSGE and GVAR. Chapter 5 begins with a short demonstration of the smaller VAR models and their limitations, thus showing the need for larger, macro models. Chapter 6 also looks at the popular GARCH type models and show empirical tests on the assessment of these models. GARCH models are often used for modelling volatility. This chapter provides an option for the reader to use when estimating the expected risk of financial instruments in part II. Chapter 7 examines all major types of macro models such as GVAR, FAVAR and DSGE and how are they constructed, tested, and used for forecasting. The large scale models are notoriously difficult to estimate, and this has been treated with extensive care. Chapter 8 shows an experiment on how to validate and compare model performance. A forecasting contest was conducted between GVAR, FAVAR and DSGE models.

Part III is more practical and focuses on how to apply the models to use. Chapter 10 discusses how to formulate portfolio risk and reward and forecasts. Chapter 11 focuses on trading rules and how to backtest them. The last three chapter shows how to backtest a trading strategy with the aforementioned portfolio criteria of risks and reward. It also shows how forecasts can be translated into an actual trading position. The final backtesting chapters 13 and 14 show that trading with accurate forecasts is much more profitable. The reader is advised to use the excel workbook when reading these chapters.

The workbook shows how the backtest can be applied to check whether a strategy would be profitable, given the historical data and trends. The first sample given is a simple backtest for testing one position strategy. This allows the reader to hold one position at any time, either buying or shorting. Therefore the reader's net position can either be short (-1), no holding (0) or long (+1). The indication of buy or sell here is indicated by the underlying strategy, which is described in the book. Once a signal is given, the reader will either buy or sell the underlying security. The profit and loss for each trade are calculated, and cumulative return is also calculated to indicate whether the strategy worked. Performance metrics are also calculated to provide a comprehensive picture.

The second part of this workbook is a backtest template that allows multiple positions. It also includes portfolio management criteria and tools that were mentioned in chapter 10. This allows the trader to backtest if holding multiple positions within the same instrument is a better strategy or not. Detailed portfolio criteria are also in place to adjust the position size to be traded, according to the risk criteria as stipulated at the start. This part was designed with flexibility in mind so that the reader can test multiple scenarios with the same dataset but with different criteria.

Chapter 2

Portfolio Theory and CAPM

2.1. Introduction

The traditional aim of portfolio theory is to deliver a maximized return for the investor given a level of risk. The return of the portfolio is then related to the risk of the portfolio. If the unit of return achieved is bigger than the unit of risk, then the portfolio is achieving better than the expected return given by the equivalent unit of risk. This chapter aims to introduce the classical framework of portfolio theory and also the workhorse model that relates the return and risk together, named the capital asset pricing model (CAPM). Discussion is focused on whether the CAPM is still applicable and the implication for us when we are bringing in macroeconometric models as the forecasting tool.

The goal of this chapter is to provide a background in portfolio theory based on the mean-variance paradigm and its implication for integrating macroeconometric forecasts into this traditional framework. This is achieved by first introducing the capital asset pricing model and its variant, such as a multifactor model that can be used to determine assets that are most sensitive to macroeconomic events. The ability to differentiate assets that are particularly sensitive to economic events proves the justification of producing correct economic forecasts. This chapter begins with an overview of the CAPM, a literature review on the critique on CAPM and a short philosophical approach to theory-making in economics, and an evaluation of empirical evidence in the end. It can be concluded that despite the poor empirical records but knowing the limitations of CAPM, it should remain as the main framework to be used for portfolio management as it continues to give a clear way of thinking and designing a portfolio.

2.2 Portfolio Theory and Capital Asset Pricing Model

The capital asset pricing model (CAPM) is possibly the most popular and used in financial management. The model was built by Sharpe (1964) and Lintner (1965) based on the mean-variance paradigm developed by Stuart and Markowitz (1959) earlier. The recognition for the works on the CAPM is not only recognized in academia but also has a wide range of applications in the financial industry, such as risky asset valuation and decision making in corporate policies, etc. As noted in Sharpe's paper, one of the main contributions is its market equilibrium theory approach to construct the model. Prior to Sharpe's model, virtually all investment models were constructed based on the investor's rational decision and behaviour (e.g. Tobin, 1958, etc.) rather than from the perspective of the overall market. It is important to note that CAPM was a logical extension to the financial theory of investment uncertainty and portfolio selection. The implication is that the model inherited a lot of the assumptions (unrealistic but justifiable) that were prevalent at those times but are heavily criticized in more recent literature. Since its origin in the 1960s, a vast literature has been devoted to developing new models with relaxed assumptions and others testing whether the model holds in reality. Despite the critiques opposing and empirical evidence provided against the model, CAPM remains a popular tool used by financial managers (Graham and Harvey, 2001; Greenwood and Shleifer, 2014) and is taught in universities. A quick survey can confirm that it occupies a significant portion in finance textbooks and standard finance curriculum. The debate on whether CAPM is dead is the epitome of other recurring debates in economics and finance. Stating 'CAPM is dead' is an easy option considering the empirical evidence against it. But to what extent can we say it is dead while the persistence of its existence lingers in both literature and industry? This may suggest there is still value left, and it warrants an explanation.

2.3 The CAPM Model

The original CAPM was proposed in Sharpe (1964) and Linter (1965). Essentially the model provides a framework that explicitly links the expected return of an asset based on the systematic risk—beta—defined by covariance and variance. This allows the user to determine what return should an asset be given a certain amount of risk. It adopted the market equilibrium theory approach with a set of assumptions about the market, participants, and their subsequent behaviours. The simplified assumptions allowed an elegant model to be constructed, but it also undermined its validity and subsequent critiques. The assumptions will be deliberated in the next section. Naturally, notations and terminology in Sharpe (1964) and Linter (1965) have changed since their inception, but the definitions remain the same. The CAPM model is presented below with notations taken from the standard form:

$$E(R_i) = R_f + \beta_i(R_m - R_f) \qquad (2.1)$$

Where:

$E(R_i)$ - The expected return on the capital asset i predicted by the model.

R_f - The risk-free rate of return. Examples include bank fixed saving rates guaranteed by government and bonds issued by a secure government.

β_i - The beta coefficient of asset i.

R_m - The return of the market.

$R_i - R_f$ - Extra return in excess of the risk-free rate.

$R_m - R_f$-The risk premium, which is the excess return above the risk-free rate.

In this model, the relationship between expected return and beta is linear. In other words, the higher risk the asset is, the higher its expected return is. Beta (β_i) is defined as a statistics or an index that measures the changes of return for asset i with respect to the changes of return for a chosen market. Therefore, the beta of the market is always going to be 1. Beta became a measure of systematic risk (the movement of the return of an asset). For example, an asset beta of 0.7 means it has 30% systematic risk less than the market.

The assumptions of CAPM

Sharpe's paper in 1964 titled "theory of market equilibrium under conditions of risk" gave birth to CAPM. At this point, the reader should be reminded that CAPM is an equation that summarised Sharpe's theory. Like all theories, Sharpe's theory is a system of interrelated ideas that had its roots in other theories. In particular, the CAPM is built on the expected utility theory and portfolio selection (Stuart and Markowitz, 1959). Unsurprisingly, the CAPM assumed and inherited most assumptions that were proposed in those theories. Like all models in economics, assumptions are a necessary part of the modelling process as a complete representation of reality is not possible and unnecessary. The assumptions of theory allow CAPM to be built in a simple but versatile way that predicts asset return and beta. However, unrealistic assumptions also undermine the validity of the model. Some assumptions of the CAPM are explicitly stated, e.g. portfolio selection, while others are more implicit, e.g. homogeneous beliefs. In essence, the assumptions can be summarised in three themes i) Equilibrium asset markets; ii) portfolio selection by mean-variance criterion; and iii) homogeneous beliefs of investors.

Equilibrium in asset markets

The CAPM assumes that the asset markets are in equilibrium. In general, this implies the asset prices are determined by supply and demand with no friction. Markets are frictionless, meaning no transaction costs and no restrictions on trades. Unsurprisingly, transaction costs such as taxes, trading fees, bid-ask spread and illiquidity costs exist in the real-world (see Ortiz-Molina and Phillips, 2014) for illustration on real assets and seminal paper on transaction costs in the stock market by Demsetz (1968). These factors will ultimately deter trading strategy that requires constant buying and selling such as momentum and day trading and effect on asset prices (Barclay et al., 1998). The costs also impose a big challenge for individual investors with smaller capital (Barber et al., 2009). The bid-ask spread is the difference between the buying and selling price, which is composed of the broker's margin and asymmetric information (Glosten et al., 1993). The spread exists as transaction costs to the traders. Amihud and Mendelson (1986) found that asset prices (hence asset returns) are positively related to the bid-ask spread; this further renders the assumption of no transaction costs unrealistic. New extensions were developed with relaxed assumptions. Fama and French (2007) argue that tastes and taxation can affect prices as it does consumption goods. After-tax CAPM was investigated later with contributions from Litzenberger and Ramaswamy (1982), which looked at the effects of tax, short selling and other factors on asset prices. More specific assumption include voluntary ownership of assets at market prices. This may be stating the obvious, but there are stock markets that only allow buying and not selling, such as the early 1990s stock exchanges in China as it was seen as unpatriotic (Coase and Wang, 2016). Recent intervention (see China Daily[1]) of the Chinese government to ban selling by large investors will immediately invalidate this assumption. The assumption is unrealistic, but its merit is in suggesting that if market friction is low, then the predictions from CAPM are more likely to hold true.

In addition to the assumptions above, CAPM's market portfolio is, in theory, the market of all types of assets, including assets that are not traded legally, such as drugs and illegal labour. As the true market portfolio is unobservable, this led to the Roll's critique that empirical studies could never test the CAPM; therefore, it is unfalsifiable. The model also explicitly assumes that investors can borrow unlimited funds at a fixed interest rate. As noted in Linter (1965), this is a mathematical convenience. This subsequently relaxed in Black CAPM (Black, 1972). All assumptions above entail the ideation of a frictionless market that has strict restrictions on transaction costs. However, results from modified versions of the CAPM with relaxed transaction costs assumptions show that the predictions are similar to those predicted by the Sharpe- Linter CAPM (Vayanos, 1998). Therefore it can be argued that the assumptions are unrealistic but not unreasonable given the similar results.

2.4 Portfolio selection by mean-variance criterion

Critiques of the CAPM in this theme comes in two related ideas: investors are not rational and investors do not judge purely on mean-variance. CAPM assumes that all investors decide their portfolio by the mean-variance criterion established in Stuart and Markowitz (1959), implying investors select investments solely on expected return and the variance of return (risk). This

---

[1] Govt to issue new rules to regulate share sales by top investors. Available: http://en.people.cn /business/n3/2016/0106/c90778-8999795.html. Last accessed 01-04-2016.

entails whether an investor's portfolio is efficient. As the portfolio is further diversified, idiosyncratic risk is mathematically possible to approach zero. Therefore the implication is if a portfolio is diversified enough, investors no longer need to worry the individual asset variances. Rather, the investor should pay attention to the covariance between assets. This can be easily violated in reality as investors are irrational (Akerlof and Shiller, 2010) and exhibit animal spirits such as overreaction and over-concentration of assets in one sector etc. Other critiques come in the claim that not all investors are risk-averse, and some are risk-seeking. Therefore utility for investors is different, and beta (variance) cannot be used as an index for risk. Contributions from prospect theory by Kahneman and Tversky (1979) have changed the linearity of risk and return. Instead, the investors make decisions based on the potential losses and gains rather than the expected risk, as suggested in CAPM. This, in turn, undermines the validity of portfolio selection is similar to that predicted by the Sharpe- Linter CAPM. Therefore it can be argued that the assumptions are unrealistic but not unreasonable given the similar results.

Homogenous beliefs of investors and static model

In (Fama and French, 2007), the authors stated that standard asset pricing models such as Sharpe-Lintner CAPM, Intertemporal CAPM (Merton, 1973), consumption-based model (Lucas, 1978) and after-tax CAPM all share the assumption that investors know and agree on the risk and return of all assets. Undoubtedly the assumption is unrealistic, but it has opted for its simplified mathematics. This assumption is relaxed, and Fama and French (2007) proposed a new model that takes disagreement between investors into account. It is understandable that the original CAPM was developed as a static model as it allowed subsequent extensions to build on it. It is sufficient to a short time horizon, but empirical tests from Harvey (1989) and Campbell and Vuolteenaho (2004) have shown that the predictive power of CAPM is significantly undermined as returns are not consistent and time-varying. This led to new CAPM models developed in Bollerslev et al. (1988), which takes into account time-varying covariances.

2.5 An Empirical assessment of CAPM

Having examined the theoretical critiques of the CAPM model, this section turns to the results given by empirical assessments. The goal of empirically assessing the model is to test whether the model should be rejected and to provide information on the model itself that could be useful for further research. From the literature, the CAPM has had a bad track record in empirical assessments. One is therefore tempted to reject the works as worthless, judging on theatrical and empirical results and the claim CAPM is dead. But it is never straightforward in economics and social sciences that a model will give 100% correct predictions as in physical sciences. If a falsifiable theory has not been falsified under scrutiny, then it will be accepted as true (Popper, 2005). Even though it is more complicated than this in practice given the types of experiments and data to be collected. The principle of falsifiability applied to sciences is well justified (Rosenberg, 2011). Falsificationism is, however, deemed to be inapplicable, as some have argued. This is not for the support of not carrying out empirical works, but rather an economic theory should be not rejected purely based on empirical tests, as the initial conditions are numerous and it is impossible to specify all factors in a test condition. In the case of CAPM, the original model is reduced to a single parameter: beta, which determines the expected return under a set of restrictive assumptions. This is evident in the evolution of the CAPM model. If the Shape-Linter model is unrealistic, than a newer version will be made with adjusted assumptions and parameters. In the following section, the evidence from empirical works will be examined. In the end, we conclude what sense we can make of the debate.

Time series

The goal of time-series econometric analysis of the CAPM is to see how beta fits the data. Recall that the original CAPM,

$$E(R_i) = R_f + \beta_i(R_m - R_f) \tag{2.2}$$

is a simple linear model that allows the security market line to be plotted on a two-dimensional graph where the intercept is R_f and the steepness of the line is determined by beta. Following the approach in Jensen (1968), if we substitute excess return $R_i - R_f$ to the left, then we have

$$R_i - R_f = \beta_i(R_m - R_f) \tag{2.3}$$

To make this model empirically testable, Jensen introduced an intercept for residuals, later developed by Black et al. (1972), in which the paper found evidence against CAPM using monthly data on NYSE. The econometric model becomes:

$$R_i - R_f = \alpha + \beta_i(R_m - R_f) + \varepsilon \tag{2.4}$$

The logic behind the test is, if the excess return is strictly given by beta, then intercept α must equal to zero. The null hypothesis of the test was $\alpha = 0$, therefore if α is not 0, then CAPM does not hold. To empirically test this model, the values of R_i, R_f and R_m are needed. As these values are theoretical in basis, in reality, they are approximated by using short-term government debt as a risk-free rate (although not 100% risk-free as sovereign default is possible); average market return such as the FTSE 100 in a sample period and the return of the particular stock/portfolio. The trouble that these are approximations and therefore a 'true market portfolio' is never fully achieved gave rise to Roll's critique (1977). This can be sidestepped by specifying that the empirical tests are conditional upon the portfolio and depends on the chosen market.

From the logic of Jensen's test, it is easy to see that as we put more terms as independent variables, then we are testing whether those independent are influential in explaining the excess returns. In a seminal paper by Fama and French (1992), the authors found that size and book-to-market equity had impacts in explaining the excess returns. In addition, the authors also found that beta is flatter than it should be, meaning less than expected, given an increase in the unit of beta. This further undermines the validity of the CAPM model. Similarly, these methods allow other easily calculated financial ratios to incorporate into the model. Results from Banz (1981) and Litzenberger and Ramaswamy (1982) all suggested beta itself does not fully explain excess return.

Cross-Section

In the cross-section approach, the main investigation is focused on the relationship of beta with the excess returns. Therefore it is the test for the security market line. This allows the readers to see whether CAPM holds for a particular asset, as Fama and French (2004) pointed out from earlier empirical tests like Blume and Friend's (1973). Two problems arise when testing CAPM with the cross-section method. It explained that using individual security for estimating beta to explain excess return will lead to measurement errors. This is notable, as when considering the framework of the mean-variance paradigm, investors are not rewarded by idiosyncratic risks. Therefore focusing on individual stocks does not justify the claim that CAPM / beta is dead. This can be overcome by using portfolio returns rather than a single asset. On the other hand, industry effects are prevalent to a particular type of stocks such as those in a cyclical industry, e.g. oil and gas, commodities etc. This may cause heteroskedasticity in residuals which undermine the results of the regression. It is easy to find research that rejects the CAPM because either the beta is too small or the intercept is too large. This often is the result of errors in estimated variables. The concepts of alpha and beta are man-made and require approximation when selecting the underlying securities. This inevitably leads to error, as Roll's criticism (1977) suggests because it can never fully reflect the true market portfolio. Another interesting point to note is that CAPM asserts the relationship between risk and reward is linear. Therefore it cannot apply to instruments that are not linear in pay-offs, such as options and other derivatives.

2.6 Multiple Factor Models

The empirical evidence that the literature has provided indicates that CAPM beta does not completely explain the cross-section of asset returns. This strongly suggests that there are at least one of even more factors that are missing from the model. Naturally, this leads to economists extending the model into a more general framework that allows multiple factors to be included. The Arbitrage Pricing Theory (APT) developed by Ross (1976) allows multiple risk factors to be included, and this is commonly referred to as simple multiple factor models. Numerous factors are available, and some are more well defined and documented than others, such as the small size factor (i.e. on average, companies with small capitalization will give a higher return on average due to the size and price of the company). In general, factors can be split into three types such as macroeconomic, fundamental and statistical. For example, Fama and French proposed a three-factor model with beta, market capitalization and book-to-price ratio to describe prices. Various well-documented factors such as small-company factor, momentum, and growth have been discussed to explain the returns of certain assets. This discovery was quickly then sold to various product development teams at financial institutions and subsequently offered to investors as collective investment vehicles such as the Global Value Factor by Vanguard Asset Management would see a pool of company stocks and only buy companies that have a low value, e.g. have lower prices relative to their fundamental measures of value (factors such as low price-to-book or price-to-earnings ratio, estimated future earnings and operating cash flow) etc.[2]

Of the three types of factor models above, macroeconomic factor models are particularly intuitive and relevant for using macroeconometric models for forecasting. It is intuitive to think that certain stocks are more sensitive to macroeconomic data than others. For example, an oil price increase will see an increase in the oil producer's share price due to higher revenue for their products. Lower interest rates will also increase the share price rise as companies will have a lower burden on servicing their loans and increase the possibility of using leverage to expanding their revenue streams. It is also true that certain stocks will be more sensitive than others, and some stocks will react very differently. The oil price increase will see an increase in share price for oil producers but opposite for airliners as they are the main consumer of fuels which would imply an increase in the cost. Some commonly used macroeconomic factors include shock in short term interest rate, change in

---

[2] For the details of the fund: https://www.vanguardinvestor.co.uk/investments/vanguard-global-value-factor-ucits-etf-usd-accumulating

industrial production (benchmark such as Industrial Production Index), change in inflation, change in term spread and commodity prices such as oil, corn, wheat, etc., depending on the particular stocks the investors are interested in. However, the estimation of macroeconomic factor models isn't quite as straight forward as economic factors tend to move together, i.e. if the oil price increases, therefore it is likely that inflation would also respond to it by moving higher. This co-movement of macroeconomic factors would deem the non-collinearity assumption invalid for econometric estimation. Therefore it is also up to the econometrician to define and refine the macroeconomic factor data and to estimate their relevance by separating the factors into differentiable and independent variables; for more about different types of multi-factor models, see the literature.

2.7 Conclusion

The literature for the original CAPM proved to be useful for later research, and there are numerous useful extensions, which are now available albeit in different forms (such as intertemporal CAPM). It is the criticism of CAPM that gave rise to the development of Arbitrage Pricing Theory (APT), which is more generalized and allows a mix and match of variables that could explain the excess return. In fact, CAPM is considered to be a special case of APT as it is much narrower. The value from theory seems to come from the selection of factors. If we can learn something from this model, it is that the selection of causal factors in economics and financial markets, in particular, is extremely difficult as the data is not only fuzzy but also time-varying and reacts to new research. Knowing the limitations of CAPM is enough to render its use in the industry. One possible reason for it to have remained as a popular model in the industry is perhaps the reliance on the mean-variance paradigm, and this forces fund managers to spread out in order to avoid idiosyncratic risks and focus more on the covariances between the assets in the portfolio.

This chapter has shown that it is possible to use the CAPM and its variant forms to construct the framework for portfolio management based on the mean-variance paradigm. Not only should the investors adopt a basic, simple market factor, but if estimated properly, investors can obtain excess returns by forecasting correctly for macroeconomic events and take advantage of the forecasts by trading stocks that are particularly sensitive to economic events based on the analysis from a macroeconomic factor model.

Chapter 3

Asset Return Predictability

3.1 Introduction

It is not a myth that there is a wide debate between supporters and critics of EMH, as evident by the Nobel Prize winners of Shiller and Fama, who won the Nobel Prize in Economics for 2013, whose opinions differ tremendously. In spite of the debate, it is evident that the EMH has gained popularity in both academia and has been adopted in the financial industry. The main claim of EMH is that prices reflect all available information; therefore, the implication is that investors cannot beat the market by going through the extra analysis and spending money on finding extra information. This rationale has contributed to the rise of passively managed and tracker funds that passively track stock indices rather than 'beat the market' by active management (Malkiel, 2003). This is due to the assumptions that investors are rational and will act upon the information received; therefore, the market would be so competitive that no one could profit in the long-run. The theory has since been developed and criticized by academics and practitioners; nevertheless, it is still the main tool in modern finance (Malkiel, 2005). The central idea of EMH is that asset price fully reflects all information, including insider and outside. A stock market is likely to be more efficient, as it has higher trading volumes, liquidity, and also regulations imposed upon. Investors can infer from the efficiency of the market to the macroeconomy; in other words, larger economies tend to have more efficient stock markets. This chapter looks at the literature on whether asset return is predictable and presents an empirical study using data from some small European stock markets to test this theory. In the end, the implication is also discussed on how the investor should use macroeconometric models in light of the evidence (or belief) in EMH.

This case study looks at the smallest stock markets in Europe, and we test whether they are weak-form efficient. The selection represents small economies in Europe (including EU members who adopted the euro, i.e. Estonia and those who haven't—Croatia, Czech Republic and Iceland) and non-EU members—Ukraine is included to represent the small minority of non-EU members in Europe. At the time of writing, the stock markets in Croatia, Czech Republic, Iceland, and Ukraine had completely collapsed as a result of the financial crisis in 2008. Only Estonia and the UK have recovered since. Foreign investment inflows in these five countries also differ dramatically. The weak form of the efficient market hypothesis (EMH) is tested across five small

European economies: Croatia, Czech Republic, Estonia, Iceland, and Ukraine. Data from the United Kingdom as used as a comparison. These five countries are represented by their respective stock exchanges. The time frame spans from 2008 to 2019, as this period covers the financial crisis and also the euro crisis. Empirical tests used include parametric tests -Augmented Dickey-Fuller test; autocorrelation test; variance ratio test; and non-parametric runs test. Results from parametric tests show that the weak form efficiency is rejected across all five countries. On the other hand, runs test suggest that all countries satisfy the weak form efficiency. Based on literature reviews and empirical results, the paper is inclined to conclude weak form efficiency should be rejected for these five countries during this sample period; however, the result is ambiguous.

3.2 Literature review

Before the theory of EMH, there has been a tremendous interest in randomness and price since the 16th century, such as the work of Cardano titled *The Book of Games of Chance*. However, the application to finance did not appear until the mid-19th century. The very bedrock of EMH is the random walk hypothesis, first postulated by Bachelier in 1900 in his PhD thesis titled '*Théorie de la spéculation*', which was inspired by his experience in Bourse de Paris. However, his theory did not gain popularity until half a century later, in 1955 when the notion of 'stock prices are random' quickly caught on and papers from Working (1958), Roberts (1959), and Osborne (1959) that prices follow Brownian motion and are random. A seminal book by Malkiel (2013) focused on the randomness of stock market prices, and empirically confirmed the theory of random walk hypothesis. Since then, it became the foundation that EMH was built upon. During the 1970s, research in this area produced definite papers which would benefit future generations. In his paper, Fama (1970) reviewed the notion of efficient capital markets and built the theory of EMH, which was built upon his earlier work in Fama et al. (1969) that suggested stock prices adjust efficiently to new information. EMH states that the price of security should fully reflect all the information available, whether insider or not. In his seminal paper, Roberts (1959) distinguished the EMH as a weak and strong form which was later adopted in Fama et al. (1969). The taxonomy of weak-form efficiency, semi-strong form efficiency and strong-form efficiency became the standard. The conjecture of weak-form EMH is that prices of securities fully reflect historical information of past prices. This implies that no investors can gain excess returns with this information rendering technical analysis useless but given some hope to fundamental analysis. In comparison, semi-strong form efficiency implies that all public information is known and reflected in the prices; therefore, no investors can generate excess returns. Lastly, the strongest of all EMH claims and also hardest to test empirically is the strong-form, where public and private information is known and reflected in the price. Empirical tests on EMH, particularly the weak-form, have been published extensively, and many studies are found not in favour of the predictions of EMH. The early empirical support for EMH has led Jensen (1978) to claim that 'there is no other proposition in economics which has more solid empirical evidence supporting it than the EMH'. Although many research papers supported the EMH—such as Cowles (1944), Working (1949), and Kendall and Hill (1953)—not all were in support. In a literature review of EMH, Sewell (2011) noted that the only paper prior to 1960 which found the market was significantly inefficient was from Slutzky (1937). As more granular data and new empirical models appear, EMH seems to be challenged even more. Levy (1967) divided EMH into three forms and focused on three methods of the testing theory, of which two are employed in this paper, namely serial correlation and runs test. The testing of serial correlation became popular for EMH. This method began in Cowles (1944), which found significant autocorrelation in indices of stock prices. After the Black Monday crash in 1987, more papers found EMH do not hold. In Fama and French (1988), negative autocorrelations for stock returns were found, thus rejecting the strong form of EMH. In Campbell et al. (2012), the authors devised a new method of variance ratio test (which is adopted in this paper) and strongly rejected the EMH. The bulk of the tests are carried on major stock exchanges such as the NYSE and LSE, and smaller emerging markets are neglected (Mobarek and Keasey, 2000). Testing of EMH in emerging or less developed stock markets is often in weak-form as it is more convenient as data sources are likely to be incomplete and sensitive information is likely to be leaked before public announcements (Mobarek and Keasey, 2000). One of the nature of emerging markets is the information availability compared to developed markets; it is explained that "prices in emerging markets cannot be assumed to fully reflect all available information". This is due to reasons like poorer regulation of corporate announcements and financial reporting and, to some extent, the poor interpretation of financial information. As the theory of EMH is fully dependent on the information being received and acted upon by investors, Grossman and Stiglitz (1977) proposed a new model in which, as more investors receive more information, the market becomes more efficient. However, the information they receive is only partial; thus, obtaining further information could pay off when the uninformed investors do not have this advantage. Information in the emerging market is likely to be more expensive to obtain e.g. via private network and personal relationships. This can be seen as blat (Russian-speaking and influenced countries) and guanxi (Chinese), which can be loosely translated as personal connections (Michailova and Worm, 2003). Other factors that could impact the efficiency of markets include transaction costs, regulations by the government such as red-tapes, foreign ownerships, investor protections, ease of borrowing etc. (Bushman and Smith, 2003). There are many methodologies to quantify and rank these impacts. One of the most cited rankings is the ease of doing business by the World Bank Group.

Figure 3.1: Ease of doing business ranking by World Bank Group.

Ease of doing business ranking	
UK	6
Estonia	16
Iceland	19
Czech Republic	36
Croatia	40
Ukraine	83

Source: http://www.doingbusiness.org/rankings

From the table above, the UK is a lot easier to doing business (as judged by the regulations, getting credit, contract enforcements, taxes and investor protections etc.) than those studies in this paper. From this perspective, it is expected that those markets are likely to be less efficient than the UK. The empirical results from testing emerging stock markets are mixed. Smith (2013) found that weak-form EMH for European emerging stock markets was rejected using variance ration and autocorrelation tests. Compared to established markets, there are not as many academic papers on testing these markets. For Croatia, Sonje et al. (2011)[1] found that the Croatian stock market was inefficient. However, the authors conclude that it was mainly to the financial crisis, and arguably although not conclusively, the Croatian stock market was more efficient before the crisis. A literature review on the testing weak-form efficiency of Czech capital markets has found that the Czech market is less efficient than developed markets. On the other hand, virtually no paper is found on the Icelandic market. Similarly, little literature is found on Estonia and Ukraine. Although Kvedaras and Virmantas (2002)[2] found evidence to reject EMH for all Baltic States markets, the market was still in its infancy during the 2000s; therefore, the conclusion is less certain for the future. In Khrapko (2013), the author tested the weak-form EMH and found evidence to support EMH with the Kendall test but results from autocorrelation and variance ratio test were ambiguous.

---

[1] https://hrcak.srce.hr/index.php?id_clanak_jezik=106565&show=clanak
[2] http://citeseerx.ist.psu.edu/viewdoc/download?doi=10.1.1.475.6507&rep=rep1&type=pdf

3.3 Empirical testing of EMH

The data used in this chapter are the main indices by five small European economies, namely Croatia, Czech Republic, Estonia, Iceland, Ukraine and the UK, for comparison. The period is from 30/11/2008 to 10/04/2019. Due to the relatively small market capitalization of these exchanges, they tend to have one respective stock index only (except the UK). Therefore the indices should reflect the main activities in their stock markets. Weekly data is adopted rather than daily or monthly. This is due to the fact that these exchanges operate in different time zones and will have missing data on different dates inevitably (such as holidays). This is further complicated by the different institutional ownership and political associations and, therefore, their trading and indexing methods used to calculate the data (Harris, 2003). Similar studies also use weekly stock indices for the same arguments (Fama and French, 2004). The definition of asset return used in this paper is one-period simple return in the natural log:

$$Rt = Log(Rt/Rt - 1) \tag{3.1}$$

where Rt is the return of asset after holding one period (week). The natural log transformation was first introduced by Mandelbrot (1963) as it contained better statistical properties. This chapter uses stock index returns instead of the index values to test EMH. This is due to the fact that indices are likely to be non-stationary in the long-run and they are not scale-free. Using returns allows the user to normalize the different indices, thus enabling comparisons. This is reinforced by Campbell et al. (2012) and Tsay (2002) that most studies involving financial assets tend to use asset returns than their prices. By taking the log form, the time series yield continuously compounded returns (Bollerslev, 1986).

The movement of the stock exchange returns is shown in the figures. All six exchange returns follow a similar mean-reversing pattern to 0% but also exhibit continuous clustered volatility. One striking example is from the Icelandic exchange, as its returns plummeted drastically during the beginning of the financial crisis in 2008. The impacts are smaller in other exchanges, however. The correlation matrix is calculated and it shows that except for the Icelandic index, all five indices exhibit strong correlation. This is particularly strong with the UK and the Czech Republic with a 0.61 correlation coefficient. Despite the strong correlation, it has little implication as it does not suggest causality. Descriptive statistics and a plot for the maximum and minimum returns is illustrated in the next figure. Not surprisingly, Iceland experienced the lowest return as it was affected by the financial crisis the most. The Ukrainian index also exhibits the largest volatility with the highest return. The large kurtosis and skewness statistics suggest that all indices are not normally distributed. This is further reinforced by the Jarque-Bera test as the probability values are all lower than 5%, thus rejecting the null hypothesis of data being normally distributed.

3.4 Methodology

Unit root test

If stock index returns are weak-form efficient, then it must be stationary. A stationary time series should have two properties where its mean and variance are constant over time, and the value of covariance between time rt and rt+1 should depend only on the distance between the time periods, not the time itself. If a time series is not stationary, then weak-form efficient is rejected. In this case, the augmented Dickey-Fuller (ADF) non-stationarity test is used. The null hypothesis of the test is the time series is non-stationary. Autocorrelation test: further to the concept of stationarity above, it specifies that a series should not be serially correlated. This means the linear dependence between two periods of return, such as rt and rt+1, should have no correlation. This is carried out by using the autocorrelation function (ACF). For testing an individual ACF, t statistics are often employed. But in our case, we require to test several autocorrelations of the return series and check whether they are zero. The Q statistic (Ljung and Box, 1978) is often used for deciding whether the series is autocorrelated. The Q statistic is given as below:

$$Q(m) = T(T+2) \sum_{l=1}^{m} \frac{p^2}{T-l} \qquad (3.2)$$

The null hypothesis is a strong condition in which all autocorrelation coefficients are zero; therefore, the series is not autocorrelated. It follows the Chi-squared distribution with m degrees of freedom. The decision rule is if the p-value from the test is less than, say, 5% then it is rejected, therefore implying that the series is autocorrelated.

Variance Ratio Test

The last parametric test carried out is the VR test. It was proposed by Campbell et al. (2012). The test was developed to test the random walk hypothesis, and the authors strongly rejected that US weekly stock market returns follow the random walk hypothesis during the sample period. The logic of the test is that if a time series Y is a random walk, say in weekly frequency and has a variance of s, then the variance in monthly frequency should be four times larger. It also allows assumptions of homoscedastic and heteroskedastic in the series. The null hypothesis of the test is that the series follows a random walk.

Figure 3.2: Weekly stock market returns (in natural log)

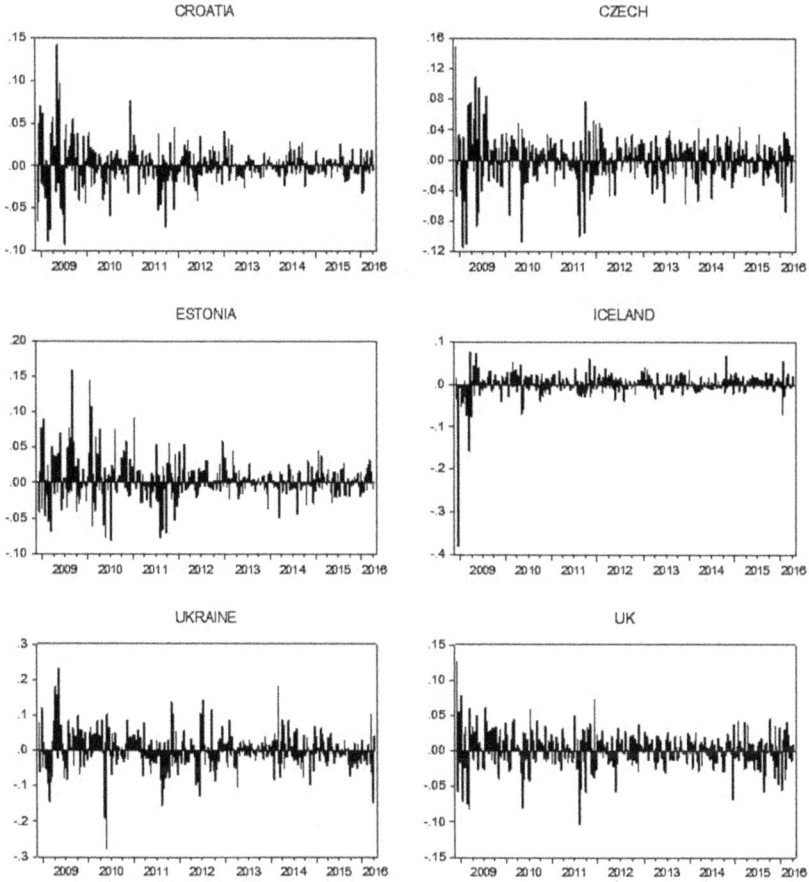

Figure 3.3: Correlation Matrix of stock exchange returns

	Croatia	Czech Rep	Estonia	Iceland	Ukraine	UK
Croatia	1					
Czech Rep	0.34319	1				
Estonia	0.439939	0.311081	1			
Iceland	9.74E-02	0.13692	1.05E-01	1		
Ukraine	0.406192	0.447167	0.359144	2.14E-01	1	
UK	0.356974	0.609124	0.327417	0.048805	0.398292	1

Figure 3.4: Descriptive statistics

	Croatia	Czech Rep	Estonia	Iceland	Ukraine	UK
Mean	-0.00008	0.00049	0.00321	0.00104	-0.00042	0.00129
Median	-0.00106	0.00103	0.00108	0.00171	-0.00324	0.00307
Maximum	0.14191	0.14753	0.15968	0.07552	0.23199	0.12585
Minimum	-0.09217	-0.11449	-0.08056	-0.38083	-0.27682	-0.10282
Std. Dev.	0.02320	0.02915	0.02732	0.02876	0.05100	0.02443
Skewness	0.50995	-0.08250	1.08199	-6.52557	-0.01771	-0.09777
Kurtosis	9.00492	6.85731	8.76690	84.78586	7.25904	6.06047
Jarque-Bera	595.13420	239.11800	608.61890	110034.0000	291.00720	150.86760
Probability	0.00000	0.00000	0.00000	0.00000	0.00000	0.00000
Sum	-0.03111	0.18853	1.23380	0.40123	-0.16113	0.49528
Sum Sq. Dev.	0.20665	0.32623	0.28664	0.31752	0.99889	0.22909
Observations	385	385	385	385	385	385

Figure 3.5: Chart showing the maximum and minimum return from the stock exchanges

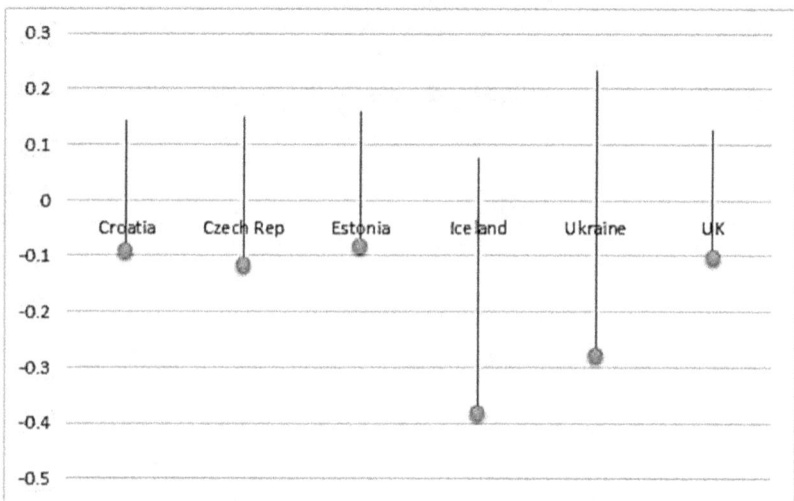

Runs Test

The runs test was formulated by Wald and Wolfowitz (1940), and it does not assume the distribution of the data. The null hypothesis is that the series is a random variable. It requires the user to count the 'runs', which is the period of consecutive stock returns with the same sign (+/-). It is then determined by comparing to the expected run in such series. The expected runs are given by the equation below. If the expected runs below is statistically different from the actual runs, then the test is rejected.

$$E(r) = \frac{(2N_1N_2)}{N} + 1 \qquad\qquad (3.3)$$

Figure 3.6: Summary of ADF test results

	t-Statstic	Prob
Croatia	-16.6122	0.0000
Czech Rep	-19.7860	0.0000
Estonia	-11.7570	0.0000
Iceland	-18.7616	0.0000
Ukraine	-11.0136	0.0000
UK	-22.1509	0.0000

3.5 Empirical results

All tests were carried out in Eviews. Original outputs can be found at the end of the chapter.

Unit root test

Augmented Dickey-Fuller tests were carried to check the stationarity of the series. The original outputs for all indices from EViews are attached. The table below shows the summary of ADF test results on all indices

All t-statistic values are larger than the critical values at 1%, 5% and 10% levels. This is reinforced by the 0.000 probability suggesting the rejection of the null hypothesis of non-stationarity, implying all series are stationary. Autocorrelation Test Next test employed is the autocorrelation test with the Ljung-Box Q-statistics. All original outputs, including the correlogram, are displayed in the appendix. The null hypothesis is that there is no serial correlation in the series. If the probability is above 5%, then we fail to reject the null hypothesis. The tests used 36 lags, and their respective p-values are displayed. Visually judging from the figure, which shows the p-values for the series, it is obvious that most series and their lags are below the 5% limit. Here, an interesting result is observed. As the FTSE 100 has 20 lags with a p-value above the 5% limit (67% of all lag), suggesting that its returns are a lot less predictable. The Tallinn exchange also has less but significant 33% of p-values being accepted as not autocorrelated. This is in stark contrast with the Eastern European markets of Croatia (0%), the Czech Republic (10%) and Ukraine (0%). On the other hand, the Icelandic index has 17% of p-values being autocorrelated.

Variance Ratio Tests

This test was first proposed by Lo and MacKinlay (2014) to test whether the time-series follow a random walk. The null hypothesis for each series: the stock index returns is a weak form of the efficient market. If the probability is less than 5%, then the null hypothesis is rejected. For each series, VR is carried out twice; one for the assumption of homoscedastic and another for heteroskedastic. As shown in the table, all test results reject the hypothesis of weak-form efficient except the OMX Iceland All-share Index, under the heteroskedastic assumption where its p-value is 0.06; therefore, the null hypothesis is not rejected. There is a very good chance that this is due to the impacts of the financial crisis on the Icelandic exchange in 2008, where it experienced large drops and volatility.

Figure 3.7: Showing p-values of the indices

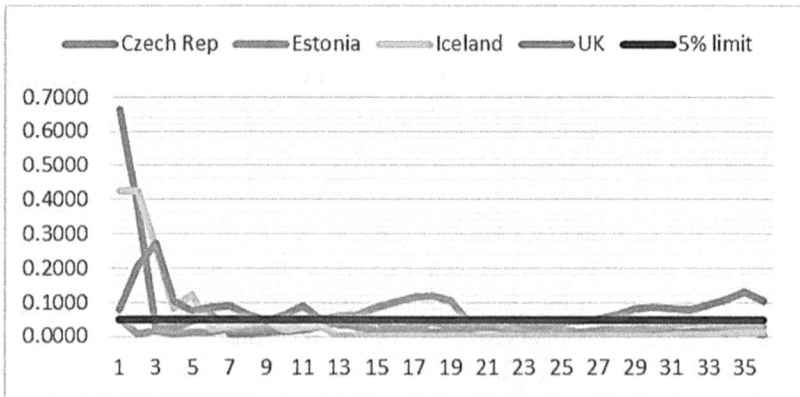

Runs Tests

As suggested by the Jarque-Bera tests, all indices are not normally distributed. Therefore the non-parametric method may be more suitable; as the name suggests, it does not assume the distribution of the series. The null hypothesis of the test is that the series follows a random walk. The results here show that all indices pass the test as their p-values are above 5%. Therefore the test indicates that all these markets follow a random walk. The results show that all indices pass the test as their p-values are above 5%. Therefore the test indicates that all these markets follow a random walk.

3.6 Implication on Portfolio Management

The results from various studies on EMH are often not conclusive. The implication of managing one's portfolio largely rely on the conviction of an investor's belief in this theory. If one is convinced by it and that it believes that EMH is correct and that no additional effort would yield extra returns then but yet the investor would still like to participate in the asset market (mainly due to attraction to the historical returns); then the investor shall be satisfied by market returns only. This investor's position on the portfolio management then should only use instruments that are designed to bring returns, such as index-based ETFs, mutual funds or managed funds that have a large position containing main market indices such as S&P500 that are large and diversified enough and will deliver a market returns almost identical to an index that the fund is tracking. In this scenario, it is worth asking what it means for the investor to use macroeconometric forecasts if EMH is true? In this case, the primary use of macroeconometric forecasts should be to dictate the timing of purchasing and selling of investments. Although the investor is happy with market returns alone, it does not, however, always receive the market return if the investor is investing across multiple periods and not with a lump sum at the start of the investment horizon. This is particularly important if the investor is young and has a long investment horizon (from 10 to 30 years). This implies that the capital to be used at the start of the investment horizon is likely to be low (without endowment from third parties nor own capital), and capital from employment or other remunerations will only be gained from later periods (such as post-graduation). This implies that the investor will invest gradually and at different timing; therefore, it is still important to time the investment, i.e. adhering to the famous adage: buy high and sell low. This will require constant balancing to the portfolio, and it is the benefit for the investor to have an advantage in forecasting and timing the subscription and redemption of investments.

On the other hand, if the investor does not believe in EMH or not in its strongest form then, it is even more important for the investor to forecast the future movements of different assets in order to gain an extra return. Logically this investor would also believe and be convinced by the evidence as presented from multi factors model that there are factors (such as macroeconomic variables) that determines asset movements (such as oil price increase on an oil producer). In this case, the rationale for using macroeconometric models are even stronger, as it can be used to dictate the decisions to buy and sell. This is particularly important if the asset is from a market that is considered to be less efficient.

Figure 3.8: Summary of p-values for autocorrelation test with Q statistics (36 lags)

P - Values

Croatia	Czech Rep	Estonia	Iceland	Ukraine	UK
0.0010	0.6640	0.0530	0.4250	0.0060	0.0780
0.0010	0.3790	0.0070	0.4250	0.0000	0.2040
0.0000	0.0250	0.0140	0.2580	0.0000	0.2720
0.0010	0.0230	0.0070	0.0810	0.0000	0.1030
0.0020	0.0440	0.0120	0.1230	0.0000	0.0730
0.0010	0.0670	0.0130	0.0210	0.0000	0.0850
0.0010	0.0070	0.0230	0.0310	0.0000	0.0910
0.0020	0.0060	0.0220	0.0360	0.0010	0.0640
0.0010	0.0110	0.0290	0.0470	0.0010	0.0460
0.0000	0.0150	0.0450	0.0170	0.0000	0.0630
0.0000	0.0190	0.0380	0.0250	0.0000	0.0900
0.0000	0.0300	0.0510	0.0300	0.0000	0.0500
0.0000	0.0410	0.0610	0.0010	0.0010	0.0320
0.0000	0.0250	0.0650	0.0000	0.0010	0.0360
0.0000	0.0170	0.0870	0.0000	0.0020	0.0440
0.0000	0.0180	0.1000	0.0000	0.0030	0.0240
0.0000	0.0240	0.1160	0.0010	0.0040	0.0300
0.0000	0.0110	0.1180	0.0000	0.0060	0.0400
0.0000	0.0150	0.1030	0.0000	0.0020	0.0290
0.0000	0.0220	0.0400	0.0010	0.0000	0.0280
0.0000	0.0280	0.0510	0.0000	0.0000	0.0360
0.0000	0.0230	0.0210	0.0000	0.0000	0.0470
0.0000	0.0200	0.0270	0.0000	0.0000	0.0320
0.0000	0.0070	0.0160	0.0000	0.0000	0.0310
0.0000	0.0090	0.0220	0.0000	0.0000	0.0410
0.0000	0.0040	0.0130	0.0010	0.0000	0.0440
0.0000	0.0050	0.0170	0.0010	0.0000	0.0540
0.0000	0.0070	0.0230	0.0010	0.0000	0.0650
0.0000	0.0070	0.0220	0.0020	0.0000	0.0820
0.0000	0.0100	0.0280	0.0020	0.0000	0.0860
0.0000	0.0110	0.0320	0.0030	0.0000	0.0820
0.0000	0.0150	0.0410	0.0040	0.0000	0.0800
0.0000	0.0180	0.0430	0.0050	0.0000	0.0940
0.0000	0.0180	0.0290	0.0070	0.0000	0.1090
0.0000	0.0230	0.0270	0.0100	0.0000	0.1320
0.0000	0.0040	0.0290	0.0120	0.0000	0.1040

Figure 3.9: Number of p-values above 5% threshold

Number of P-value accepted	0	3	10	5	0	20
Proportion of accepted	0%	10%	33%	17%	0%	67%

Figure 3.10: Results from VR tests

	Homoskedastic		Heteroskedastic	
	z-statistics	Probability	z-statistics	Probability
Croatia	8.5772	0.0000	4.4520	0.0000
Czech Rep	10.2503	0.0000	6.1167	0.0000
Estonia	10.0894	0.0000	5.9796	0.0000
Iceland	9.8918	0.0000	2.3883	0.0660*
Ukraine	10.0224	0.0000	5.0750	0.0000
UK	10.5340	0.0000	6.7018	0.0000

Figure 3.11: Runs test results

	Croatia	Czech	Estonia	Iceland	Ukraine	UK
Runs	185	197	183	189	183	197
p value	0.406059	0.70873	0.493529	0.653583	0.390559	0.67674

The case study results are broadly in line with literature on emerging markets, such as those which used similar methods. References cited that used the same methods, i.e. autocorrelation, variance ratio, and runs test, are largely the same as this study, particularly those investigating emerging markets. The evidence from the autocorrelation and variance ratio test implies that the return series are not random. On the other hand, results from the non-parametric runs test did not reject the weak-form efficient EMH for all markets. This is perhaps not too surprising as the first two methods, autocorrelation and variance ratio, use a parametric method that assumes the distributions of the time series. As demonstrated, the return series are volatile, particularly in Iceland due to the financial crisis; therefore, they won't be normally distributed. It seems that the impact of 2008 is still lingering in these stock exchanges, and it has an impact on this analysis. To further investigate, it would be interesting to test daily data, although requiring a lot of cleaning and interpolation as non-trading days are different across countries. As the Icelandic and Estonia exchange were both acquired by NASDAQ OMX in 2008 during the height of the financial crisis, it is no surprise that the impact on them was significant. Other the other hand, Croatia and Czech had a long history with data available. This allows further research that could incorporate inter-temporal data with different periods (e.g. before and after crisis etc.) In the end, research on the Ukrainian stock exchange is few as data is relatively little and information is harder to obtain. The geopolitical problems in Ukraine also further marginalized the stock exchange as it does not integrate with the rest of Europe. The EU sanction on Russia has a huge implication on the Ukrainian stock market as the market has a strong tie with Russia. Another interesting fact is that it was owned by the Moscow Exchange (49%) until recently as the relationship became dire. The contradictory results from the tests are also faced by similar research in this area. Although this cannot strongly conclude that weak-form efficiency EMH does not apply to these markets, the final verdict tends towards rejecting the hypothesis as the results are also found in the literature. One thing is more certain: these markets are less efficient than the UK market in comparison.

3.7 Appendix - ADF and Autocorrelation test

Figure 3.12: Zagreb Crobex Index

	t-Statistic	Prob.*
Augmented Dickey-Fuller test statistic	-16.61218	0.0000
Test critical values: 1% level	-3.447169	
5% level	-2.868848	
10% level	-2.570730	

Autocorrelation	Partial Correlation		AC	PAC	Q-Stat	Prob
.|*	.|*	1	0.171	0.171	11.360	0.001
.|.	.|.	2	0.069	0.041	13.227	0.001
.|*	.|*	3	0.115	0.100	18.418	0.000
.|.	*|.	4	-0.035	-0.076	18.904	0.001
.|.	.|.	5	-0.030	-0.023	19.255	0.002
*|.	*|.	6	-0.109	-0.112	23.896	0.001
.|.	.|*	7	0.030	0.085	24.253	0.001
.|.	.|.	8	-0.042	-0.053	24.962	0.002
*|.	.|.	9	-0.081	-0.049	27.580	0.001
*|.	*|.	10	-0.104	-0.113	31.840	0.000
*|.	*|.	11	-0.169	-0.126	43.166	0.000
*|.	.|.	12	-0.093	-0.043	46.598	0.000
.|.	.|*	13	0.008	0.076	46.626	0.000
.|.	.|.	14	-0.007	-0.006	46.646	0.000
.|.	.|.	15	0.020	0.006	46.807	0.000
.|.	.|.	16	0.032	-0.016	47.229	0.000
.|.	.|.	17	0.065	0.043	48.931	0.000
.|.	.|.	18	0.051	0.031	49.979	0.000
.|*	.|.	19	0.077	0.070	52.368	0.000
.|*	.|*	20	0.146	0.089	61.076	0.000
.|.	.|.	21	0.044	-0.028	61.854	0.000
.|.	.|.	22	0.023	-0.029	62.078	0.000
.|.	.|.	23	0.022	0.002	62.277	0.000
.|.	.|.	24	-0.016	0.009	62.377	0.000
*|.	*|.	25	-0.109	-0.090	67.320	0.000
.|.	.|.	26	-0.063	-0.012	68.943	0.000
.|.	.|.	27	-0.042	-0.028	69.683	0.000
*|.	.|.	28	-0.070	-0.013	71.747	0.000
*|.	.|.	29	-0.072	-0.030	73.895	0.000
.|.	.|.	30	-0.065	-0.015	75.663	0.000
.|.	.|.	31	-0.033	0.001	76.114	0.000
*|.	*|.	32	-0.122	-0.106	82.383	0.000
.|.	.|.	33	-0.032	-0.013	82.811	0.000
.|.	.|.	34	-0.025	-0.034	83.072	0.000
.|.	.|.	35	0.037	0.050	83.644	0.000
.|.	.|.	36	0.034	-0.032	84.139	0.000

Figure 3.13: Prague Stock Exchange Index

	t-Statistic	Prob.*
Augmented Dickey-Fuller test statistic	-19.78603	0.0000
Test critical values: 1% level	-3.447169	
5% level	-2.868848	
10% level	-2.570730	

Autocorrelation	Partial Correlation		AC	PAC	Q-Stat	Prob
.|. |	.|. |	1	0.022	0.022	0.1889	0.664
.|. |	.|. |	2	0.067	0.067	1.9414	0.379
*|. |	*|. |	3	-0.138	-0.141	9.3403	0.025
.|. |	.|* |	4	0.071	0.075	11.309	0.023
.|. |	.|. |	5	0.016	0.031	11.415	0.044
.|. |	.|. |	6	0.031	0.000	11.801	0.067
*|. |	*|. |	7	-0.140	-0.128	19.502	0.007
*|. |	.|. |	8	-0.068	-0.061	21.319	0.006
.|. |	.|. |	9	-0.022	0.003	21.507	0.011
.|. |	*|. |	10	-0.037	-0.070	22.065	0.015
.|. |	.|. |	11	-0.041	-0.040	22.740	0.019
.|. |	.|. |	12	0.008	0.031	22.763	0.030
.|. |	.|. |	13	0.028	0.030	23.082	0.041
.|* |	.|. |	14	0.087	0.067	26.131	0.025
*|. |	*|. |	15	-0.081	-0.100	28.773	0.017
.|. |	.|. |	16	0.054	0.058	29.963	0.018
.|. |	.|. |	17	0.030	0.046	30.338	0.024
.|* |	.|. |	18	0.100	0.039	34.433	0.011
.|. |	.|. |	19	-0.027	-0.021	34.719	0.015
.|. |	.|. |	20	-0.006	-0.003	34.734	0.022
.|. |	.|. |	21	-0.027	0.017	35.038	0.028
.|. |	.|. |	22	0.072	0.044	37.178	0.023
.|. |	.|. |	23	0.068	0.070	39.063	0.020
*|. |	*|. |	24	-0.110	-0.109	44.079	0.007
.|. |	.|. |	25	-0.040	-0.004	44.727	0.009
*|. |	*|. |	26	-0.106	-0.082	49.398	0.004
.|. |	.|. |	27	0.004	-0.029	49.404	0.005
.|. |	.|. |	28	0.007	0.028	49.426	0.007
.|. |	.|. |	29	-0.060	-0.063	50.946	0.007
.|. |	.|. |	30	0.001	0.028	50.947	0.010
.|. |	.|. |	31	0.040	0.041	51.618	0.011
.|. |	.|. |	32	-0.017	-0.058	51.739	0.015
.|. |	.|. |	33	-0.034	-0.035	52.228	0.018
.|. |	.|. |	34	0.055	0.045	53.530	0.018
.|. |	.|. |	35	-0.015	-0.040	53.627	0.023
.|* |	.|* |	36	0.144	0.104	62.498	0.004

Figure 3.14: OMX Tallinn Index

		t-Statistic	Prob.*
Augmented Dickey-Fuller test statistic		-11.75696	0.0000
Test critical values:	1% level	-3.447214	
	5% level	-2.868868	
	10% level	-2.570740	

Autocorrelation	Partial Correlation		AC	PAC	Q-Stat	Prob
.|* |	.|* |	1	0.098	0.098	3.7594	0.053
.|* |	.|* |	2	0.126	0.117	9.9370	0.007
.|. |	.|. |	3	0.043	0.021	10.659	0.014
*|. |	*|. |	4	-0.096	-0.119	14.250	0.007
.|. |	.|. |	5	0.033	0.045	14.674	0.012
.|. |	.|. |	6	-0.063	-0.046	16.231	0.013
.|. |	.|. |	7	0.008	0.016	16.256	0.023
.|. |	*|. |	8	-0.065	-0.071	17.914	0.022
.|. |	.|. |	9	-0.041	-0.020	18.569	0.029
.|. |	.|. |	10	-0.017	-0.009	18.680	0.045
*|. |	.|. |	11	-0.069	-0.049	20.599	0.038
.|. |	.|. |	12	0.029	0.028	20.928	0.051
.|. |	.|. |	13	0.042	0.055	21.651	0.061
.|. |	.|. |	14	0.052	0.035	22.744	0.065
.|. |	.|. |	15	-0.018	-0.056	22.878	0.087
.|. |	.|. |	16	-0.040	-0.044	23.523	0.100
.|. |	.|. |	17	0.039	0.055	24.127	0.116
.|. |	.|. |	18	0.053	0.071	25.263	0.118
.|. |	.|. |	19	0.067	0.034	27.067	0.103
.|* |	.|* |	20	0.113	0.086	32.291	0.040
.|. |	.|. |	21	0.028	0.007	32.607	0.051
.|* |	.|* |	22	0.108	0.095	37.388	0.021
.|. |	.|. |	23	-0.032	-0.051	37.800	0.027
*|. |	*|. |	24	-0.089	-0.093	41.061	0.016
.|. |	.|. |	25	-0.017	0.006	41.176	0.022
*|. |	.|. |	26	-0.093	-0.043	44.729	0.013
.|. |	.|. |	27	-0.017	-0.016	44.854	0.017
.|. |	.|. |	28	-0.008	0.028	44.882	0.023
.|. |	.|* |	29	0.059	0.096	46.347	0.022
.|. |	.|. |	30	0.014	-0.003	46.430	0.028
.|. |	*|. |	31	-0.041	-0.069	47.137	0.032
.|. |	.|. |	32	-0.012	-0.044	47.199	0.041
.|. |	.|. |	33	-0.047	-0.017	48.141	0.043
.|* |	.|* |	34	0.086	0.085	51.302	0.029
.|. |	.|. |	35	0.060	0.038	52.851	0.027
.|. |	.|. |	36	0.045	0.019	53.708	0.029

Figure 3.15: OMX Iceland All-Share PR Index

		t-Statistic	Prob.*
Augmented Dickey-Fuller test statistic		-18.76160	0.0000
Test critical values:	1% level	-3.447169	
	5% level	-2.868848	
	10% level	-2.570730	

Autocorrelation	Partial Correlation		AC	PAC	Q-Stat	Prob
.|.	.|.	1	0.041	0.041	0.6372	0.425
.|.	.|.	2	0.053	0.051	1.7105	0.425
.|*	.|.	3	0.077	0.073	4.0300	0.258
.|*	.|*	4	0.104	0.097	8.2957	0.081
.|.	.|.	5	0.031	0.017	8.6649	0.123
.|*	.|*	6	0.126	0.112	14.913	0.021
.|.	.|.	7	0.035	0.012	15.382	0.031
.|.	*|.	8	-0.053	-0.079	16.473	0.036
.|.	.|.	9	0.039	0.021	17.090	0.047
.|*	.|*	10	0.107	0.087	21.599	0.017
.|.	.|.	11	-0.028	-0.038	21.910	0.025
.|.	.|.	12	0.046	0.036	22.769	0.030
.|*	.|*	13	0.181	0.170	35.845	0.001
*|.	*|.	14	-0.081	-0.101	38.460	0.000
.|*	.|*	15	0.087	0.076	41.502	0.000
.|.	.|.	16	0.017	-0.033	41.625	0.000
.|.	*|.	17	-0.041	-0.072	42.291	0.001
*|.	*|.	18	-0.100	-0.098	46.382	0.000
.|.	.|.	19	0.046	0.001	47.233	0.000
.|.	.|.	20	-0.001	0.021	47.233	0.001
*|.	*|.	21	-0.108	-0.085	52.022	0.000
.|.	.|.	22	-0.059	-0.064	53.442	0.000
.|.	.|.	23	-0.045	-0.038	54.271	0.000
.|.	.|.	24	-0.051	0.008	55.355	0.000
.|.	.|.	25	0.037	0.021	55.909	0.000
.|.	.|.	26	0.025	0.021	56.171	0.001
.|.	.|.	27	-0.030	0.043	56.551	0.001
.|.	.|.	28	-0.010	-0.017	56.595	0.001
.|.	.|.	29	-0.011	-0.009	56.647	0.002
.|.	.|.	30	0.001	0.018	56.647	0.002
.|.	.|.	31	-0.018	0.015	56.791	0.003
.|.	.|.	32	0.003	-0.016	56.796	0.004
.|.	.|.	33	-0.034	0.000	57.292	0.005
.|.	.|.	34	-0.003	0.041	57.297	0.007
.|.	.|.	35	-0.006	-0.015	57.313	0.010
.|.	.|.	36	-0.036	-0.028	57.881	0.012

Figure 3.16: Ukrainian Equities Index

		t-Statistic	Prob.*
Augmented Dickey-Fuller test statistic		-11.01364	0.0000
Test critical values:	1% level	-3.447214	
	5% level	-2.868868	
	10% level	-2.570740	

Autocorrelation	Partial Correlation		AC	PAC	Q-Stat	Prob
.|* |	.|* |	1	0.139	0.139	7.4784	0.006
.|* |	.|* |	2	0.161	0.144	17.537	0.000
.|* |	.|. |	3	0.109	0.073	22.198	0.000
.|. |	.|. |	4	0.035	-0.009	22.684	0.000
.|. |	*|. |	5	-0.060	-0.094	24.109	0.000
.|. |	.|. |	6	0.024	0.030	24.328	0.000
*|. |	*|. |	7	-0.082	-0.071	26.998	0.000
.|. |	.|. |	8	0.024	0.051	27.220	0.001
.|. |	.|. |	9	-0.061	-0.053	28.703	0.001
*|. |	*|. |	10	-0.089	-0.083	31.831	0.000
*|. |	.|. |	11	-0.084	-0.054	34.669	0.000
.|. |	.|. |	12	-0.032	0.004	35.077	0.000
.|. |	.|. |	13	-0.034	0.018	35.542	0.001
.|. |	.|. |	14	0.032	0.041	35.966	0.001
..|. |	.|. |	15	0.007	0.002	35.984	0.002
..|. |	.|. |	16	0.024	-0.002	36.219	0.003
.|. |	.|. |	17	0.010	-0.008	36.259	0.004
.|. |	.|. |	18	-0.010	-0.022	36.300	0.006
.|* |	.|* |	19	0.111	0.126	41.360	0.002
.|* |	.|* |	20	0.125	0.100	47.751	0.000
.|* |	.|. |	21	0.076	0.023	50.103	0.000
.|* |	.|. |	22	0.115	0.044	55.555	0.000
.|* |	.|. |	23	0.108	0.054	60.374	0.000
.|. |	*|. |	24	-0.060	-0.098	61.853	0.000
.|. |	.|. |	25	0.057	0.058	63.217	0.000
.|. |	.|. |	26	-0.033	-0.017	63.662	0.000
.|. |	.|. |	27	0.010	0.030	63.701	0.000
.|. |	.|. |	28	-0.009	-0.009	63.737	0.000
*|. |	*|. |	29	-0.107	-0.114	68.551	0.000
.|. |	.|* |	30	0.025	0.103	68.812	0.000
.|. |	.|. |	31	-0.029	-0.014	69.156	0.000
*|. |	*|. |	32	-0.133	-0.087	76.669	0.000
.|. |	.|. |	33	-0.008	0.018	76.693	0.000
.|. |	.|* |	34	0.060	0.082	78.232	0.000
.|. |	.|. |	35	-0.035	-0.041	78.759	0.000
.|. |	.|. |	36	0.054	0.027	79.981	0.000

Figure 3.17: FTSE 100 Index

		t-Statistic	Prob.*
Augmented Dickey-Fuller test statistic		-22.15091	0.0000
Test critical values:	1% level	-3.447169	
	5% level	-2.868848	
	10% level	-2.570730	

Autocorrelation	Partial Correlation		AC	PAC	Q-Stat	Prob
*|.		*|.		1	-0.090	-0.090	3.1139	0.078
.|.		.|.		2	-0.013	-0.021	3.1747	0.204
.|.		.|.		3	-0.043	-0.047	3.9061	0.272
*|.		*|.		4	-0.098	-0.108	7.6976	0.103
.|*		.|.		5	0.078	0.058	10.092	0.073
.|.		.|.		6	-0.050	-0.045	11.094	0.085
.|.		*|.		7	-0.055	-0.073	12.292	0.091
.|*		.|.		8	0.079	0.064	14.736	0.064
*|.		.|.		9	-0.079	-0.063	17.198	0.046
.|.		.|.		10	-0.031	-0.064	17.573	0.063
.|.		.|.		11	-0.015	-0.024	17.662	0.090
*|.		*|.		12	-0.092	-0.091	21.041	0.050
.|*		.|.		13	0.085	0.034	23.915	0.032
.|.		.|.		14	-0.048	-0.043	24.826	0.036
.|.		.|.		15	0.039	0.026	25.451	0.044
.|*		.|*		16	0.094	0.078	29.053	0.024
.|.		.|.		17	-0.036	-0.003	29.575	0.030
.|.		.|.		18	0.019	-0.001	29.725	0.040
*|.		*|.		19	-0.079	-0.067	32.239	0.029
.|.		.|.		20	0.060	0.069	33.700	0.028
.|.		.|.		21	-0.030	-0.062	34.065	0.036
.|.		.|.		22	0.017	0.026	34.188	0.047
.|*		.|*		23	0.083	0.088	37.045	0.032
.|.		.|.		24	-0.058	-0.051	38.444	0.031
.|.		.|.		25	0.012	0.019	38.504	0.041
.|.		.|.		26	-0.048	-0.037	39.459	0.044
.|.		.|.		27	-0.027	-0.005	39.765	0.054
.|.		.|.		28	0.028	-0.003	40.097	0.065
.|.		.|.		29	0.009	0.020	40.129	0.082
.|.		.|.		30	-0.047	-0.049	41.053	0.086
.|.		.|.		31	0.058	0.024	42.462	0.082
.|.		.|.		32	-0.056	-0.020	43.808	0.080
.|.		*|.		33	-0.027	-0.068	44.114	0.094
.|.		.|.		34	0.027	0.042	44.433	0.109
.|.		.|.		35	-0.005	0.018	44.444	0.132
.|*		.|.		36	0.077	0.026	46.995	0.104

Part II:
Macroeconometric Models

Chapter 4

Historical Perspectives on Macroeconometrics

4.1 Modelling the economy

As economies grow bigger and more interconnected, the conduct of economic policy also became more complex as it is harder to understand in terms of the transmission mechanism and also the impact on other economic components such as output and employment. Since the inception of macroeconomics in the 1930s, a large part of the subject is devoted to the empirical analysis and application of economic policies. As a practice, economic policy can be viewed as a series of action implemented by institutions such as the government and central bank, with the intention to influence the behaviour of the economy. However, it can also be understood as an academic discipline that provides analysis and guidance on how economists should determine the course of action. Essentially the goals of economic policy can be divided into three types: resource allocation, income distribution, and macroeconomic stabilization, as pointed out in Musgrave et al. (1989). It is to these aims that economic policies were designed, and by themes associated with them, we can further classify them into fiscal policy, monetary policy Lubik and Schorfheide (2007) Bénassy-Quéré et al. (2010). Like any other disciplines, theories and tools created and implemented have changed throughout time. To properly understand the nature of economic policy and the transmission, economists and policymakers utilize macroeconometric models to organize their thinking and disentangle the interrelationships between variables such as inflation and interest rates.

Before the 1930s, the main type of state intervention (i.e. economic policy actions) was confined to the uses of taxes, import/export tariffs, provision of public goods, money regulation and antitrust laws when there is a market failure; as stipulated by classical and neoclassical economics in the vein of Pigou and Marshall. From the 1940s to the 1970s, the Keynesian paradigm dominated the period and saw the domination of policies designed for macroeconomic problems during the post-war period, such as income distribution, inflation, exchange rate etc. By increasing or lowering tax and also spending on the economy, the government has the power to influence the economy by shifting the aggregate demand and the level of economic activity. It is also used during the peaks and troughs of business cycles in order to stimulate or stabilize the economy. Essentially Keynesian thought was a theory on spending from the government in order to boost aggregate demand, thus reducing employment and lifting the economy. However, the stagflation due to the first and second oil crisis during the 1970s and 1980s saw the focus switched from unemployment to inflation. Policymakers were confronted by a situation that never happened before. The eventual policy response was a combination of tight monetary policies with high-interest rates to control prices, neutral fiscal policies, supply-side and structural reforms to reduce costs to increase the efficiency of the private sector. This, in turn, increased the competitiveness of the private sector and reduced the cost of doing business. In other words, it was market-oriented polices and no longer was the domination of the fine-tuning fiscal policies of the previous era. Despite the magnificent and seemingly unstoppable growth from the 1980s, it was disrupted by the Great Recession beginning in 2007. The capital market liberalization contributed to the rapid spread of the crisis around the world and sectors that are not directly involved in the financial market. The collapse of major banks and corporations essentially stopped the borrowing and lending market as confidence was lost. This crisis challenged some of the prevent thoughts from the previous free-market paradigm. Institutions designed to avoid the crisis failed; thus, the credo that markets are themselves efficient and self-correcting and therefore, regulation is not needed was reconsidered in Acocella et al. (2016, p.103). This has ushered a new era of economic thinking and also policymaking, as exemplified by Quantitative Easing (QE) in major developed countries.

As the brief description above has shown, the economic environment has changed many times and will continue to change in perhaps a different way. It is the goal of the modeller to capture these dynamics. Often sudden, unexpected shocks such as that during the 1970s and the recent financial crisis in 2007 has shown that the data recording such events exhibited properties such as structural breaks or trends that could be difficult to model. As a result of this challenge, different types of modelling approaches were developed, each with its peculiar strengths.

It is a daunting endeavour to model the economy, let alone the world economy, with all the complexities and interrelations of the individual economies. Depending on the modeller's purpose for the model, he can either create a mental, perhaps a heuristic model of the economy by taking into the relationships between different types of economic indicators. On the other hand, the more laborious but rigorous approach is to create a quantitative model with the relationships among the economic variables. The second has been the dominant approach among major institutions and the economics profession. Macroeconometrics, the field of enquiry devoted to modelling the economy with the tools of econometrics, has developed an arsenal of large scale and complex models for forecasting the direction of the economy and for the analysis of alternative economic policy.

Like any other academic disciplines, it has a fair share of controversies and different schools of thoughts with widely different approaches. The methodologies and the associated models employed have been changing not only due to advance in the tools but also the underlying monetary policy rules and conditions differed tremendously in the past few decades. Although the protagonist in this study is the GVAR model, there are a few other approaches followed by academics and practitioners in the industry. Current approaches to modelling the global and national economy include large-scale simultaneous equation models (SEMs) and dynamic stochastic general equilibrium modelling (DSGE), and Vector Autoregressive (VAR). As the reader will see, the GVAR is closely related to the VAR modelling approach proposed by Sims (1980). It is not a coincidence that GVAR also inherited some of the theoretical aspects of this approach but also differ significantly in its ability to be applied to a large and complex set of data.

In light of the failure of previous macro models, many solutions have been put forth, and one of the most promising approaches is via the method of Global Vector Autoregressive (GVAR) since its creation in 2004 in Pesaran, Schuermann and Weiner (abbreviated as PSW) 2004. The GVAR approach is closely related to the VAR modelling approach proposed by Sims (1980) but provided a relatively simple yet effective way of modelling interactions in a complex high-dimensional system such as the global economy. Other existing large models, such as the simultaneous equations model (SEM) and dynamic stochastic general equilibrium model (DSGE), are often incomplete and do not present a closed system, which is required for simulation analysis Chudik and Pesaran (2016). Compared to empirical DSGE models, which can model a few countries but often do not treat them as a whole system, GVAR provides a more complete method that allows the user to include many countries under a single large model while explicitly allow interactions among the countries.

GVAR's capability to accommodate many individual countries, their respective economic variables, and modelling them in one coherent framework has been very attractive to study the effects of economic shocks from one economic variable of a country to other variables in the rest of the model. For example, Chudik and Pesaran (2016) have pointed out that GVAR is one of the main techniques used to understand interlinkage across individual countries. Numerous applications can be found at policy institutions such as the International Monetary Fund (IMF), European Central Bank (ECB) etc.

It is no surprise that macroeconometric modelling has since occupied the heart of decision-making by major institutions such as government agencies, industrial and financial institutions. In an extensive and perhaps the only recent survey of macroeconometric models by Welfe (2013), we can see that the major users of these models are governments and central banks. While the macroeconometric models are often created by said institutions, there are also models created by private companies such as Oxford Economics and NIESR[1] and are sold to institutions such as investment banks and asset managers. Depending on the purpose of the model, the methodology used for construction would also be different. Macroeconometric modelling has undergone many changes in the past twenty to thirty years, driven not only by developments in economic and econometric theory but also the changing economic circumstances Garratt et al. (p.3 2006a)[2].

Throughout the history of model building, we can see that a modeller can either begin building from economic theory or statistical description of the data. For example, a simple, unrestricted VAR model is often considered to be 'atheoretical' as it is a simple system comprised of a stochastic process for modelling the linear interdependencies among multiple time series and does not rely on an *a priori* economic theory to determine the structure of the model. On the other hand, a complex DSGE model is constructed based on microeconomic theory and provides an explicit inter-temporal general equilibrium model of the economy based on optimising decisions made by households and firms[3]. Depending on

---

[1] See: https://www.oxfordeconomics.com/ and https://www.niesr.ac.uk/

[2] For a detailed review on the history of macroeconometric modelling see Qin (2013). For the actual models used or are being used by institutions, the reader can be directed to an excellent and perhaps the only survey Welfe (2013). Public information is also sometimes available via working papers or model documentation published online. Summary of the methodology and the actual equations used in the macro models are sometimes available (although may not be up to date). Such as the SEM model at Office for Budget Responsibility in the UK: http://obr.uk/docs/dlm_uploads/Final_Model_Documentation.pdf
Another example is the current suit of macro models used at the Bank of England is DSGE COMPASS and is subject for examination by academia. See https://www.economics.ox.ac.uk/materials/papers/15157/832- hendry–muellbauer.pdf and https://academic.oup.com/oxrep/article/34/1-2/287/4781814
GVAR as currently used at the Federal Reserve and the European Central Bank can be seen in: https://www.dallasfed.org/~/media/documents/institute/wpapers/2014/0180.pdf
https://papers.ssrn.com/sol3/papers.cfm?abstract_id=2302511

[3] For detailed review on the history of macroeconometric modelling see Qin (2013). For the actual models used or are being used by institutions, the reader can be directed to an excellent and perhaps the only survey Welfe (2013). Public information are also sometimes available via working papers or model documentations published online. Summary of the methodology and the actual equations used in the macro models are sometimes available (although may not be up to date). Such as the SEM model at Office for Budget Responsibility in the UK: http://obr.uk/docs/dlm_uploads/Final_Model_Documentation.pdf
Another example is the current suit of macro models used at the Bank of England is DSGE COMPASS and is subject for examination by academia. See https://www.economics.ox.ac.uk/materials/papers/15157/832- hendry–muellbauer.pdf and https://academic.oup.com/oxrep/article/34/1-2/287/4781814

the purpose of the model (whether it is for forecasting or policy analysis etc.), the methodology also differs tremendously. As Granger (1999, p.16-17) puts it:

One can find advocates at two extremes, some saying that theory contains the only pure truth and so has to be the basis of the model, even to claiming that all 'residuals' have to have theoretical explanations, leaving little place for stochastics, uncertainty, or exogenous shocks to the systems. At the other extreme, some econometricians have thrown up their hands in despair when trying to find a use for theory and so build 'atheoretical' models based just on examination of the data and using any apparent regularities and relationships found in it. Most applied economists take a middle ground, using theory to provide an initial specification and then data exploration techniques to extend or refine the starting model, leading to a form that better represents the data.

The synthesis between theory and empirical data has taken four main forms according to Garratt et al. (p.6 2006a)., namely large scale SEM, unrestricted and structural VAR, DSGE and structural cointegrating VAR (also known as CVAR and when applied to a global setting becomes a GVAR).

SEM models have a long history and were developed during the early years at the Cowles Commission in the 1940s by Haavelmo (1944) and Klein (1947). As they have been the first and also the staple macro models in the literature, the term 'macroeconometric models' often refers to these types of models directly, like in Valadkhani (2004).[4] One of the prominent examples of the SEM model is the Project LINK model. It was constructed in 1968 as a project to integrate the existing macroeconometric country models into a world system. The application of the model was for supporting the studies into the properties and impacts of the international transmission mechanism Welfe (2013, p.242). Countries included in the model grew from 7 in the 1960s to 80 in 1995 and 176 in the 2016 vintage of the World Economic Forecasting Model (WEFM, which succeeded the LINK model at the United Nations[5]). The number of equations describing each country also grew enormously from 1500 to circa 30000 Klein et al. (1999) (precise

---

GVAR as currently used at the Federal Reserve and the European Central Bank can be seen in:
https://www.dallasfed.org/~/media/documents/institute/wpapers/2014/0180.pdf
https://papers.ssrn.com/sol3/papers.cfm?abstract_id=2302511

[4] It should be noted that, there are many terms referring to this type of model in the literature. Nomenclatures include traditional macroeconometric model, Klein model, Cowles Commission model and simultaneous equation model. However, in this thesis, we only use SEM when referring to this type and macroeconometric model is the umbrella term covering all kinds of macro models.

[5] Details of the WEFM model: https://www.un.org/development/desa/dpad/wp-content/uploads/sites/45/publication/2016_Apr_WorldEconomicForecastingModel.pdf

figures are not published for the 2016 vintage of WEFM.) By their nature, they are hard to evolve because of their sheer size. Essentially they have followed the tradition of the Cowles Commission, making a distinction between exogenous and endogenous variables and imposing restrictions, often on the short-run dynamic properties of the model, in order to achieve identification Garratt et al. (2006b, p.14). Large-scale SEM models were under heavy criticisms during the 1970s by Lucas (1976) and also Sims (1980) due to their methods of identification and accuracy in forecasting. The demise of the SEMs led to the development of real business cycle models Kydland and Prescott (1982), which became the core of the DSGE literature. It relies on a deep structural microeconomic foundation in order to bypass the Lucas critique (see part 1.3.2 for more details). It also saw the development of the VAR model by Sargent and Sims (1977) and Sims (1980), which took the opposite direction by focusing on the data.

Secondly, following the methodology developed by Doan et al. (1984), Litterman (1986), and Blanchard and Quah (1988), there are unrestricted, Bayesian, and 'structural' vector autoregression (SVAR). Compared to the large scale SEM, VAR offers a much simpler and manageable framework typically consisting of a handful of countries and no more than five variables (limited by the curse of dimensionality, see 1.4). In the literature, VAR and Bayesian VARs (BVAR) are primarily used for forecasting as the model captures the dynamics of the data very well when specified correctly. However, most estimates from a simple VAR provide little 'economic meaning', and this requires restriction imposed on the model in order to be used for policymaking (such as scenario and counterfactual analysis). The structural VAR approach aims to provide the VAR framework with structural content through the imposition of restrictions on the covariance structure of different types of shocks. This allows distinction made between shocks with temporary effects from those with permanent effects. The modeller can then refer to economic theory to interpret these effects. This approach does not attempt to model the structure of the economy in the form of specific behavioural relationships as SEM does. However, the mean culprit is the limitation on size, which rendered it undesirable for global macroeconomic analysis.

The third approach, DSGE methodology, was originally employed in the Real Business Cycle literature Kydland and Prescott (1982) and has become the essential tool for macroeconomic analysis. The DSGE approach came as a response to Lucas critique (1976) to build a macroeconomic model based on microfoundations that are not affected by policy changes. Instead of modelling individual markets as was done traditionally, DSGE model the economy as a whole (represented by the behaviour of representative economic agents), thus achieving *general equilibrium.*

The fourth approach is the GVAR, which began as a long-run structural method akin to co-integrating VAR, but with more emphasis on using theory for determining long-run relationships and data for the short-run.

4.2 Literature review on macroeconometric approaches

4.2.1 Early macroeconometrics and SEMs

The development of macroeconometrics was largely due to research works done on fundamental econometrics (as described above) at the Cowles Commission from the 1940s to 1950s. This is referred to as the consolidation period, which saw the foundation of econometrics established and gradually became the mainstream econometrics. For a comprehensive treatment of various macroeconometric models developed and their history, see Qin (2013) and Welfe (2013) for a detailed exposition of the major models being used around the world. Shorter works that summarise the changing paradigm in macroeconometric from the Cowles Commission to later DSGE and VAR can be seen in Pesaran (1990) Valadkhani (2004).

In particular, the work of Haavelmo (1944) was foundational and became the 'textbook' standard. The works from this period by the Cowles Commission is often referred to simply as the Cowles Commission approach or the traditional approach. The main output of this period was a methodology known as simultaneous equation models (SEM). Although Lucas's (1976) and Sims's (1980) critiques largely ended the domination of the SEM, they are still being used today.[6] As computing capability developed, SEMs are being applied on more than just one country—like the Klein Model or the LINK model, which contain hundreds of equations and modelling dozens of countries. Gradually these models contain a very large set of equations that described the local and international economies and were known as the large-scale SEMs. These large-scale SEMs shared some important features comprised of three basic building blocks Garratt et al. (2006b): equilibrium conditions, expectations formation, and dynamic adjustments such as the archetype used in Klein et al. (1999).

---

[6] Such as NiGEM developed by NISER, HM Treasury and Bank of England. Summary of the methodology and the actual equations used in the macro models are sometimes available (although may not be up to date). Such as the Office for Budget Responsibility in the UK: http://obr.uk/docs/dlm_uploads/Final_Model_Documentation.pdf But for certain, there is a much larger literature on macro models created or used by public institutions. For example, the current suit of macro models used at the Bank of England is DSGE COMPASS and is subject for examination by academia. See https://www.economics.ox.ac.uk/materials/papers/1515 7/832-hendry–muellbauer.pdf and https://academic.oup.com/oxrep/article/34/1-2/287/47 81814 for example.

Prominent examples of large-scale models include Klein et al. (1999), Ando et al. (1969), Brayton and Mauskopf (1985) for a model of the US economy, Murphy's (1988) model for Australia, and the variety of models constructed for other central banks and authorities, see Welfe (2013) for more details.

4.2.2 Consensus on macroeconometrics disintegrated

The Cowles Commission (CC) approach to empirical research was often referred to as the traditional strategy, which combined theory and evidence (Hylleberg and Paldam 1991). However, the consensus on the proper way of carrying out empirical research as developed by the CC was disintegrated during the 1970s. As pointed out in Pesaran and Smith (1995), there are three shocks to the demise of the CC approach. Firstly it was thought that the SEMs did not represent the data. This led to an increased emphasis on testing the models, such as diagnostic and misspecification tests, and there was less focus on the estimation of the models and poor forecasting performance of the SEMs during the stagflation. Secondly, in conjunction with the rational expectations revolution by Muth (1961) and Lucas's critique (1976), it was thought to be devastating to the CC approach as it completely undermined its relevance and its usage on policy evaluation.

Rational expectation, as outlined in Muth (1961), outlined that the traditional models did not consider the full information available by the agents regarding the expectation of the future. Instead, the models treated the agent's future expectations as a simple extrapolation from the past (particularly the most recent past), and therefore this is irrational. A rational agent should use all available information, including now and the expected future, and therefore the forecast error (when all information are used to make this forecast) should only present arbitrary events that cannot be predictable. The assumption of a perfect rational expectation is unrealistic, given that most households do not (and cannot, due to time and cost) evaluate all information before acting on the future, but there are agents with strong incentive to consider all available information such as investment banks and asset manager as forecast error can be costly. The rational expectation led to the Lucas critique (1976).

During the stagflation period in the late 1960s and early 1970s, the usual output-inflation relationship no longer held with a high inflation rate, economic growth rate slowing, and while unemployment remains high. The behavioural equations representing the economic agents such as the consumers and suppliers in the traditional approach relied on the statistical relationship between economic variables. The role of the SEMs for the policymakers was to evaluate the impact of the economic policy changes, e.g. by changing an exogenous variable such as money supply. However, Lucas noted that this way of modelling the macroeconomy based on aggregate variables cannot be done.

Suppose that policymakers would like to raise interest rate in order to curb inflation, with the amount of interest rate to be raised *I* estimated in an SEM model (which uses historical data) to derive the likely reduced inflation by this raise, say *Y*. However, rational workers would have expected this raise and have already requested a pay rise in order to hedge against expected inflation thus increasing inflation. The original macroeconometric model, which estimated the interest rate *I* to be raised to reduce inflation by *Y*, is useless as the economic agents have optimal decision rules, which altered the structure of the econometric models (from which the estimated impacts are derived). Therefore in order to evaluate the impact of economic policy, Lucas suggested that the variables in the model must be structural in the sense of policy-invariant, such as tastes and preferences, which are unlikely to change due to policy changes. In Lucas's words,

> given that tile structure of all econometric model consists of optimal decision rules of economic agents, and that optimal decision rules vary systematically with changes in the structure of series relevant to the decision-maker, it follows any change in policy will systematically alter the structure of econometric models (1976, p.41).

The impetus from Lucas's critique resulted in the wide adaptation of the rational expectations in SEMs. Besides, given the difficulty to estimate these models and the prohibitively high requirements on the data to fulfil order condition identification of the model parameters in the 1970s and even now. As concluded by Brayton et al. (1997), 'large-scale macromodels are by their nature slow to evolve.' When commenting on SEMs, Garratt et al. (2006a) concluded that despite the imaginative attempts to combine theory and data into a large-scale macreconometric model, it remains a formidable task to fulfil this task. Therefore as noted in Qin (2013), many have given up on SEMs to macro modelling and started new approaches such as DSGE and VAR.

4.2.3 Identification problem of SEMs

Without a doubt, the SEMs have dominated for such a long time as they have been quite impressive in their scales and the detailed description of the economy via numbers of behavioural equations. However, as seen above, Lucas's critique was proved to be destructive to SEMs. At the same time, Sims's seminal paper "Macroeconomics and Reality" (1980) criticised the identification strategy in SEMs and outlined a specific attack on the identification strategy used in large scale SEMs and famously remarked it as 'incredible'. As noted in Sargent and Sims (1977), there was already work criticising SEMs' identification, particularly in Liu

(1960), which argued that the number of restrictions required to identify large-scale SEMs far exceeded those the economic theory can provide. This implies that large-scale SEMs are unidentified instead of overidentified, as usually assumed in the literature. Pesaran and Smith (1995, p.64) noted a proliferation of estimation techniques such as IV, 2SLS, 3SLS etc., created for simultaneity and overidentified models by the Cowles Commission.

The crux of Sims's paper and Sargent and Sims (1977) was attacking the identification strategy used on the SEMs regarding the 'identification problem'. SEMs often suffered from what is called the identification problem—referring to the inability to identify an estimate of the value for the equation parameters, such as when there are common variables in multiple equations. This problem has been acknowledged early on, like in Koopmans (1949). The Cowles Commission's approach towards this problem was by using introducing different exogenous variables in each equation, thus allowing the system of simultaneous equations to be overidentified and fulfilling the order and rank conditions of identification. Given that many structural-form equations (in the sense that the parameters in the equation are derived from economic theory) are not directly observable, they are normalised into reduced-form equations which can be estimated; the problem is, of course, the loss of economic meaning. As emphasised in Sims (Ibid.), this normalisation is indeed acceptable. However, the problem is, in order to fulfil the ability to identify the whole system of simultaneous equations by adding exogenous variables on each individual equation basis, how much are the equations representing theory? Not only the consistency of economic theory is sacrificed, but also the exogenous variables on the right-hand side are also arbitrary and cannot be relied on to uncover the structural model. As summarised in Pesaran and Smith (1995, p.65), 'the traditional strategy ... did not represent the data ... did not represent theory ... the models were ineffective for practical purposes of forecasting and policy evaluation.'

4.2.4 Vector Autoregressive models

Recall that exogeneity was a crucial property to the selection for the right-hand side equation and to the identification in SEMs. However, the concept of the exogenous (explanatory) variable is a lot more controversial, and it depends on the modeller's choices Pesaran (1990, p.18). For example, the Cowles Commission's approach to exogeneity was based on economic intuition. Furthermore, the modeller can choose the definition of exogeneity, e.g. viewed as a property of a proposed model (Koopmans 1950) or as weak and strong exogeneity regarding the distribution of observable variables (Engle, Hendry, and Richard 1983). For example, the unrestricted VAR proposed in Sims (1980) does not differentiate endogenous nor exogenous variables, while GVAR in

Chudik and Pesaran (2016) uses the weak-exogenous assumption for other country variables (see section 1.4.1).

In light of this, the unrestricted VAR approach introduced by Sims abolished the differentiation on endogenous and exogenous variables and treated all as in the system. Instead, variables are explained based on their lagged values and those of other variables as specified by the modeller. This is at the polar opposite to large-scale models as there is no economic theory used in its construction, although the modeller can select economic variables to be included in order to have economic meaning. Instead of the large complex equations in SEMs, VAR is created for modelling a small set of macroeconomic variables. This is achieved by using a VAR specification and also emphasises on statistical fit on the data. The conjunction with impulse response analysis also allows the user to investigate the dynamic response of the system to shocks 'without having to rely on "incredible" identifying restrictions, or potentially controversial restrictions from economic theory' (Garratt et al. 2016, p.16). Compared to SEMs, VAR models allow the rich, dynamic structure of the data 'to speak for itself' (Hoover et al. 2008) instead of being restricted by theory and prior beliefs. Due to the flexibility and ease of estimation, unrestricted VAR models are particularly well used in forecasting.

It should be noted that the stationarity of the data to be fed into VAR is particularly important. Based on the World decomposition theorem (see Hamilton 1994, p.108-109) states that any zero-mean covariance stationary process can be represented as the sum of a deterministic component and a stationary process possessing an infinite order moving average (MA) representation Garratt et al. (p.17 2006a). From this, impulse response functions can be derived for each variable, then the Cholesky decomposition of the covariance matrix is used for the VAR model's shocks, and this allows the MA representation to be written in terms of orthogonalised innovations.

Apart from forecasting, Sims' VAR was also created for policy evaluation, and this is done via impulse response analysis with orthogonalised impulse response function (OIRF) and orthogonalised forecast error variance decomposition (OFEVD). In general, the impulse response function measures the time profile of the effect of exogenous shocks on the expected future values of the economic variables in the VAR model. For example, the modeller could 'forecast' the effects of 1 standard deviation increase in interest on other economic variables such as real GDP, inflation, etc., extended into future time based on the historical data fed into the model. This is akin to a conceptual experiment in which the policymakers could test the response from changing the policy variable (such as interest rate as mentioned above) on the rest of the variables in the model. However, there are some problems with this approach. The computed orthogonalised impulse responses are not unique and depend on the causal ordering of the economic variables. This causal ordering implies a restriction on the economic variables to be chosen in the model, and the order itself is formed based on the modeller's. The identification strategy used in Sims' VAR (1980), as well as in Sims (1992), were both recursive ordering, which requires the modeller to choose the exogeneity of the variables and rank them in order in order to restriction the causality of the shock from one variable to another. For example, weather is likely to affect industrial output and therefore supply, but it is not true the other way, as weather is unlikely to be affected by industrial output and supply (although this assumption could be challenged as climate change could affect output and other economic variables). As the number of variables increased in the VAR model, the user is required to determine the recursive order of each. This is clearly not feasible if there are many variables and countries to be determined. As well as OIRF, OFEVD also relies on Cholesky decomposition. In light of this problem, Koop et al. (1996) provided the concept of generalised impulse response function (GIRF), which is applicable to both linear and non-linear models and circumvent the problem of the dependence of the orthogonalised impulse response to the ordering of the variables (Pesaran and Shin 1998, Pesaran 2015). This recursive ordering also implies that the original unrestricted VAR requires economic theory in order to place the restrictions to be imposed on the variables in order to be identified in the model. It is clear that at least some economic theory is required in order to achieve meaningful restrictions, and this is the approach taken in Structural VAR (SVAR). The seemingly random restrictions imposed, as outlined above, have been the main problem. Due to the lack of economic, unrestricted VAR was referred to as 'non-structural' and 'atheoretical', which did not sit well with many such as Cooley and Leroy (1985). Works in Bernanke (1986), Blanchard and Watson (1986) and Sims (1986) considered a priori restrictions on contemporaneous effects of shocks and developed the framework of SVAR. This contrasts with the unrestricted VAR that economic rationale is now explicitly used for covariance restrictions used. This avoids the use of arbitrary identifying restrictions associated with OIR, as seen above.

4.2.5 Dynamic Stochastic Equilibrium models

The DSGE approach methodology was originally employed in the Real Business Cycle literature Kydland and Prescott (1982), which has since become the essential tool for macroeconomic analysis. The DSGE approach came as a response to Lucas's critique (1976) to build a macroeconomic model based on microfoundations that are not affected by policy changes. Instead of modelling individual markets as was done traditionally, DSGE models the economy as a whole (represented by the behaviour of representative economic agents), thus achieving *general equilibrium*. As the idea is to look at the economy as a whole, and variables are always linked in a multiple and complex relationship; therefore, the usual *ceteris paribus* can be bypassed with this approach.

As mentioned previously, a macroeconomic model can be built from either theory or data, while in practice, most models are built with a mixed proportion in theory and data. Unrestricted VARs and the Structural VARs, as illustrated in the above section, make minimal use of economic theory as it is confined to the restrictions imposed on the model and interpretation of the results. Large scale SEMs utilise economic theories but tend to be in modular form in specific parts of the model; therefore, it raised important issues of inconsistent theory. As a remedy to this problem of inconsistent theory and response to the Lucas critique, DSGE models were developed using a general equilibrium approach to model the whole economy based on 'deep parameters' of the economic agents, e.g. households, firms and government etc. This approach has since become the mainstream and staple tool in macroeconomics until the financial crisis during 2008/2009, which received heavy criticisms and calls for reform, such as in Kocherlakota (2010), Korinek (2017), and Stiglitz (2018). However, Christiano et al. (2017) gave an excellent rebuttal to the critics by illustrating and summarising the DSGE literature and aimed at some common criticisms such as the lacking of the financial sector in a DSGE model (which some works addressed before the crisis and even more post-crisis).

A classic example of an early DSGE model is the Real Business Cycle (RBC) model by Kydland and Prescott (1982) and Long and Plosser (1983). These early models assumed an economy populated by representative agents who operate in perfectly competitive markets in a stochastic environment with uncertainty such as labour or technology shocks. The fluctuations in the economy are considered to be an efficient response to the exogenous shocks; for example, Kydland and Prescott (1991) claimed that 70% of business cycle variation in output reflected the efficient response of the economy to technology shocks. The implication on economic policy is clear that there was no need for any form of government intervention as government policies aimed at stability the business cycle would be welfare-reducing, therefore, counter-productive (Christiano et al. 2017). Broadly defined, DSGE models can be classified into either New Classical DSGE models or New Keynesian models. Typical New Classical DSGE models are based on the assumption of a perfect competition environment, while New Keynesian models included imperfect competition features such as the existence of adjustment costs in the investment process, liquidity constraints, or rigidities in the determination of prices and wages Christiano et al. (2017). These two types of models differ in their additions, but the core is that both are grounded in the microfoundation of the behaviour of economic agents.

The core structure of a typical DSGE model is relatively simple. In contrast to the SEM, the basic block of a DSGE model consists of three main types of economic agents: households, firms and the government. An additional economic agent can also be added, such as a central bank or foreign countries. The economic agents in the DSGE model are represented in the sense that their behaviour is optimising, i.e. an agent maximises a given objective function (such as a utility function consists of consumption and leisure where the consumer has to trade-off) given resource or rule restrictions such as a budget constraint. Depending on the assumptions of the model, the behavioural functions for respective agents can also be modelled differently. Thus by observing the basic rules of different economic agents and model them based on such rules with their respective objective functions, competitive equilibrium can be derived, meaning that all markets (goods, services, capital and labour market) are in equilibrium.

The basis of the DGE model (without the stochastic element) was initially developed in the 1920s by Ramsey (1927, 1928) and extended by Cass (1965), which is better known as the Ramsey growth model. It is a neoclassical model of economic growth with a finite number of agents with an infinite time horizon, meaning that agent's decisions are made on an infinite time basis such that the agents will live forever, therefore, making consistent choices. The intuition behind this assumption is that agencies such as the government, although they do not exist indefinitely, their *revealed decisions* are made on the assumption that they will exist indefinitely. The assumption of the infinite horizon can be dropped and instead employ an overlapping-generations model (OLG), in which there is a continual entry of new households and agents into the economy (Diamond, 1965). Another important assumption is that agents are also completely alike; therefore, it is a *representative* agent model. This assumption is often employed in the DSGE literature in which the behaviour of households, families or consumers have identical preferences (with respect to their own group) and can be modelled as representative agents. This assumption that all households or firms are the same—and which does not resemble reality—has caused many criticisms in the literature (such as Stiglitz 2018) and has entailed a long and endless debate in economic philosophy and methodology such as in Friedman (1968), on whether the assumptions should represent the reality or is the prediction from the model enough. Nonetheless, it allows us to analyse the behaviour and reactions from the economy as a whole and provides a neat and basic benchmark case for other alterations on the assumptions to be compared with.

Another important aspect of DSGE is the element of time. DSGE explicitly allows time into the model as when a shock (such as technological shock) enters into the economy; macroeconomic variables do not return to the equilibrium instantly but change slowly over time, which could produce complex reactions as the economy is in a stochastic environment and is subject to a variety of shocks such as technological, productivity, consumption, etc. This is the assumption in the RBC literature, which explicitly includes an exogenous variable (which is assumed to follow a stochastic process) into the deterministic version of the model. From this, the model can be estimated (or calibrated), and the modeller can then carry out numerical experiments such as inducing an economic shock to observe the dynamic changes in the economic variables. Economists and policymakers often employ this approach to determine the effect of changing a policy variable on other variables.

One of the complaints on the DSGE model is the lack of financial variables and also the housing sector included in the model. However, Christiano et al. (2017) rebutted and summarised other papers in the literature that incorporated financial frictions and the housing sector into their models. Examples include Iacoviello (2005) and Iacoviello and Neri (2010), where the authors studied the effect of shocks on the housing sector when the value of housing constraints household borrowing. Liu et al. (2013) also used a DSGE model to study the interaction of land and house prices over the business cycle, and Berger et al. (2015) developed one with financial frictions to analyse the response of consumption to changes in house prices.

Regarding DSGE for forecasting, Edge and Gurkaynak (2011) have found that DSGE models are very poor for forecasting GDP growth and inflation, but it was mainly due to the wrong specification of the model and concluded the failure of the forecast for the financial crisis should be not used to judge models. Earlier, Adolfson et al. (2007) and Edge et al. (2010) compared DSGE with other less complex models such as VAR for forecasting performance and found that simple VAR and VECM are better at forecasting, particular with Bayesian estimation techniques, see Herbst and Schorfheide (2015), DSGE model can also be used for forecasting. However, Gürkaynak et al. (2013) compared the standard, mainstream DSGE model in Smets and Wouters (2007) with a typical simple AR model and VAR model with out-of-sample data and found that DSGE models are poorer for short-run forecasting but better in the long-run.

Both the DSGE modelling approach and the structural cointegrating VAR approach represent attempts to combine theory and evidence to obtain models that will be useful for policy- and decision-makers. The differences in approach reflect modellers' strength of conviction on different aspects of theory and evidence. So, the structural cointegrating VAR approach assumes that we understand how the economy works in the long-run with some degree of confidence and allows the theory to inform this aspect of modelling. But it is less sure on the short-run dynamics and so turns to the evidence on these. In comparison, the DSGE approach emphasises the use of theory in the modelling of both the short-run and long-run.

4.3 The structural cointegrating VAR approach and Global Vector Autoregressive

Recall that the main justification of Sim's VAR approach is the indifference on both the endogeneity and the exogeneity of the variables. This logic also applies to the GVAR but with a modification. Given the general nature of interdependencies in the world economy, it is supposed that all country-specific variables and common global observed factors such as oil and commodity prices should be treated as endogenously (as part of the system, i.e. a closed world economy). However, this is also the largest culprit for the undesirability of using unrestricted VAR for global macroeconomic modelling. The straightforwardness of unrestricted VAR models is constrained by its computational limitation. As the variables of interest and the size of economies also increased in our model, the parameters in each equation of the model to be estimated follow the rule of mp(N+1) (See Garratt et al. 2006a), which implies that if we have six macro variables, 31 economies, and a lag order of 2, this means we will need 384 parameters to be estimated for each equation. This is practically impossible as there isn't enough data series for such estimation. This problem has become known as 'the curse of dimensionality.' While it is possible in principle to extend the modelling strategy to cover the same m variables in each of, say, N +1 separate economies, in practice, this would involve the estimation of a co-integrated VAR involving around mp(N+1) parameters in each equation of the model to be estimated (where p is the order of the VAR). If there are five variables modelled in each economy, 20 economies, and a lag order of 2 is used, at least 210 parameters to be estimated in each equation are generated, which is clearly infeasible for the data series that are available. In our model, the aim is to understand the transmission of shocks across economies and time. However, using VAR is infeasible, as shown above, due to the proliferation of unknown parameters to be estimated. The method proposed in Sims (1980) to solve the curse of dimensionality is to impose a set of restrictions on the VAR model so that the model can be estimated. However, as mentioned in section 1.3.4, this method requires extensive time to impose an order to the variables, which can be inconsistent, and the result is also not unique. It is clear that the method to model a large system based on individual VAR models (each representing one country) is very attractive but is hurdled by the curse of dimensionality.

To tackle this problem, the framework of Global VAR (GVAR) was conceived in Pesaran et al. (2004), which provided a relatively simple yet effective way of modelling large and complex systems such as the world economy. Although, as the reader can see, GVAR is not the only model available for modelling the world economy. Its strengths are dealing with the curse of dimensionality in a theoretically coherent and statistically consistent manner (Pesaran 2015; Chudik and Pesaran 2016). In comparison, GVAR provides a complete and closed system that allows simulation analysis with empirical data accommodating multiple countries while other alternative modelling strategies do not (Granger and Jeon 2007).

The introduction of the GVAR model was in Pesaran et al. (2004). The authors created a model that was originally developed in the aftermath of the 1997 East Asian financial crisis to quantify the effects of macroeconomic conditions from a national and global perspective. The basic framework was further expanded upon in Dees et al. (2007), where more countries and data are used, and more discussion on handling issues such as structural breaks more clearly. It should be noted that GVAR itself is a continuation of the works on co-integrating VAR, like Johansen's (1988) and Hoover et al. (2008), but with an emphasis that the long-run relationship between economic variables are determined by macroeconomic theories; thus, it was referred to as a long-run structural approach (or structural cointegrating VAR approach) in Garratt et al. (2006a). The book by Garratt et al. was a culmination of the research on this long-run structural approach, containing a detailed chapter comparing this approach with large scale SEM, DSGE and unrestricted VAR. However, although the application of GVAR was already published in Pesaran et al. (2004), there is only a short mention of the GVAR approach at the end of chapter 3 as the rest of the book was focusing on modelling a single country with the long-run structural approach. To clarify, the GVAR approach is a generalised and expansion on the long-run structural approach that allows multiple countries (or units) to be modelled under the same framework. The readers are encouraged to review this publication as the details on how macroeconomic theories are incorporated into GVAR and the detailed comparison between alternative models are lacking in more recent and more cited publications such as di Mauro and Pesaran (2013a), Pesaran (2015), Chudik and Pesaran (2016).

Since then, there have been numerous applications of the GVAR approach developed over the past decade. The GVAR approach has also found its way into policy institutions, including the International Monetary Fund (IMF) and the European Central Bank (ECB), where this approach is one of the main techniques used to understand interlinkages across individual countries such as Dées et al. (2007), Chudik and Fratzscher (2011), Al-Haschimi and Dées (2013), Greenwood-Nimmo et al. (2013), Cesa-Bianchi et al. (2013), and Eickmeier and Ng (2015). Particular mention is also needed for The GVAR Handbook, edited by di Mauro and Smith (2013). It is a collected work focused on the application of the GVAR mainly pitched to academics and also policymakers. The book provides an interesting collection of empirical applications from 27 contributors with backgrounds in major central banks, thus illustrating how the model is being used

at their respective institutions. This handbook provides a historical background of
the GVAR approach (Chapter 1), describes an updated version of the basic DdPS
model by Dees et al. (2007) (Chapter 2), and then provides seven applications of
the GVAR approach on the international transmission of shocks and forecasting
(Chapters 3–9), three finance applications (Chapters 10–12), and five regional
applications. The applications in the handbook span various areas of the
empirical literature. Chapters on the international transmission on forecasting
investigate, among others, the problem of measuring output gaps across
countries, structural modelling, the role of financial markets in the transmission
of international business cycles, international inflation interlinkages, and
forecasting the global economy. Finance applications include a macroprudential
application of the GVAR approach, a model of sovereign bond spreads, and an
analysis of cross-country spillover effects of fiscal spending on financial variables.
Regional applications are also plenty, such as investigating the increasing
importance of the Chinese economy, forecasting the Swiss economy, imbalances
in the euro area, regional and financial spillovers across Europe, and modelling
interlinkages in the West African Economic and Monetary Union. In the rest of this
section, we first review the long-run structural approach methodology before
embarking on the GVAR method and some literature applications.

4.3.1 Long-run structural approach

As mentioned above, the long-run structural approach (or structural
cointegrating VAR) is a precursor to the GVAR method as GVAR was an
extension that allowed the application of the long-run structural to multiple
countries. As stated in Garratt et al. (2006c),

> [the long-run structural] approach is based on the desire to develop a
> macroeconometric model that has transparent theoretical foundations,
> providing insights on the behavioural relationships that underlie the
> functioning of the macroeconomy. Implicit in the modelling approach
> is the belief that economic theory is most informative about the long-
> run relationships, as compared to the short-run restrictions that are
> more contentious. The approach is based on the desire to develop a
> macroeconometric model that has transparent theoretical foundations,
> providing insights on the behavioural relationships that underlie the
> functioning of the macroeconomy. Implicit in the modelling approach
> is the belief that economic theory is most informative about the long-
> run relationships, as compared to the short-run restrictions that are
> more contentious.

At the outset, it is clear that the philosophy behind this approach is using macroeconomic theory in the long-run while 'letting the data speak' in the short-run as often in the cointegrating literature such as Hoover et al. (2008) but with a much stronger emphasis on the long-run with macroeconomic theory. This is in strong contrast to the ad-hoc and modular theories applied in large-scale SEMs and coherent but more restrictive DSGE models (thus limiting short-run dynamics as restricted by theory). While the approach is focused on the long-run restrictions, it is also possible to impose short-run restrictions to test and investigate specific theories (such as the impact on monetary shocks in the short-run) without impact the long-run restrictions (or vice versa).

The approach begins with an explicit statement of a set of long-run relationships between the macroeconomic variables in the system. The long-run relationships among the variables are derived from macroeconomic theory and are then embedded within a VARX (vector autoregressive with exogeneity) model. The works on VARX was originally developed by Gali (1992), Crowder et al. (1999) and later fully developed by Pesaran et al. (2001b, 2006) and applied to national and global macroeconometric modelling in Pesaran et al. (2004). The main difference between an unrestricted VAR, as in Sims (1980), is that VARX is augmented with weakly exogenous or long-run forcing (as defined in Engle et al. 1983) foreign variables such as oil price, metal prices which are global and used by many other countries. This is built on the assumption that the individual macroeconomic series is not stationary and have a unit root. The long-run relationships are then derived from the theory associated with the cointegrating relationship between the variables, and the existence of these cointegrating relationships imposes restrictions on a VAR model as a VARX (Garratt et al. 2006a, p.7). This assumption can be tested, as shown in di Mauro and Smith (2013), and this assumption is often correct. The economic rationale behind this is that each small country, relative to the world economy and mathematically, allows multiple countries to be stacked together as a single GVAR model in order to be solved later.

Compared to the cointegrating VAR advanced by Johansen (1991), the long-run structural approach places more emphasis on macroeconomic theory in order to explicitly state cointegrating relations with the VARX models. The usual cointegrating VAR begins with an unrestricted VAR and then impose restrictions on the long-run relations later in the analysis without a clear, a priori view of the economy's structural relations. While the latter works relatively well for a system with only one cointegrating relationship among the variables. It is often very difficult, if not impossible, for this to be applied when there are more than two cointegrating relations (Garratt et al. 2006c).

The long-run structural approach explicitly requires the modeller to determine the long-run relationships in the form of individual VARX models (e.g. if there are ten countries in the model, then there will be 10 VARX models, each representing one country). When the models are estimated, the model possesses transparency that is often lost in the large-scale SEM, and the approach here is much easier to interpret. Another important advantage of this approach is the clarified relationship between the short- and long-run restrictions of the model, allowing analysis of the effects of shocks much clearer. Combing the use of GIRF (for details, see 1.3.4) eliminates the needs to order variables in the system. Compared to alternative methods, this avoids some of the difficulties, such as rigid economic theory and imposing restrictions that often result in poor data fit.

4.3.2 Global Vector Autoregressive model

The exposition of the approach in Garratt et al. (2006c) was primarily aimed at modelling a single open economy, and the authors used the UK as an example and linked the national economy to the world via a VARX model augmented with foreign country economic variables. This also allowed analysis of shocks which the authors used impulse response functions to interpret the results. This approach was further developed when combing multiple countries into a single GVAR model. For example, Pesaran et al. (2004) and Dees et al. (2007) showed how this can be done.

The GVAR approach can be described as a two-step process. The first step is built on the long-run structural approach above. This step assumes that there are N+1 countries in the global economy, indexed by i = 0, 1,. . ., N, and the aim is to relate a set of country-specific variables, e.g. GDP, inflation, interest rates, etc. that are of interest to the modeller. As the model contains a large number of variables, it is best to represent using linear algebra as per the standard convention in the literature. The vector of interest denoted as **x** collects the macroeconomic variables specific to the individual countries of interest indexed by i and over time, indexed by t=0,1,...,T. It also imposes the assumption of weak exogeneity of foreign country-specific and global variables. In other words, it assumes that the individual economy is actually relatively small in terms of the world economy except for the special case of the US (Dees et al. 2007). The weak exogeneity is then tested empirically to see whether this assumption holds. Specifically, an individual country (economy) is represented by a VARX model (or in its error-correction form VECMX), which links the domestic economy (defined by a range of domestic macroeconomic variables) to foreign economies (defined by corresponding foreign variables), which are treated as weakly exogenous. The domestic and foreign economies are then linked via weights matrices which match the international linkages in trade.

For example, the weight of Britain (domestic) is expected to have a large trade with the EU countries such as Germany (foreign); therefore, it will have a larger weight than, say, Malaysia. It should be noted that, similarly to the framework of an unrestricted VAR, the VARX model can also be written in its error-correction form VECMX, which allows the differentiation of short and long-run effects. In particular, the long-run effects being treated as co-integrating. The individual VECMX models are estimated separately for each country i, based on reduced rank regression (see Pesaran (2015), thus identifying the long-run effects or I(1) relationships that exist within and across the domestic variables and also the foreign economic variables. Thus, the total number of co-integrating relations, the speed of adjustment for each country can be derived and given economic meaning.

The second step then stacks all individual country models together in a theoretically consistent manner that can be solved as a whole (for a brief introduction see di Mauro and Smith (2013) and full derivation of the method see Chudik and Pesaran (2016). The solution can be used for scenario analysis and forecasting, as is usually done with alternative DSGE or VAR models. The GVAR model has numerous applications that are catered for policymakers, such as traditional shock analysis and conditional forecasting (see di Mauro and Pesaran 2013b for a number of applications and also Pesaran 2015 for a brief review of applications in the literature). Although the primary interest mentioned so far are based on individual countries with the world economy, this is not necessary as the basic units in a GVAR can be organised as regions (a collection of local countries etc.), industries, banks or sectors in any given economy. For example, papers from the ECB uses a mixed cross-section GVAR model for country data to link with firm-level data (such as banks; Gross and Kok 2013, 2016). Although the individual models are estimated country by country, shocks can be transmitted across countries as each individual is connected to other foreign countries via the weight matrix. Therefore there are three channels of shock transmissions, namely via 1) direct dependence of domestic variables on foreign variables (and also lagged values), 2) dependence of the region-specific variables on common global exogenous variables such as oil and material prices, and 3) non-zero contemporaneous dependence of shocks in region i on the shocks in region j (Garratt et al. 2006c, p.64).

4.3.3 Empirical applications

The GVAR developed in Pesaran et al. (2004)[7] was intended to analyse credit risk among multiple countries. As indicated in The GVAR Handbook, there have been many applications developed since the initial publication. As mentioned previously, the ability to model many countries and their respective variables under a single, theory consistent model that allow scenario analysis and conditional forecasting has been proven to be very popular among central bankers. Publicly accessible works from central banks with the GVAR method include Ng and Eickmeier (2013), where the authors were interested in the credit supply shocks propagation via the GVAR method; it was further expanded in 2015 to identify the specific US shocks (Eickmeier and Ng 2015). Chudik and Fratzscher (2011) from the European Central Bank also used the approach for the global transmission of the financial crisis from 2007 to 2009 with the GVAR model. Similar to those principles of the GVAR modelling laid down in Dées et al. (2007), Chudik and Fratzscher also employed the now standardised global model-identification of shocks and impulse response analysis procedure. Although the GVAR has its main application in international shock transmission, it is also capable of carrying out other applications in economics and finance; Favero (2013) at Deutsche Bank used it to model and forecast government spread in the Euro area. Melecky and Podpiera (2012) at the World Bank, for example, used it for macroprudential stress testing for central banks in central and southeastern Europe. In another ECB paper, Bussière et al. (2009) used the GVAR model to model global trade flows and the GIRFs to stimulate shocks. In more recent papers, Gross and Kok (2016) built a mixed-cross-section GVAR model that included 23 sovereigns and 41 international banks, for which the authors modelled their credit default swap spreads. The paper concluded that should large shocks of a size similar to the euro crisis in 2011/2012 occur, the effects would have been more pronounced and more synchronised across the countries and banks.

Due to its versatility in accommodating multiple countries and economic variables, many applications have been published regarding international transmission and forecasting. For example, Garratt et al. (2016) looked at the

---

[7] Although the GVAR approach is conceptually simple, it requires some programming skills since it handles large-data sets and it is not yet incorporated in any of the mainstream econometric software packages. Fortunately, an open-source toolbox developed by Smith and Galesi together with a global macroeconomic data set, covering the period 1979–2013, can be obtained from the web https://sites.google.com/site/gvarmodelling/. This toolbox has greatly facilitated empirical research using the GVAR methodology and appeared to be the standard and only toolbox available for GVAR.

performance of the G7 economies in relation to global recessions. Galesi and Sgherri (2013) developed a GVAR model containing 27 countries in Europe and key economic powers such as China, Japan, and the US and assess the relevance of international spillovers following the slowdown in US equity prices. Specifically, each country model is linked to others by a set of foreign variables such as bilateral bank lending exposures. The authors found that asset prices are the main channel through which shocks are transmitted in the short-run while cost and credit supply are more important in the long-run. In Galesi and Lombardi (2013), the authors assessed the extent to which oil and food price shocks transmit to the inflationary outlook and the real economy with the GVAR model. The paper found that there are direct inflationary effects of oil price shocks affecting most developed countries but less for emerging economies. The food price increase also has significant inflationary effects but particularly pronounced for emerging economies. In another paper, Greenwood-Nimmo et al. (2013) used a GVAR model for scenario-based forecasting and counterfactual analysis. The applied used probabilistic forecasting to analysing global imbalances with conditional probability for a given event or a combination of events and found that GVAR models are particularly well-suited to scenario-based analysis when there are rich datasets. The research focused on more regional interlinkages are also seen in Han et al. (2016), Chen et al. (2017), Cashin et al. (2017b), Dreger and Zhang (2014), Feldkircher and Korhonen (2012), Ma et al. (2012), and Osorio and Unsal (2013), which looked at the impact on the rise of the Chinese economy to other countries in particular. Other regional applications also include ASEAN Tan (2016), European Union (Castrén et al., 2010, Backé et al., 2013, Dragomirescu-Gaina and Philippas, 2015, Feldkircher, 2015, Hájek and Horváth, 2016), Japan (Ganelli and Tawk, 2017), Middle East (Mensi 2017), Nigeria (Oyelami and Olomola 2016), Swiss (Katrin 2013) and the US economy (Georgiadis 2016 and Subrahmanyam 2016), etc. In a unique study by Cashin et al. (2017a), the paper investigated the impacts of El Niño weather shocks (measured by the Southern Oscillation Index, SOI) on world economies. As weather events are exogenous in nature, their shock has a profound impact, and the authors found that considerable heterogeneities in the responses of the shock, with many experiences a short-lived fall in economic performance while others experience a growth-enhancing effect due to an increase in short-term commodity price increases.

4.3.4 Canonical GVAR model for shock transmission

Although there are many different types of GVAR and its applications in the literature, most began in the now-canonical paper by Dées et al. (2007), which laid out the identification, estimation and specification strategy to build a

GVAR model. In di Mauro and Smith (2013), the authors reintroduced this model and updated it with the latest data to 2013. This section examines the model in this paper and its finer technical details, particularly regarding the specification that was not discussed before.

The model in this study describes the relationships between and across 33 countries from 1979 q1 – 2013 q1, extending the study in Dées et al. (2007) by seven quarters. The current model contains 33 countries, of which eight eurozone countries are grouped into Euro Area and treated as one country (in the sense of a separate VARX model). This list of the countries in the model consists of the US, China, Japan, UK, Euro area (Germany, France, Italy, Spain, Netherlands, Belgium, Austria, Finland), Canada, Australia, New Zealand, Sweden, Switzerland, Norway, Korea, Indonesia, Thailand, Philippines, Malaysia, Singapore, India, South Africa, Turkey, Saudi Arabia, Brazil, Mexico, Argentina, Chile and Peru. As it stands, it contains the bulk of the world output at around 90% (di Mauro and Pesaran, 2013, p.18). It is not surprising that due to data quality and availability, semi-emerging economies such as Russia, Nigeria, Pakistan, and Vietnam are not selected. It should also be noted that, due to the strict requirement of the data, most African countries are not included in the model. The variables included in each individual VARX model for both domestic and foreign countries are real output, inflation, real exchange rate, real equity price, short-term interest rate, long-term interest rate. The common global variables also included oil price, raw material, and metal prices.

Recall that a generic VARX (p,q) model has lag orders p for domestic lag order and q for foreign variables. The exact lag orders to be selected are similar to those employed in time series literature with the Akaike information criterion (AIC) or the Schwarz Bayesian criterion (SBC). This is embedded in the GVAR toolbox, and the largest values from AIC or SBC are selected for the lag orders. The table would give the lag orders selected by either AIC or SBC, whichever value is the highest. It should be noted that it does not matter whether the lag orders of p and q are equal.

Unit root tests are then used to identify short-run and long-run relations (as in cointegration). Like many other papers in the literature, the Augmented Dickey-Fuller test is used instead of the older standard Dickey-Fuller test. The ADF test was carried out at 95%, implying if the test statistic for the variable is more negative than the critical values, then it will be rejected as there is no unit root. The test was carried out on level, differenced, and twice differenced, with trend and without trend on all variables. The test results indicate most variables have either I(0) or I(1) characteristic, which is expected for the GVAR approach. The next step is the identification of the cointegrating relationships within the individual models. The rank of cointegrating relationships for each model is then computed using Johansen's trace and maximal eigenvalue statistics (see Pesaran et al. 2000).

Testing for weak exogeneity. As mentioned before, the main assumption in the GVAR approach is the weak exogeneity of the foreign variables x^* with respect to the respective VARX model. As described in Pesaran et al. (2004), this assumption is compatible with a certain degree of weak dependence across the residuals. Following the work on weak exogeneity testing by Johansen (1991), the weak exogeneity assumption implies no long-run feedback from x to x^*, suggesting that x^* error correction terms of the individual country VECMX models do not enter in the marginal model of x^*. This implies we can consistently estimate the VARX models individually and later combing together to form the GVAR. The proof of weak exogeneity implication on x^* can be seen in Pesaran (2015, p.569). The test is a regression model described in Harbo et al. (1998). The regression was run on the foreign variables in the VARX models real output, inflation, equity price, short-term interest rate, long-term interest rate, as well as the global variables such as the price of metal, oil, and raw material with 5% significance level. Based on all 208 regression runs, only nine variables (4.3%) cannot meet the assumption. This result is a slight increase from Pesaran (2004). As a result, the foreign long-term interest rate would not enter Australia, Brazil, and Turkey in the VARX models.

Another important property in the time-series analysis is the disruption from structural breaks. Having considered the integrated series in the previous section and the possible violations of weak exogeneity and its treatment, we now turn to one of the most fundamental econometric modelling problems. So far, we have shown that the problems mentioned above can be mitigated but unfortunately, similarly to other time-series / econometric models, the GVAR is also susceptible to structural breaks. The core concept of structural breaks is straightforward; it refers to the unexpected sudden shift of the time-series. Consider a daily stock price time series where a sudden shift is very common due to stock split, unexpected announcements, overnight trading, oversea stock exchange performance etc. This renders the original time-series model unreliable as the time-series shifted unexpectedly and are therefore not within the range of the forecast; this also implies forecast errors with be greater. The problem of structural breaks has been discussed extensively in the literature since the 1960s by Quandt (1958, 1960), who proposed the Sup F test that calculates the likelihood ratio test for a change in model parameters and identifies the break date. The Sup F test was quite adaptable but only worked on univariate regression; nevertheless, it became the basis for future research. In the GVAR literature—mainly those in Pesaran and Timmermann (2004),

Pesaran et al. (2006), Dees et al. (2007), Pesaran et al. (2009)—there has been an extensive discussion of the problem. The GVAR Handbook surveyed the existing strategy that was employed. These include several test statistics to assess the structural stability of the estimated coefficients and error variances of the individual VARX / VECMX models. Specifically, the survey indicated the methods used are (p.21): the maximal OLS cumulative sum (CUSUM) statistic, and its mean square variant by Ploberger and Krämer (1992); a test for parameter constancy against non-stationary alternatives by Nyblom (1989); as well as sequential Wald type tests "of a one-time structural change at an unknown change point specifically"; also the QLR statistic by Quandt (1960), the MW statistic Hansen (1992), and the APW statistic Andrews and Ploberger (1994).'

Although structural breaks occur more in the current model, overall, it is similar to those described in the literature. As Dees et al. (2007) concluded, they are mostly from the error variances that would not impact the application with impulse responses despite the evidence for some structural breaks. It is based on the bootstrap method for median and confidence boundaries rather than just point estimates. It would not be surprising to find that the dates are mostly related to episodes of financial distresses as it is when volatility dominates.

The main application of the VAR models for dynamic analysis is from the impulse response function (IRF) and also variance decompositions. In particular, the IRF can answer scenario-type what if questions such as the effect of a negative shock on the equity price of GDP in the US. Essentially the IRF calculates the effects of shocks on the path of the selected variables. Consider a generic univariate series where the series begins with a value of 0 and takes on a shock of vt. If we assume the shock happened at $t=1$, then the series would become v. By using recursive substitution, we can define the time path of y following the initial shock as the impulse response function. In order words, it displays what happens to the variable y after a certain shock over time. This is, of course, rather simple as it involves only one variable. However, if there is more than one variable in the system, then it becomes significantly more difficult to discover the shocks, i.e. identifying where is the shock coming from. This problem is commonly referred to as the identification problem.

In light of this difficulty, Pesaran et al. 2014, Pesaran and Smith (2006) and other GVAR literature have mainly adopted the generalised IRF (GIRF) approach proposed by Koop et al. (1996). The GIRF is no longer relying on the ordering of the variables. The studies used GIRFs to study the dynamic properties of the global model and graphs presenting the time-persistent profiles from different shocks applied were shown in the end, indicating the effects of a particular shock on another variable. For example, the paper presented three different scenarios, 1) Negative one standard error real equity price shock from the US on real GDP, 2) Positive one standard error oil price shock on real GDP, and 3) Positive one standard error increase of US real interest rate on inflation.

In the case of negative one standard error equity price from the US, it is clear that it will negatively impact the largest economies, including China, Japan, the Euro area, Korea, Saudi Arabia, and the UK. Upon the impact, the strongest effect is on South Korea, which could lead to an estimated 1% fall in its GDP. The heavy potential lost is mostly due to the trading weights of Korea with the US. It is also alarming that Korea's heavy influence by the US equity market, which could lead to a long term effect of more than 2% downfall in real GDP.

In the second scenario, a positive oil price shock of one standard error magnitude was used to shock the world economies on their real GDP. During this simulation, the Latin American countries in the existing model are combined to a single region and compared to three other areas, namely Euro, the UK and the US. Although both the UK and the US are net oil exporters, the rising price of oil price will temperately boost the economy in the forms of the energy sector, but soon after two quarters, the impact becomes negative as it chases up with the price in the wider economy. The result from the GIRFs for the UK and US exhibit similar behaviour of the oil shocks in the 1970s and 2000s.The case of the Euro is poor; with an initial decrease in its GDP that could cost up to 3% of the output and does not stabilise until a year later. The ultimate winner here is the Latin American group, as many are oil exporters, including Brazil, Peru, and Venezuela, but similarly, the effect is diminished by the end of the first year, although it does accumulate an average growth from 5% to 1% as it stabilises.

The last scenario is a positive shock to the real US interest rate on the real inflation rate. Here we have four different areas: Argentina, Canada, Euro and the US. From the shape of the graph, Argentina appears to be largely indifferent with an equal size of confidence intervals on both sides. Although it is possible, it should be noted that the lack of the debt information in the model had significantly discounted the effect, which saw Argentina defaulting on its debt in 2014 as it could no longer increase the cost of refinancing. The graph for Canada is more plausible as the US is its largest trading partner; thus, it would increase its inflation rate. This is also shown in the case of the Euro. While domestically, the US would receive a sharp growth of inflation up to 0.2% until its later stabilisation.

4.3.5 Monetary policy shock in GVAR

From the example of the canonical model above, it is easy to see that the choices are almost infinite as there are no particular methods on which variables to act as an exogenous shock on all other variables in the model. However, in order for an analysis to have any economic meaning, the modeller must posit a relevant question and, according to the GVAR, let macroeconomic theory determine the long-run and the data to reveal the short-run. As seen before, GVAR is particularly well adapted for shock transmission and analysis. Although the concept of a shock is quite intuitive, the definition is often ambiguous. The concept to be adopted in this chapter, as well as the often unstated definition in many papers, is the one used in Ramey (2016) and originally suggested in Bernanke (1986, p.52-55), which indicated that a shock should be primitive exogenous forces that are uncorrelated with each other and they should be economically meaningful. Another important aspect is that the shock should be unexpected.

While many potential applications are using GVAR, the analysis of monetary shock is particularly important and proven to be challenging to the modelling literature. In this last section, we briefly review the background of monetary policy and its transmission mechanism and identification strategy used in the GVAR approach. In the end, we also point out some research directions.

During recent decades, the global economy has become more intertwined with trade and financial integration. Therefore the importance of spillover effect of shocks from one country, say a monetary shock in the US, is likely to affect other foreign economies than just itself. For example, Rey (2015) and Bekaert et al. (2013) argued that financial conditions and growth worldwide are driven by a global financial cycle, which appears to be determined by monetary policy in the US. As the variables involved in fiscal policies such as taxes have direct and immediate effects on consumers and investors, the design and implementation of fiscal policies are often highly politicised. This is in contrast to monetary policy, which is often seen as more opaque by the public and is often blamed by politicians as central bank decisions are perceived as less transparent Issing (2005). For example, Favero et al. (2011) have found that fiscal policy multipliers and the effects are heterogeneous in nature and are determined by debt dynamics, degree of openness of the economies and fiscal reaction functions across the countries in the study. Although the typical instrument of monetary policy is confined to altering interest rate and reserve requirement, the actual mechanism on how it affected the economy via different channels such as asset prices and/or credit effects etc. (see table 4.1).

Table 4.1: Table adapted from (Boivin et al., 2010)

Neoclassical Channels		*Non-Neoclassical Channels*	
Channel	Description	Channel	Description
Interest rate / cost-of-capital / Tobin's q	Changes in short-term policy rates affect the user cost of capital for consumer and business investment	Regulation-induced credit effects	Restrictions on financial institutions (e.g., deposit rate effects ceilings, credit restrictions) affect spending
Wealth effects	Changes in short-term interest rates affect discounted present values and/or Tobin's Q for various types of assets, and these changes in the market value of assets induce changes in consumption	Bank-based channels	Banks play a special role in addressing problems of asymmetric information. Thus, decreases in bank's lending capacity impact spending
Intertemporal substitution	Changes in short-term interest rates affect the slope of the consumption profile	Balance-sheet channel	Changes in net worth associated with the asset price effects of monetary actions influence external finance premia facing firms and households
Exchange rate effects	Changes in short-run policy interest rates induce changes in the exchange rate through uncovered- interest parity and/or portfolio balance effects		

Understanding how monetary policy affects the economy is important as it is essential to evaluate and set policy instrument, e.g. short term interest rate, and assess the timing and effect of the policies on the economy. Monetary policy is typically carried out by the monetary authority such as a central bank or currency board. Depending on the mandates given to the central bank, monetary policies usually target the inflation rate and/or interest rate to ensure the trust of the currency. Some central banks, such as the Fed, are dual-mandated to aim for price stability and maximum sustainable employment. In contrast to a fiscal policy where the policymakers have a wide choice of instruments to choose from, in general, there are two conventional instruments by central banks, such as managing the short-term interest rates and changing the reserve requirements for commercial banks. This allows the central bank to conduct either expansionary or contrary policy depending on the period it is in the business cycle. An unconventional tool such as quantitative easing was used by major central banks during the Great Recession from 2007 as short term interest rates were approaching zero, hence the risk of a liquidity trap.

Understanding the central bank's mandate is important as this affects the identification strategy in the model. For example, Georgiadis (2016) studied global spillovers from US monetary shocks with a GVAR model with 61 countries from 1999 to 2009. The authors identified the US monetary shock by imposing sign restrictions on the responses of output growth and inflation which was originally used in Ng and Eickmeier (2013). The sign restrictions approach to orthogonal (structural) shock identification consists of constructing impulse response functions for a large number of candidate shocks that are all orthogonal. In the end, it reports some statistic of this set of impulse response functions via graphs of persistent time profile. In an earlier paper, Georgiadis (2015) studied the transmission of euro area monetary policy across EU member states and used sign restrictions to identify the shocks. The author found that the effects of EU and US monetary policy shocks are heterogeneous across countries. For example, countries with foreign output effects larger than the domestic effects for many countries. In the European case, countries with more wage and fewer unemployment rigidities are found to exhibit stronger output effects.

In another paper, Feldkircher and Huber (2016), the authors found that US monetary shocks have the most pronounced effects on real output internationally. The authors examined the international transmission of aggregate demand, supply and monetary policy shocks from the US economy on foreign countries. Instead of the plain GVAR, the authors used a Bayesian version which was coupled with a specific prior that allows for variable selection at the country level. Structural shocks were identified via constraining impulse response functions in the US model. The authors also examined the transmission channel on how US shocks were spread. It was found that financial channels are particularly important as the response of domestic interest rates tend to be strong in the short-run. Trade channel was also found to be significant as real effective exchange rates tend to appreciate an expansionary US aggregate demand shock. The paper concludes that the patterns found in the impulse response functions are well in line with the economic theories regarding these types of shocks.

In a survey of monetary transmission mechanisms, Boivin et al. (2010) identified the ways monetary shocks are transmitted via either neoclassical and/or non-neoclassical channels. The table above summarises the channels. The authors found that neoclassical links between variables, such as short-term interest rates, asset prices, long-term interest rates, equity prices and exchange rate, etc., have remained steady from traditional macroeconometric, public-models such as the Fair model or Penn-MIT SSRC MPS Model and also modern DSGE models. However, non-neoclassical channels such as credit-based channels have remained outside of the main models. One future direction of research suggested by the paper is the role of non-neoclassical channels in understanding economic fluctuation and monetary policy. The paper compared how different types of macroeconomic models (i.e. SEM, DSGE and FAVAR) incorporated these channels policies.

4.4 Concluding remarks.

To conclude, we have reviewed the main macroeconometric models that have been used by academics and policymakers in policy analysis. Particular attention was paid to how macromodelling has evolved and the implication on the types of models to be used. To recap, we began at the early macroeconometric models, which were large scale SEMs that dominated until the 1970s. We then considered the disintegration of how economists model the world economy as implicated by Lucas and Sims. Since then, two strands of modelling approaches were used, namely DSGE and VAR. Having reviewed these two models, including their identification strategy and specification, GVAR was presented in which detailed discussion was made on the methodology and applications. A canonical form of the GVAR model was also presented to illustrate the common formation and the applications for transmission analysis.

In the final section, the reader can see that the GVAR approach was used to identify monetary (and other) shocks and estimate their impacts in different scenarios. We also noted that similar models that were covered previously were also applied to this problem. In particular, Boivin et al. (2010) provided a detailed review of how shocks are transmitted via different channels and how different models were used to model these dynamics. We have reviewed a few other publications that were focused on the monetary shocks with GVAR; however, what is lacking is that there are no comparisons made between GVAR and other models in this area. Although there are similar models such as SVAR and FAVAR which were compared, comparative studies on GVAR have been lacking, perhaps due to its relatively recent adoption in the literature.

Another interesting topic to be investigated is the strategy of shock identification. As seen in the previous review, the strategy used in GVAR have so far been limited to Cholesky decompositions and sign restrictions. It would be very useful to compare with other identification methods that are commonly used, such as contemporary restrictions, factor-augmented VAR (FAVAR) and estimated DSGE models Ramey (2016).

The comparison and potentially integration of GVAR and DSGE approx is also appealing. Noted by Chudik and Pesaran (2016, p.190), GVAR provides a coherent reduced form of VAR representation of the global economy, and the solution of DSGE is a VAR model; therefore, it will be useful to bring these two modelling methods together. For example, Dees et al. (2014) and Smith (2013) began works in the direction and considered a number of issues such as the measurement of steady states in the DSGE model, short-run analysis of shocks and also identification and estimation in light of rational expectation. Upcoming research could continue this line of enquiry by constructing a DSGE, FAVAR, GVAR with the same data and compare the impulse response functions generated from macroeconomic shocks.

Chapter 5

Methodology of Macroeconometric Models - Small Models

5.1 Introduction

The last chapter reviewed and compared major classes of macroeconometric models from a historical perspective. In two continuous parts, the aim is to compare the models in a more formal, methodological setting where the actual specification, estimation and identification strategy will be examined. The main focus of this chapter (part 1) is to examine the relationship between GVAR and other comparable large models such as Factor-Augmented VAR (FAVAR) and DSGE models with a detailed comparison. In chapter 3, a presentation of two experiments was carried out to compare the similarities and differences from these three different approaches for policy shock analysis. This chapter focuses on the exhibition of the methodology behind these different approaches and the framework from which policy shocks are transmitted through the models. The actual setup and configuration (data, specification, estimation, diagnostics) and experiments are carried out in chapter 3, following the first theoretical comparison of models in this chapter.

5.2 VAR models

Before illustrating the GVAR approach, we begin with the unrestricted or reduced form of the VAR model and then show the structural VAR model, which allows identification of impulse response analysis for shocks. However, as documented by the curse of dimensionality, the restrictions needed for identifying the SVAR model become infeasible as there are not enough data series for estimation. In light of the big data environment we are in now, where data series can run into infinitesimal frequency or extended very far back in time, a few approaches have been made to handle this problem. One is the GVAR approach, and another is the FAVAR approach.

5.2.1 Unrestricted - reduced form VAR model

The VAR model is a simple and widely used model for multivariate time series analysis. It consists of a system of regression equations - equation 2.1 below shows a basic VAR model of order 2 (with two lags). This model below shows that the y matrix at time t simply equals parts of its lags (t-1 and t-2) plus a stochastic element ut containing this equation's residuals (elements that could not be fitted). Using this in an economic context, for example, we have the three economic variables, say real GDP growth Δ_t, inflation rate π_t and interest rate i_t. In this case, the VAR model simply regresses three variables using their own lags as well as the lags of every two other model variables, thus rendering the exclusion of the incredible identification of the traditional SEM approach (Sims, 1980).

The model:

$$y_t = A_1 y_{t-1} + A_2 y_{t-2} + u_t \tag{5.1}$$

where

$$y_t = \begin{pmatrix} \Delta_t \\ \pi_t \\ i_t \end{pmatrix}, A_i = \begin{bmatrix} a11,i & a12,i & a13,i \\ a21,i & a22.i & a23,i \\ a31,i & a32,i & a33,i \end{bmatrix}, u_t = \begin{pmatrix} u_{1t} \\ u_{2t} \\ u_{3t} \end{pmatrix}, i = 1,2 \tag{5.2}$$

The model above is also known as a reduced form, defined as the current values only depend on its lagged values and other lagged model values. As seen above, it is a neat way of capturing the dynamic for a system of related time series data. This VAR model can also be seen as a finite-order approximation of its underlying data generating process (DGP). As seen in the literature, the VAR models have been proven to be very useful for summarising the data, forecasting, and applied for cointegration analysis should such a long-run relationship exist. Except for the estimated parameters A_1 and A_2 (using standard methods such as least squares or maximum likelihood), which tell us how much the current Y values depend on the previous lags. However, the VAR model does not inform much meaningful economic relationship among the variables.

5.2.2 Structural VAR model

The VAR(p) model above has shown us that it could summarise the data well; however, it does not tell the relationship between the variables at time t, i.e. the instantaneous relations.

$$B_0 y_t = B_1 y_{t-1} + \ldots B_p y_{t-p} + w_t \tag{5.3}$$

Consider the equation model above, which contains three more terms, namely: B_0, B_1 and B_p. Here the B_0 matrix represents the instantaneous relations among y_t and B_i, $i = 1, 2\ldots p$ representing the slope coefficients. Here we also have a $K \times 1$ vector w_t, representing a vector of mean zero structural shocks, which is serially uncorrelated with a diagonal covariance matrix Σ_w of full rank number of shocks coinciding with the number of variables. An important assumption (given correct estimation) is that these structural shocks in w_t are unrelated to other elements in the vector. This fact implies that independent movement in the vector can be assigned to the particular element in w_t caused by that shock. The structural shocks cannot be recovered from equation 3, given that there are more parameters to be estimated then equations available in the system. However, if a restriction is applied for the elements in B_0, then the structural shocks can then be recovered from the reduced form model. For example, using the examples above, we have three economic variables, i.e. real GDP growth t, inflation rate π t and interest rate. We would like to know the effects of an interest rate shock on these variables for a central bank. This is not feasible as there are not enough equations for the estimation of the unknown parameters. However, if we place a restriction on the B_0 such that we have:

$$\begin{pmatrix} a_{12} & 0 & 0 \\ a_{21} & a_{22} & 0 \\ a_{31} & a_{32} & a_{33} \end{pmatrix} = B_0 \tag{5.4}$$

In this case, we assume that the central bank sets interest rate by looking at the fluctuation in real GDP growth Δ_t, inflation rate π_t only while interest rate i_t is the instrument it uses. Restriction (set to zeros) is then applied to the elements in B_0 that there would be no contemporaneous impact of i_t on i_t but only from Δ_t and π_t. Given the data and the restriction applied, we can recover the structural shocks by multiplying the SVAR model with the inverse of B0, namely $B0-1$. It is now clear to see that we only need B_0. Therefore if the matrix B_0 can be solved so that we can obtain the estimates of B_1 and B_i, $i = 1, 2...p$ and $w_t = B_0 u_t$, we can then say that the SVAR model can be identified. This is commonly referred to as the identification problem in the macroeconoemtric literature[1]. It is now easy to see that any meaningful interpretation of an SVAR analysis rests on the credible identification applied. Using the example from Sims (1992), recursive ordering was used to obtain the Cholesky factor for the identification, which relies on the ordering of the economic variables; for example, interest will first affect equity price, then inflation and in the end, GDP growth. The recursive ordering allows identification, but the values from such order are not unique and could also be criticised as ad hoc, depending on the economic reasoning used.

---

[1] For standard demonstration of the identification in SVAR see (Favero, 2001) and technical summaries of various identification strategies in (Kilian and Lütkepohl, 2017).

5.2.3 Curse of dimensionality

As a rule of thumb, the minimum number of restrictions needed for estimating the SVAR model is the difference between the number of unknown and known elements.

Although that restriction enables the estimation of the SVAR model, it is also the largest culprit for the undesirability of using the VAR for global macroeconomic modelling. Typical global models constructed with the traditional SEM approach often contain hundreds of variables and equations. Therefore we can see that straightforwardness of VAR models is constrained by its computational limitation. As the variables of interest and the size of economies also increase in the model, the parameters in each equation of the model to be estimated follow the rule of $mp(N+1)$ (see Garret et al. 2004), which implies explicitly, if we have six macro variables, 31 economies and a lag order of 2, this means we will need 384 parameters to be estimated for each equation. This is practically impossible as there isn't enough data series for such estimation. This problem has become known as 'the curse of dimensionality.'

Due to this limitation, the typical VAR models are used for a small set of variables for analysis. However, there is a motivation to incorporate more variables and the relevant data into the VAR model. Consider measuring the output gap, for example. The notion of output gap does not have a direct economic measurement as it is made up of a host of individual economic variables such as industrial productions in various industrial sectors. As such, there is often no single economically equivalent variable that could be used when this notion encapsulates many individual variables. In this case, there is no clear rule to exclude any potentially relevant variables in the model, but this would render the normal VAR model inestimable. If variables are ignored due to computational difficulties, then the result could be a VAR model that is informationally deficient and misspecified. Another motivation for employing a larger VAR model is the desire to have more understanding of policy shocks on a more disaggregated level for a specific sector in relation to the whole economy. For example, Bernanke et al. (2005) proposed the FAVAR method for identifying the impact of monetary policy on individual industries.

In general, there are two approaches to this problem; one is via Factor-Augmented VAR; the other is the Global VAR approach. Essentially the FAVAR model shrinks the large dimensional datasets into common factors but summarising the information contained within. These factors are then used in the VAR model, which could also be used for policy analysis with impulse responses analysis.

Another approach, namely the DSGE models, are motivated from a different angle, starting with microeconomic theory and then fit the data around such theoretical models. However, due to its limit on computation, most models in the literature are for 1 or 2 countries only and with a high aggregation. Due to this reason, it is hard to compare the VAR type models with the DSGE models. The two approaches may appear to be completely different, but there have been works trying to combine both.

Chapter 6

Methodology of Modelling Volatility
- GARCH Models

6.1 Introduction

Many economic and financial time series exhibit volatility in certain periods and happen in clusters. Such time series often have constant unconditional variance, but the variances are conditionally heteroskedastic in some time periods. During the last great recession that began in 2008, major stock markets suffered massive losses and increased volatility due to the financial crisis. This is also true for the 2020 virus pandemic, which caused stock market crashes in the world. From an investor's point of view, although knowing the long-run (unconditional variance) variance of his portfolio is useful, but the investor may want to know the conditional variance at a particular period rather than the overall variance as it contains little information when it comes to forecasting tomorrow's volatility for his share. Furthermore, there is often an autocorrelation in a security's returns. In Mandelbrot's words (1962): 'large changes tend to be followed by large changes-of either sign-and small changes tend to be followed by small changes.' This particular phenomenon of stock's returns triggered LTCM's crisis due to its failure to forecast the herd behaviour in shareholders (2005). From an investor's point of view, knowing the overall variance (hence its risk) of his shares at time T is not particularly helpful if he wishes to sell his positions at T+1. In this philosophy, Robert Engle (1982) designed the ARCH model to handle such heteroskedasticity in the data and enable investors to model and forecast the conditional variance. In this paper, we tested four models, namely below. This chapter first introduces the models then show empirical tests that were completed to demonstrate their working mechanism.

1) ARCH (1);

2) GARCH (1, 1);

TARCH (1, 1) and

GARCH-in-mean (1, 1).

6.2 Literature review

Although models in time series analysis are powerful and well designed to model the underlying stochastic process, strict requirements are often attached to such models. One of the popular methodologies, Box-Jenkins's ARMA, requires the data to be stationary; otherwise, differencing is needed (hence the integrated term 'I' in the ARIMA, see Hamilton 1989, p.360). Similarly, when dealing with a stochastic variable with a time-varying variance, a different approach was developed by Engle (1982) based on the autoregressive (AR) model. The method is called autoregressive conditional heteroskedasticity (ARCH) and later generalised by Bollerslev (1986) to become GARCH (p,q). Similar to the least squares method, ARCH became the workhorse in modelling volatility. According to the basic least squares method, heteroskedasticity in the squared residuals is treated as an error and require detection and correction using statistical methods such as Breusch and Pagan's test (1979). Engle, however, treated heteroskedasticity not as an error but as a variable to be modelled. This allows the user to model the variance and predict future variances. This application attracted many applications in the financial sector. The ARCH models became a standard tool in graduate finance and risk management textbooks such as Paul Wilmott (2006). Furthermore, the ARCH models are now part of the toolkit in analysing high-frequency data (see Engle 2000 Andersen et al. 2005, and Oral and Oral 2012). The popularity of the ARCH models is due to their application and precision. The models allow the user to calculate the conditional variance of financial time series, which 'is important when pricing derivatives, calculating measures of risk and hedging against portfolio risk' (Hansen and Lunde 2005). Application of the ARCH models is often used within conjunction with other models such as the popular Value at Risk (VaR) methodology in banking and the financial industry Giot and Laurent (2004) and Angelidis et al. (2004) along with time series methods such as ARMA which could be used to calculate the conditional volatility for VaR (Berkowitz and O'Brien 2002). The versatility and predictive power are particularly prominent in the GARCH (1, 1) model. In Hansen and Lunde (2005), the authors tested over 330 models in the ARCH family, and there is no evidence that other models outperformed GARCH (1, 1). The simple model ARCH (1) was outperformed significantly by many models as it is considered to be less flexible to capture the persistent volatility. This is no surprise as ARCH (1) was generalised by Bollerslev (1986) to deal with the problems of parameters estimation (ARCH consumes a lot of degree of freedom) and lags that are more than three periods.

Another advantage of the ARCH models is their flexibility. Since its inception in the early 80s, many extensions have been designed, allowing users to make further inferences in the data (Engle and Patton 2001). In addition to ARCH (1) and GARCH (1, 1), this chapter has tested the threshold ARCH (TARCH) model suggested by Rabemananjara and Zakoian (1993) and Zakoian (1994). The main contribution of TARCH is that it allows the asymmetry properties of positive news and negatives to be reflected in the estimation for the conditional variances. Another model that this chapter discusses is the so-called GARCH-in-mean model suggested by Engle et al. (1987). It allows the model to incorporate the notion that higher risk yields higher return into the mean equation. This is carried out by assuming the return is no longer unconditional but rather conditional on the volatility.

6.2 Data and model methodology

The data employed in this study is the daily returns of BP's share price from 02/01/2010 to 10/04/2020. During this period, there are days that BP was not traded as it was either a public holiday or other restrictions. All non-trading days are removed from the series as it may affect the analysis as the discontinuity and missing values exist. Authors such as Valadkhani (2004) recommended that using weekly data would avoid this problem. However, when transaction costs are getting low (e.g. broker fees, data feeding, access to data) and the rise of day trading and high-frequency trading, the significance of daily volatility measure is even more important. Therefore, the amended daily data is used instead of weekly. The daily return is calculated from BP's stock price listed on LSE and extracted with Zaitun Time Series. To measure the daily return, we simply take the difference between today's and yesterday's share price:

$$r = sp_t - sp_{t-1} \qquad\qquad (6.1)$$

Where r is the daily stock returns, spt is the stock price at t and spt-1 is the stock price at the previous period. Since BP is traded on the London Stock Exchange, it is traded to the nearest penny. Real monetary value (i.e. penny) is used as the measurement instead of percentages in this paper as BP's daily return in percentage is often small compared to its share price. This is because BP is a 'blue-chip' company and also a constitute of the FTSE100 (the largest hundred companies measured by market capitalisation floating on LSE); therefore, its perceived risk is less compared to companies in lower tiers such as the ATM market (Wang et al. 2011) and its price is thus less volatile. This is correct to some extent. If we compare the shares of BP, which is traded at around 300p, to Tullow Oil, which was traded around 30p at the time of writing, Tullow Oil is more likely to get a large percentage change in its price than BP, as it has a lower share price. Looking at the graph above, we can observe that the volatility is potentially greater during bad news, such as the period in early-to-middle 2010, when BP's stock price shredded over 50%. During this period, the daily returns' conditional volatility is considerably large, judging from the graph below. This will be the subject to be investigated in the TARCH section, which deals with the asymmetrical effect of good and bad news.

When we plot the daily return on the graph, we can see that the conditional volatility is very different throughout different periods. It can be observed that there are periods that involve a daily increase of 55.8p to the trough of -70p in a single day. The first period also marks the volatility clustering pattern; bigger losses bring bigger losses and vice versa. It should also be noted that most periods have relatively calm trading returns. This is supported by the histogram below, where almost 900 (66%) daily returns are in the region of ±5p. Although the distribution is almost symmetrical, it is affected by the outliers at the tails, particularly large daily return at -70p on the left. The kurtosis statistic is very large, departing from the normal distribution benchmark at

3. This suggests that the data is not normally distributed. This is also supported by the large JB statistics and probability (0.000), where both suggest the series is not normally distributed as the ARCH family models require the data to be stationary (unless Integrated GARCH, see Morana (2002). Therefore the unit root test was carried out to test the stationarity of the series. The null hypothesis is that the data has a unit root. Since the t-Statistic of -29.77 is smaller than the critical values at 1, 5 and 10%, we can reject the null hypothesis. Thus, the unit root is not present, and this is supported by the p value, which is 0.

6.4 Model estimation – ARCH (1)

Although it is suspected there are ARCH effects from visual inspection of the time series, this needs to be tested to confirm whether the series have ARCH effects, i.e. whether the time-varying variances depend on the lagged effects. A Lagrange multiplier test was run to test for the presence of ARCH effects. The first step is to regress r - BP' daily return on the constant and residuals.

After obtaining the estimated residuals, square the values. To test the first order ARCH effect, regress e^2 on its lagged values e^2 with v_t as the random term.

$$e^2_t = \gamma_0 + \gamma_1 e_{(t-1)}^2 + v_t \qquad (6.2)$$

The null hypothesis is that there are no ARCH effects implying the squared residuals do not depend on its lagged value; thus, the R^2 will be poor for the equation. On the other hand, if the R^2 is high, that implies the squared residuals depend on its lagged values. The test statistics (Lagrange multiplier / Obs*R-squared on the graph) is 184.07, larger than the 5% X^2 critical value of 3.841. This means the null hypothesis is rejected. This is also supported by the 0.00 p value for X^2. The p value for the lagged residuals also indicates that there are

ARCH effects. This is further supported by the low R^2 value. In other words, we can say there are ARCH effects in the series.

Figure 6.1: BP's price at closing

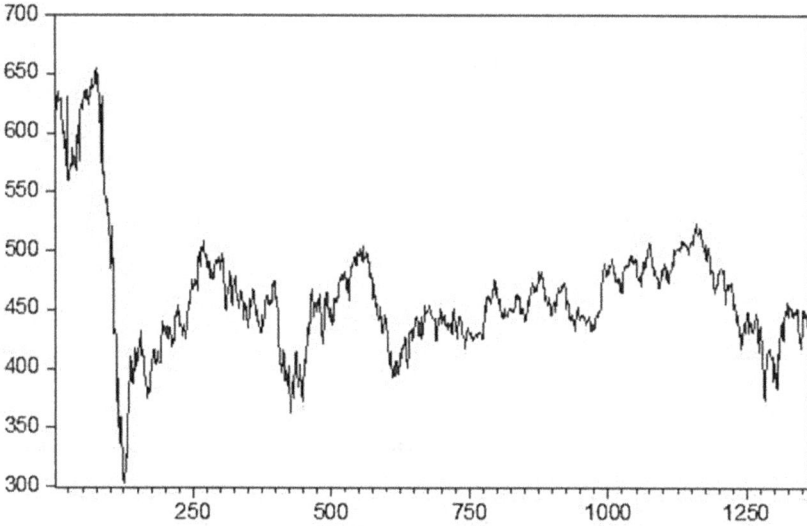

Figure 6.2: Daily return

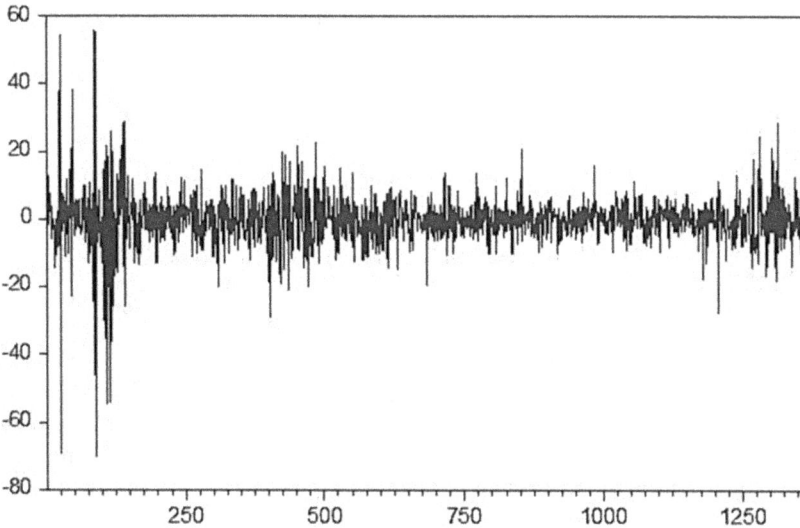

Figure 6.3: Histogram and descriptive statistics for returns

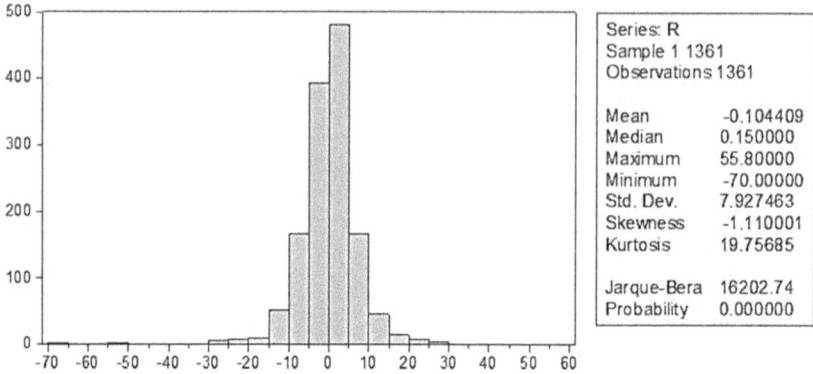

Series: R	
Sample 1 1361	
Observations 1361	
Mean	-0.104409
Median	0.150000
Maximum	55.80000
Minimum	-70.00000
Std. Dev.	7.927463
Skewness	-1.110001
Kurtosis	19.75685
Jarque-Bera	16202.74
Probability	0.000000

Figure 6.4: ADF test

		t-Statistic	Prob.*
Augmented Dickey-Fuller test statistic		-29.77930	0.0000
Test critical values:	1% level	-3.434952	
	5% level	-2.863460	
	10% level	-2.567841	

*MacKinnon (1996) one-sided p-values.

Knowing the daily return has ARCH effects, the next is to form the ARCH (1) model. The standard ARCH (1) is:

$$y_t = \Phi + e_t \tag{6.3}$$

$$e_t | I_{t-1} \sim N(0, h_t) \tag{6.4}$$

$$h_t = \alpha_0 + \alpha_1 e_{t-1}^2 \tag{6.5}$$

$$\alpha_0 > 0, 0 \leq \alpha_1 < 1 \tag{6.6}$$

The first equation is called the mean equation, where the dependent variable at t is a combination of a constant plus a stochastic part e_t. The difference between a standard autoregressive model (AR1) and ARCH (1) is the treatment of the error term e_t. In a standard AR (1) model, e_t equals constant times the lagged error term plus a random part at time t. The AR (1) in equations:

$$e_t = \rho_{t-1} + v_t \tag{6.7}$$

$$v_t \sim N(0, \sigma_v^2) \tag{6.8}$$

As we can see, the biggest difference between AR (1) and ARCH (1) is the treatment of e_t. In the ARCH (1) model, the error term is conditionally normal with $e_t|I_{t-1} \sim N(0, h_t)$. Where I_{t-1} denotes the information available at $t- 1$ and the error is distributed as a normal distribution with 0 mean and h_t variance, where it depends on a constant, plus a lagged error squared e_{t-1}^2 times a coefficient. It should be noted that the combination of α_0 and α_1 $\alpha 1$ should be less than 1; otherwise, this implies we have a non-stationary time-series which requires a different modelling method, namely IGARCH.

The results state that the average return is -0.004, although the constant term is not significant as its p value is 0.9786. The lower part gives the results for the variance equation, which states that:

$$\hat{h}_t = \alpha_0 + \alpha_1 e_{t-1}^2 = 38.505 + 0.3514 e_{t-1}^2 \qquad (6.9)$$

The ARCH effects are highly significant as the p values for both terms are 0. Here we can see that the constant α_0 is very high at 38.505. In other words, the conditional variance is 38.505, plus 35% of its squared lagged errors. We can postulate that the conditional variances will be very high for the periods when BP's price shredded more than 50%. The graph for the estimated conditional variances is shown below. This confirms that the postulate above is true as the conditional variances for those periods are remarkably high.

Taking the last BP's last daily return on t, we can forecast the estimated return and volatility at t+1 i.e. the next trading day. As the last daily return for BP is 8.05p, the conditional variance at t+1 is:

$$\hat{h}_{t+1} = \hat{a}_0 + \hat{a}_1 (r_t - (\beta_0))^2 =$$
$$8.505 + 0.3514(8.05 - (-0.00423))2 = 61.3 \qquad (6.10)$$

Therefore the conditional variance forecasted is 61.3p. If we take the square root of that, we have 7.83p. This means, based on the last daily return (lagged 1) and the constants calculated from previous returns, BP's stock price is likely to fluctuate within 7.83p on t+1. It should be noted that the constant estimated from the mean equation is insignificant. This could be because the data contained so much variation initially, affecting the mean estimate.

Figure 6.5: LM test

Variable	Coefficient	Std. Error	t-Statistic	Prob.
C	39.73955	7.045673	5.640278	0.0000
RESID^2(-1)	0.367889	0.025233	14.57984	0.0000

R-squared	0.135347	Mean dependent var	62.84142
Adjusted R-squared	0.134710	S.D. dependent var	272.1706
S.E. of regression	253.1757	Akaike info criterion	13.90751
Sum squared resid	87045007	Schwarz criterion	13.91518
Log likelihood	-9455.110	Hannan-Quinn criter.	13.91039
F-statistic	212.5718	Durbin-Watson stat	1.985303
Prob(F-statistic)	0.000000		

Figure 6.6: Results from ARCH (1) estimation

Variable	Coefficient	Std. Error	z-Statistic	Prob.
C	-0.004237	0.158134	-0.026793	0.9786
Variance Equation				
C	38.50484	0.723332	53.23259	0.0000
RESID(-1)^2	0.351398	0.030007	11.71064	0.0000

Figure 6.7: Conditional variance series

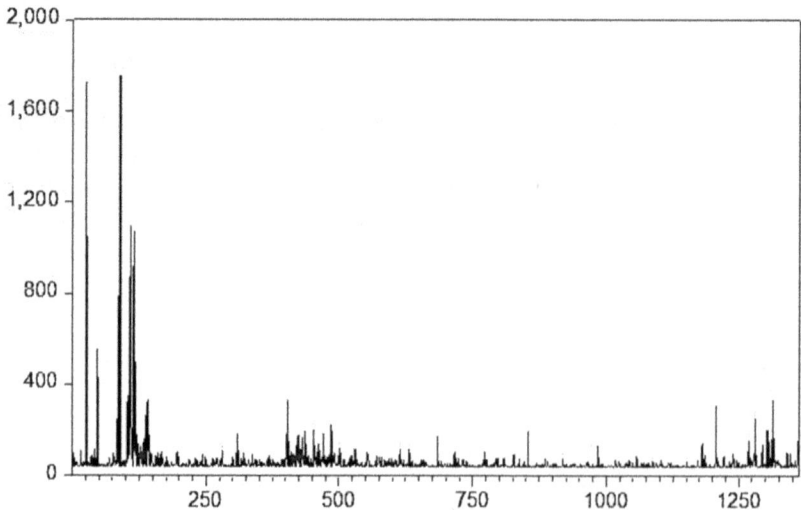

6.5 Model estimation GARCH (1,1)

This part proceeds to model the data with the popular GARCH (1, 1). The model is similar to ARCH (1) except its treatment for h_t where it is:

$$h_t = \delta + \alpha_1\, e^2_{t-1} + \beta_1 h_{t-1} \tag{6.11}$$

$$\delta = (\alpha_0 - \beta_0\alpha_0) \tag{6.12}$$

Like ARCH (1), the combined values of $\alpha_1 + \beta_1$ should be less than 1; otherwise, the series would be non-stationary or 'integrated GARCH' – IGARCH. One of the advantages of GARCH (1,1) is that it captures long lags in the shocks compare to ARCH(1). GARCH (1, 1) can capture 'similar effects to an ARCH (q) model requiring the longer lags, say q6 (Hill et al. 2011, p.526). One of the main advantages of GARCH (1, 1) is that the three parameters to be estimated (δ, α_1, β_1) capture most of the effects compared to ARCH (6), where it requires q+1=7 parameters to be estimated, therefore consuming the degrees of freedom available.

Figure 6.8: Results from GARCH (1,1)

Variable	Coefficient	Std. Error	z-Statistic	Prob.
C	0.174050	0.126527	1.375597	0.1689
Variance Equation				
C	2.509706	0.352657	7.116557	0.0000
RESID(-1)^2	0.140963	0.012959	10.87732	0.0000
GARCH(-1)	0.817755	0.015816	51.70286	0.0000

Similar to other ARCH models, the estimators are estimated by maximum likelihood method. From the results above, we have:

$$h_t = \delta + \alpha_1\, e^2_{t-1} + \beta_1 h_{t-1} =$$

$$2.510 + 0.141\, e^2_{t-1} + 0.8178 h_{t-1} \tag{6.13}$$

Where all three parameters are significant with a p value at 0.000, the series is suggested to have ARCH effects. The significance of the coefficients is also higher compared to the ones estimated in the ARCH(1), meaning the GARCH (1,1) performs better than the ARCH (1) model. To forecast the conditional variance hence the volatility for the next trading day, h_{t+1}, we use:

$$h_{t+1} = \delta + \alpha_1\, e^2_t + \beta_1 h_t =$$

$$2.510 + 0.141 * (8.050 - 0.1740)^2 + 0.818 * 81.919 = 78.266 \tag{6.14}$$

If we square the conditional variances for the next trading day, h_{t+1}, we get 8.847 as the standard deviation. The conditional variances calculated are shown below. If we compare GARCH (1, 1) to ARCH (1), we can see that GARCH (1, 1) giving more sensible estimates and less sensitive to sudden jumps.

6.6 Model estimation TARCH (1,1)

Figure 6.9: Conditional variances from GARCH (1,1)

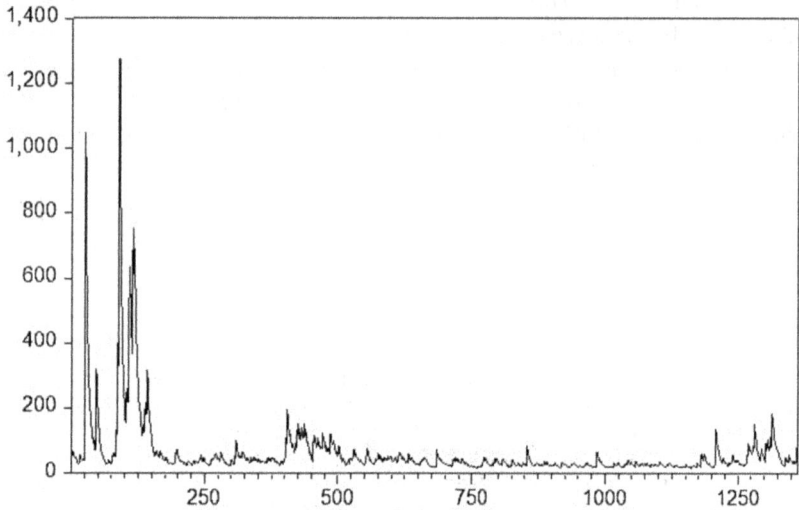

Figure 6.10: Comparing ARCH(1) to GARCG(1,1)

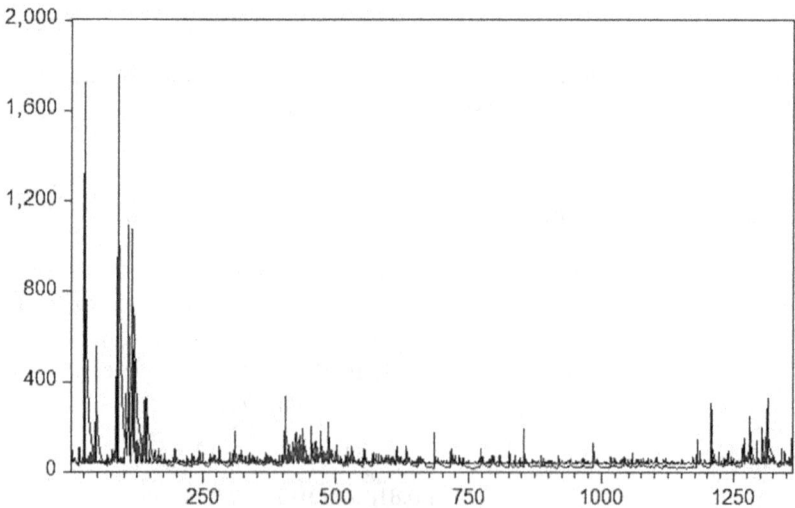

Figure 6.11: Results from TARCH (1,1)

Variable	Coefficient	Std. Error	z-Statistic	Prob.
C	0.028076	0.151137	0.185765	0.8526
Variance Equation				
C	2.222224	0.304787	7.291064	0.0000
RESID(-1)^2	0.078241	0.009573	8.173068	0.0000
RESID(-1)^2*(RESID(-1)<0)	0.106728	0.019416	5.496879	0.0000
GARCH(-1)	0.830619	0.013702	60.62033	0.0000

So far, we have used ARCH (1) and GARCH (1, 1) to model our data. Both models treat the shocks to the data as the same, implying the model is indifferent to the nature of the news. However, this is not so accurate in some circumstances. For example, certain negative news such as company facing unforeseen bankruptcy or liquidity crisis in a commercial bank will generate a much bigger shock to the share price as this is perceived as bad to investors. Therefore, threshold ARCH or TARCH is made to account for the asymmetry in negative and positive news. Compare to previous models, the conditional variance is:

$$h_t = \delta + \alpha_1 \, e_{t-1}^2 + \gamma d_t \beta_1 e_t^2 + \beta_1 h_{t-1} \tag{6.15}$$

$$d_t = \begin{cases} 1 \, e_t < 0 - Bad\_News \\ 0 \, e_t \geq 0 - Good\_News \end{cases} \tag{6.16}$$

Where γ is the term accounting for the asymmetry problem, when it is 0, the model is the same as a standard GARCH model as it cancels the terms in $d_{t-1} \, e_{t-1}^2$

The results from the re-estimations are shown above, with all estimates significant at 5%. The implications for positive and negative news are:

When the shock is positive:

$$h_t = 2.222 + 0.078 \, e_{t-1}^2 + 0.831 h_{t-1} \tag{6.17}$$

When the shock is negative:

$$h_t = 2.222 + (0.078 + 0.1067) e_{t-1}^2 + 0.831 h_{t-1} \tag{6.18}$$

This means the negative shocks will generate greater volatility by (0.078+0.1067=0.1847). If we compare this to the positive news, this clearly shows that negative news has a heavier influence on the share price.

6.7 Model estimation GARCH-in-mean (1,1)

The last model to be estimated is the GARCH-in-mean model. Similar to the previous TARCH model, the GARCH-in-mean model deals with the elements in real-world trading. In addition to estimating the coefficients, it allows us to test whether the mean return would be affected by the volatility in the shares. Intuitively, an asset that is deemed to be safe will yield a lower return, such as the UK government bond, while riskier assets such as oil company shares like BP will have a higher expected yield to compensate for the riskiness. The model is defined as:

$$y_t = \beta_0 + \alpha_1 e_{t-1}^2 + \beta_1 h_{t-1} \qquad\qquad (6.19)$$

$$e_t | I_{t-1} \sim N(0, h_t) \qquad\qquad (6.20)$$

$$h_t = \alpha_0 + \alpha_1 e_{t-1}^2 + \beta_1 h_{t-1} \qquad\qquad (6.21)$$

$$\delta_0 > 0, 0 \leq = \alpha_1 < 1, 0 \leq \beta_1 < 1 \qquad\qquad (6.22)$$

The mean return y_t is now conditional on the volatility by a factor θ rather than unconditional as in ARCH, GARCH and TARCH.

This gives:

$$r_t = -0.0018 + 0.093 \times h_t \qquad\qquad (6.23)$$

$$h_t = 0.003 + 0.081 e_{t-1}^2 + 0.108 e_{t-1}^2 + 0.827 h_{t-1} \qquad\qquad (6.24)$$

Figure 6.12: Results for GARCH-in-mean (1,1)

Variable	Coefficient	Std. Error	z-Statistic	Prob.
GARCH	-0.001850	0.005503	-0.336208	0.7367
C	0.092939	0.246982	0.376299	0.7067
Variance Equation				
C	2.278467	0.321575	7.085336	0.0000
RESID(-1)^2	0.080531	0.010846	7.425117	0.0000
RESID(-1)^2*(RESID(-1)<0)	0.108264	0.019997	5.413935	0.0000
GARCH(-1)	0.827264	0.014582	56.73166	0.0000

The results from the model show that the GARCH term in the mean equation is highly insignificant as the p value is 0.73. This implies there isn't enough evidence to prove volatility affects returns. Since the GARCH term and the constant in the mean equation are highly insignificant, we cannot determine whether the above conclusion is true. One possible reason to explain the insignificance is that the daily return varies too during the early periods (from observation 1 to 250), affecting the overall estimation of the mean return. The heavy losses in the beginning effectively wiped out all returns in the remainder of the next four years for the shareholders. From this perspective, we conclude the test above is ineffective, and the mean equation's inference is invalid. However, this does not affect the results in the variance equation, as they are all significant.

6.8 Conclusion

It is clear that ARCH (1) is more sensitive to the shocks, thus giving larger estimates. The empirical tests have decided earlier that GARCH (1, 1) is better than ARCH (1) in this case as it is more versatile and able to capture more effects with further lags. The estimates in GARCH (1, 1) also have higher significance, supporting that GARCH is superior to ARCH. However, it is not clear whether TARCH and GARCH-in-mean are better than GARCH (1, 1). When we compare the estimated return in the mean equations, all models suggest the estimates for the constant are insignificant. However, the result from GARCH is the best, with a p value of 0.169 compared to the other three models. The main advantages for TARCH and GARCH-in-mean are that they allow further inference to be drawn from the data. However, the empirical tests result is not clear whether the models worked for the dataset as it cannot estimate the mean return properly.

In general, GARCH type models are very common and often used in the industry as it gives a rather simple and intuitive understanding of volatility. When the investor is deciding the risk that he or she would like to take, it would be particularly useful to use this type of model to give an indication of the near term volatility. In part 3 of this book, the investor will have an option to provide the expected risk, i.e. volatility for the instrument. This measure can either be estimated using simple averages, although it will be less precise. Using a GARCH will be more appropriate as it contains more information.

Chapter 7

Methodology of Macroeconometric Models - Global Large Models

7.1 The GVAR approach

As seen above, VAR is infeasible due to the proliferation of unknown parameters to be estimated. In the case of FAVAR, the method to incorporate the large dataset is by estimating common factors with factor analysis, thus reducing the datasets but retaining the information within. In GVAR, for example, when modelling the world economy, each country is represented by its own equation with a VARX* model that links the domestic country with the foreign countries and a set of global variables such as oil and metal prices. In the individual model, the domestic model is linked to the foreign economies with their respective trade weights. Economically this is an intuitive approach as clearly; policy shocks from India will have a lot higher impact on its neighbours, like Sri Lanka (which has many trades directly with India), than on Paraguay, for example. Given the general nature of interdependencies in the world economy (see Pesaran and Smith 2006), it is supposed that all country-specific variables and common global observed factors such as oil and commodity prices should be treated as endogenously (as part of the system, i.e. a closed world economy). As the parameters to be estimated in the GVAR model are now restricted by the trade weights, allowing for the computation. In this sense, it is similar to the FAVAR approach by extracting 'common factors' from relative trade weights rather than statistical methods.

The GVAR objective of solving the curse of dimensionality is to impose a set of restrictions on the VAR model to be estimated practically while being consistent. The main restriction of the GVAR approach is by imposing the assumption of weak exogeneity of foreign country-specific and global variables. In other words, it assumes that the individual economy is actually relatively small in terms of the world economy except for the exception of the US (Dées et al., 2007). The weak exogeneity is then tested empirically to see whether this assumption holds. Specifically, an individual country (or economy) is represented by a VARX* model (or in its error-correction form VECMX*), which links the domestic economy (defined by a range of domestic macroeconomic variables) to foreign economies (defined by corresponding foreign variables), which are treated as weakly exogenous. The domestic and foreign economies are then linked via weights matrices which match the international linkages in trade. The second step then stacks all individual country models together in a theoretically consistent manner that can simultaneously generate forecasts for all world economic variables.

The rest of the associated parameters are similar to those in a normal VAR, which are estimated to give context to economic interpretations of the model. It should be noted that $x*it$, as a vector that captures the foreign-specific macroeconomic variables related to domestic ones, is constructed via a weight matrix. The scheme of the weight matrix can be designed to reflect the trade and/or financial linkages. For example, the weight of Britain (domestic) is expected to have a large trade with the EU countries such as Germany (foreign); therefore, it will have a larger weight than, for example, Malaysia.

As mentioned above, GVAR is a two-step process. The first was to estimate the VARX* model country by country, and the second is to stack all VARX* models together and be solved as a whole.

7.1.1 Country-specific VARX* models

The first step of the GVAR approach is the formulation of the individual VARX* (vector autoregressive with exogeneity) model for every country. In this section, we present the general methodology for advanced in Chudik and Pesaran (2016) to model individual country in the GVAR model applied to the model in this study. The approach assumes that there are N+1 countries in the global economy, indexed by i = 0, 1,. . ., N, and the aim is to relate a set of country-specific variables, e.g. GDP, inflation, interest rates, etc. that are of interest to the study. The vector of interest denoted as x it collects the macroeconomic variables specific to the individual countries of interest indexed by i and over time, indexed by t = 0, 1, . . ., T. Following the notation and definitions given in di Mauro and Pesaran (2013, p.14-17), the general individual country model VARX* (2, 2) is represented as

$$x_{it} = a_{i0} + a_{i1}t + \Phi_{i1}x_{i,t-1} + \Phi_{i2}x_{i,t-2} + \Lambda_{i0}x_{it}^* + \Lambda_{i1}x_{it-1}^* + \Lambda_{i2}x_{it-2}^* + u_{it}$$
$$(7.1)$$

x_{it} – is a vector with a dimension of $k_i \times 1$ of domestic macroeconomic variables indexed by individual country i and time as t; x_{it}^* is a vector with a dimension of $k_i^* \times 1$ of foreign macroeconomic variables indexed by individual country i and time as t; u_{it} – is a serially uncorrelated and cross-sectionally weakly dependent process. The rest of the associated parameters are similar to those in a normal VAR, which are estimated to give context to economic interpretations of the model. It should be noted that $x*it$, as a vector that captures the foreign-specific macroeconomic variables related to domestic ones, is constructed via a weight matrix. Mathematically, this is defined as:

$$x_{it}^* = \Sigma_{j=0}^{N} \, w_{it} x_{jt)} \tag{7.2}$$

where w_{ij}—i being the domestic country and j the foreign—are a set of weights that $w_{ii}=0$, and when all the weights of i and j are combined, they will become 1. The scheme of the weight matrix can be designed to reflect the trade and/or financial linkages. It should be noted that, similar to the framework of an unrestricted VAR, the VARX* model can also be written in its error-correction form VECMX*, which allows the differentiation of short and long-run effects. In particular, the long-run effects being treated as co-integrating. The individuals VECMX* models are estimated separately for each country, i, based on reduced rank regression, thus identifying the long-run effects or I(1) relationships within the domestic x_{it} and across x_{it} foreign economies, x_{it}^*. Thus, the total number of co-integrating relations and the speed of adjustment for each country can be derived and given economic meaning. The error correction form of the VARX* for country i at t, i.e. VECMX*, can be written as below:

$$\Delta x_{it} = c_{i0} - \alpha_i \beta_i' \, (z_{i,t-1} - \gamma_i(t-1) + \Lambda_{i0}\Delta x_{it}^* + \Gamma_i\Delta z_{i,t-1} + u_{it} \tag{7.3}$$

Similar to a conventional VECM model, the VECMX* model above allows for the possibility of co-integration both within x_{it} and between x_{it} and x_{it}^* and consequently across x_{it} and x_{jt} for $i \neq j$. The VECMX* models are then estimated separately for each country depending on whether the variables are weakly exogenous (or long-run forcing) or integrated of order 1, i.e. I (1). From this, the number of co-integrating relations, r_i, the speed of adjustment coefficients, a_i, and the co-integrating vectors, β_i, can be obtained (di Mauro and Pesaran 2013a, p.15).

7.1.2 Weak exogeneity

The distinction of exogeneity and endogeneity is uncommon in the VAR literature as variables are normally considered endogenous. In practice, the variables could be affected by other observable variables determined outside the system of interest. And as such, those variables are deemed as exogenous or unmodelled variables. However, the definition of exogeneity is often not precise and subjectively depends on the research question being studied. In the paper by Engle et al. (1983), formal definitions were outlined where there are different strengths of exogeneities. The variable is considered to be weakly exogenous; for instance, if we are interested in estimating a particular parameter vector γ from x_t, which is an exogenous variable, and if the estimation properties do not suffer from conditioning on x_t rather than using a full model for the data generation process of all the variables involved.

It should be noted here that the rationale behind the GVAR approach to reduce the parameters for estimation is via the assumption of weak exogeneity of the foreign variables in the individual VARX* models. This implies no feedback from the lagged endogenous variables to the exogenous variables in the VARX* model, allowing the restrictions of these lag coefficients to be zero. Effectively this is imposing a Granger non-causality from endogenous to exogenous variables. Effectively, when modelling a small open economy in a global setting, one can see that the said small economy is effectively weakly exogenous to the rest of the world. From an economic policy, the action from one country is likely to affect the rest of the world less than the rest of the world affecting that single country, thus the causality is travelling one way only, from the exogenous (e.g. rest of world or foreign countries) to endogenous (e.g. domestic country) and not the other way round, except for the USA which is usually treated as the dominant country. Such assumption of weak exogeneity is often supported in the literature such as Pesaran et al. (2004), Dées et al. (2007), and di Mauro and Smith (2013), and it can be tested via the Johansen test (Johansen 1991).

7.1.3 Solution strategy and the GVAR model

As mentioned in the introduction, the GVAR approach is a two-stage process. The first was to estimate the VARX* model country by country, and the second is to stack all VARX* models together and be solved as a whole. Below examines the solution to solve the model as outlined in di Mauro and Pesaran (ibid, p.16). Recall the generic VARX* (2,2) model above:

$$x_{it} = a_{i0} + a_{i1}t + \Phi_{i1}x_{i,t-1} + \Phi_{i2}x_{i,t-2} + \Lambda_{i0}x_{it}^* + \Lambda_{i1}x_{it-1}^* + \Lambda_{i2}x_{it-2}^* + u_{it}$$

$$(7.4)$$

Where the definitions remain the same as defined before, we now introduce a few terms to solve the model as a whole. To form the GVAR model, we first introduce a new term, z, and define it as:

$$z_{it} = (x_{it}', x_{it}^{*\prime})'$$ $$(7.5)$$

z_{it} is simply a term that combines the domestic and foreign variables to help reduce the derivation of the full GVAR model. Further introducing three more terms, where they collect the respective regression coefficients and the co-integrating term.

$$A_{i0} = (I_{ki}, -\Lambda_{i0}), A_{i1} = (\varphi_{i1}, \Lambda_{i1}), A_{i2} = (\varphi_{i2}, \Lambda_{i2})$$ $$(7.6)$$

We now have:

$$A_{i0}Z_{it} = a_{i0} + a_{i1}t + A_{i1}Z_{it-1} + A_{i2}Z_{it-2} + u_{it} \tag{7.7}$$

Country-specific trade weights w_{ij} obtained can be now used to link matrices denoted as W_i I to obtain the relationship between the domestic and foreign economies. As we have mentioned, the new term z_{it} is now:

$$Z_{it} = W_i x_t \tag{7.8}$$

Therefore we have:

$$A_{i0}W_i x_t = a_{i0} + a_{i1}t + A_{i1}W_i x_{t-1} + A_{i2}W_i x_{t-2} + u_{it} \tag{7.9}$$

Also, recall that for i = 0, 1,. . ., N, which implies the equation above is individual and country-specific and requires stacking to solve for x_t, which links all individual models together. We now introduce a few more terms to tidy up the model:

$$G_0 = \begin{pmatrix} A_{00}\,W_0 \\ A_{10}\,W_1 \\ \vdots \\ A_{N0}W_N \end{pmatrix}, \quad G_1 = \begin{pmatrix} A_{01}\,W_0 \\ A_{11}\,W_1 \\ \vdots \\ A_{N1}W_N \end{pmatrix}, \quad G_1 = \begin{pmatrix} A_{02}\,W_0 \\ A_{12}\,W_1 \\ \vdots \\ A_{N2}W_N \end{pmatrix},$$

$$a_0 = \begin{pmatrix} a_{00} \\ a_{10} \\ \vdots \\ A_{N0} \end{pmatrix}, \quad a_1 = \begin{pmatrix} a_{01} \\ a_{11} \\ \vdots \\ A_{N1} \end{pmatrix}, \quad u_1 = \begin{pmatrix} u_{0t} \\ u_{1t} \\ \vdots \\ u_{Nt} \end{pmatrix}$$

Thus

$$G_0 x_t = a_0 + a_1 t + G_1 x_{t-1} + G_2 x_{t-2} + u_t \tag{7.10}$$

As the term G_0 is a known non-singular matrix (invertible matrix). G_0 is called non–singular if there exists an $n \times n$ matrix G_0^{-1} such that $G_0 G_0^{-1} = I_n = G_0^{-1}G_0$. Thus by multiplying its inverse G_0^{-1}, the term disappears, and we now obtain the GVAR (2) model with 2 lags as where

$$x_t = b_0 + b_1 t + F_1 x_{t-1} + F_2 x_{t-2} + \varepsilon_t \tag{7.11}$$

Where the new terms collect the inverse of G_0

$$F_1 = G_0^{-1}G_1, \quad F_1 = G_0^{-1}G_2,$$

$$b_0 = G_0^{-1}a_0, b_0 = G_0^{-1}a_1 \quad \varepsilon_t = G_0^{-1}u_t$$

The GVAR model above can be solved recursively; see Pesaran (2015). To summarise, as shown above, the GVAR model allows the interactions among the domestic and foreign economies through three diverse channels. The first is the contemporaneous and lagged dependence of domestic variables x_{it} on foreign variables x_{it}^*. In addition, it also allows the effect and dependence of domestic variables x it on global weakly exogenous variables such as oil and commodity prices. This can also be used as a simulation strategy that can reveal the contemporaneous effects of shocks from country i on j.

7.1.4 Diagnostics tests

Model specification

Having described the derivation of the individual VARX* (p, q) models and their stacking to form a GVAR (p) model, we now turn to the specification of the individual models.

Lag orders of individual VARX* models

Recall that a generic VARX* (p,q) model has lag orders p for domestic lag orders and q for foreign variables. The exact lag orders to be selected are similar to those employed in time series literature with the Akaike information criterion (AIC) or the Schwarz Bayesian criterion (SBC). The main computational tools for lag order selection are currently embedded in the GVAR toolbox, automatically showing the lag orders selected by either AIC or SBC, whichever with the highest value. The table above shows the lag orders selected by either AIC or SBC; whichever value is the highest. It should be noted that it does not matter whether the lag orders of p and q are equal. Restriction on the maximum of lag order can also be imposed as a large order of lags will deplete the degrees of freedom, depending on the length of the time series.

Unit root test

A big advantage of the GVAR approach is the indifference to the stationarity / non-stationarity of the variables. However, unit root tests are still useful in the sense that it allows the identification of short-run and long-run relations (as cointegrating). Like many other papers in the literature, the Augmented Dickey-Fuller test is used instead of the older standard Dickey-Fuller test. The ADF test was carried out at 95%, implying that if the test statistic for the variable is more negative than the critical values, it will be rejected as there is no unit root. The test was carried out on level, differenced, twice differenced, with trend and without trend on all variables.

Once the unit root has been tested, the corresponding co-integrating VARX* models are estimated as VECMX*. The next step is the identification of the co-integrating relationships within the individual models. The rank of co-integrating relationships for each model is then computed using Johansen's trace and maximal eigenvalue statistics (see Pesaran et al. 2001a).

Testing for weak exogeneity

As mentioned before, the main assumption in the GVAR approach is the weak exogeneity of the foreign variables x_{it}^* with respect to the respective VARX* model. As described in Pesaran et al., 2004, this assumption is compatible with a certain degree of weak dependence across u_{it} (the residuals). Following the work on weak exogeneity testing by Johansen (1992) and Granger and Lin (1995), the weak exogeneity assumption implies no long-run feedback from x_{it} to x_{it}^*, suggesting that x_{it}^* is an error correction in terms of the individual country VECMX* models, which do not enter in the marginal model of x_{it}^* (Smith and Galesi 2014). This implies we can consistently estimate the VARX* models individually and later combing together to form the GVAR. The proof of weak exogeneity implication on x_{it}^* can be seen in Pesaran (2015, ch.23, p.569). The test is a regression model described in Johansen (1992) and Harbo et al. (1998). The test employed by Dees et al. (2007) is as follow:

$$\Delta x_{it\ell}^* = a_{ij} + \sum_{j=1}^{r_i} \delta_{ij\ell} ECM_{ij,t-1} + \sum_{k=1}^{s_i} \Phi_{ikj}' \Delta x_{i,t-k} + \sum_{m=1}^{n_i} \Psi_{im\ell ikj}' \Delta \tilde{x}_{i,\ell-m} + \eta_{it\ell}$$

$$(7.12)$$

where ECMij,t1, j = 1,2,. . .,ri are the estimated error-correction terms corresponding to the co-integrating terms found as shown in previous section. It also should be noted that $\Delta x_{it,l}^*$ is the differenced vector collection of the foreign variables. This is a F-test for the significance of $\delta_{ij,l} = 0$, j = 1,2,. . .,r_i above. While the lag orders of p and q were determined earlier via AIC or SIC.

Testing for structural breaks

Having considered the rather harmless integrated series in the previous section and also the possible violations of weak exogeneity and its treatment, we now turn to one of the most fundamental problems in econometric modelling. So far, we have shown that the problems mentioned above can be mitigated but unfortunately, similarly to other time-series/econometric models, the GVAR is also susceptible to structural breaks. The core concept of structural breaks is straightforward; it refers to the unexpected sudden shift of the time-series. Consider a daily stock price time series where a sudden shift is very common due to stock split, unexpected announcements, overnight trading, oversea stock exchange performance etc. This renders the original time-series model unreliable as the time-series shifted unexpectedly, therefore not within the range of the forecast; this also implies forecast errors would be greater. The problem of structural breaks has been discussed extensively in the literature since the 1960s by Quandt (1958, 1960), who proposed the Sup F test, which calculates the likelihood ratio test for a change in model parameters and identifies the break date. The Sup F test was quite adaptable but only worked on univariate regression; nevertheless, it became the basis for future research.

In the GVAR literature, mainly those in Pesaran et al.(2004), Pesaran and Smith (2006), Dees et al.(2007), Pesaran et al.(2009), di Mauro and Pesaran (2013), Chudik and Pesaran (2014) had extensive discussion of the problem. The GVAR Handbook by di Mauro and Pesaran (2013) surveyed the existing strategy that The GVAR literature employed. These include several test statistics to assess the structural stability of the estimated coefficients and error variances of the individual VARX* / VECMX* models. Specifically, the survey indicated the methods used are (p.21): the maximal OLS cumulative sum (CUSUM) statistic and its mean square variant by Ploberger and Krämer (1992); a test for parameter constancy against non-stationary alternatives by Nyblom (1989); as well as sequential Wald type tests 'of a one-time structural change at an unknown change point specifically'; also the QLR statistic by Quandt (1960), the MW statistic (Hansen, 1992), and the APW statistic (Andrews and Ploberger 1994).

7.1.5 Dynamic analysis

The main application of the VAR models for dynamic analysis is from the impulse response function (IRF) and also variance decompositions. In particular, IRF can answer scenario-type what if questions such as the effect of a negative shock on the equity price on GDP in the US. Essentially the IRF calculates the effects of shocks on the path of the selected variables. Consider a generic univariate series:

$$y_t = \rho y_t - 1 + v_t; \; y_t = 0 \qquad\qquad (7.13)$$

Where the series begin with a value of 0 and took on a shock of v_t. If we assume the shock happened at $t = 1$ then the series would become $y_1 = \rho y_0 + v_1 = v$. By using recursive substitution, we can define the time path of y_1 following the initial shock as the impulse response function. In order words, it displays what happens to the variable y after a certain shock over time. This is of course rather simplistic as it involves only one variable. However, if there is more than one variable in the system then it becomes significantly more difficult to discover the shocks i.e. identifying where is the shock coming from. This problem is commonly referred to as the identification problem.

The identification problem is often further complicated by the fact that, the shocks could be correlated. For example, if two shocks v_t and e_t are correlated and occur at the same time, it would be impractical to answer whether the series y_1 has been affected by v_t as the series could be affected by both shocks. The traditional impulse response function employed in the literature is Sims's orthogonalised impulse responses (OIR) (Sims, 1980) where it takes on the idea above with the assumption of the shocks being orthogonalised i.e. independent to each other. The OIR is usually employed in small VAR systems where there are small number of variables and lag orders. In addition, it also depends on the natural causal ordering of the variables in the VAR system. This particular requirement is mostly due to the use of Cholesky decomposition, which is not mathematically unique (Cochrane, 2005, p53). In summary, the standard OIR assumes that the errors are orthogonal and the response of one variable to the other shock is zero. This implies, in our GVAR model, if we are to use the OIR then it assumes shocks are not correlated to each other and are orthogonal. It further requires the order of the shocks to the system to be arranged properly in the variables. This means the dependent variable and for domestic variables vector x it has to be re-ordered so that it complies with the causal order of the shocks e.g. equity price before GDP to see the shocks. Also it is highly infeasible as one may wish to check many scenarios with the impulse response function therefore, this became a major problem for dynamic analysis. To tackle this problem, there are several methods proposed; these include Bernanke (1986), Blanchard and Watson (1986), Sims (1986) which broadly relied on reduced-form VAR (as opposed to structural VAR), which identification is possible. Particularly, they place a priori restrictions on the covariance matrix of shocks guided by economic theories. There, however, remain some issues for identification of shocks GVAR as Pesaran (2015, p.916) had shown due to the model's number of variables and lag orders. In light of this difficulty, Pesaran et al. 2014, Pesaran and Smith (2006) and other GVAR literature had mainly adopted the generalised IRF (GIRF) approach proposed by Koop e al. (1996) and Pesaran and Smith (1998).

The Generalised impulse response function (GIRF) relies on the ordering of the variables, as Pesaran (ibid.) had showed. This GIRF below is the model for one country model only. For example, to answer the question: what will happen to the UK's economy should there be a negative interest rate shock in Germany? Using the definition of the GIRF in di Mauro and Smith (2013) for a single country is given by

$$g_{\epsilon j}(h) = E(X_{t+h}|\epsilon_{jt} = \sqrt{\sigma_{jj}, I_{t-1}}) - E(X_{t+h}|I_{t-1}) = \frac{R_h G_0^{-1} \sum e_j}{\sqrt{e_j' \sum e_j}}$$

$$(7.14)$$

Where the GIRF is defined as a vector of k x1 size as g_{Ej} (h), h as the time period, j is the index of the interested country, and $E(.|.)$ being the conditional mathematical expectation with respect to the VAR model, defined as the vector of $\mathbf{x}_t$ at h period upon the shock of E_{jt} to country j at time t. The mathematical expectation is equal to the square of the shock at size σ_{jj}, pre-set to be 1 standard deviation, i.e. $\sqrt{\sigma_{jj}}$. In this case, I_{t-1} is simply referred to as the full information set at $t-1$, which is defined as the collection of vector $\mathbf{x}_t$ at $t-1$; R_h as a vector of $kxk\ G_0^{-1}$ to connect the variables Σ as the Cholesky factor; and last but not least, e_j as the sector vector that selects the element of shocks. For example, if we wish to find out the effect of 1 standard deviation negative shock to the UK economy given by the US, then we can specify this shock with the e_j mathematically, with 1 being selected; 0 not, i.e. $e_j = (0, 0, \ldots 1, 0 \ldots 0)$.

The model above is specified for a single country, and we now turn to the version which allows global or regional shocks. The model is given by:

$$g_m(h) = E(\mathbf{x}_{t+h}|\varepsilon^g_{m,t} = \sqrt{\sqrt{m' \sum m}}, I_{t-1}) - E(x_{t+h}|I_{t-1}) = \frac{R_h G_0^{-1} \sum m}{\sqrt{m' \sum m}}$$

$$(7.15)$$

Where the single country shock is ε_{jt} is replaced by $\varepsilon^g_{m,t}$, which is defined as $m^t_{\varepsilon t}$, with $\mathbf{m}$ being the vector of weights related to the global model or region. From this, the user can alter the weight specification according to the objective. The functions above allow the user to generate the time profiles of the shocks, which can be used to simulate scenarios. The final time series path given by the GIRF comes with upper and lower bounds defined by the confidence interval, e.g. 95%. This is carried out by bootstrapping, which estimates the individual models repeatedly until the solution is stable, defined as when eigenvalues are less than or equal to 1. For the technical detail, see Smith and Galesi (2014, p.149).

7.2 FAVAR model

Having examined the Global VAR approach to modelling, we now turn to the Factor-augmented VAR approach. The next few sections are devoted to the exposition of the methodologies behind the order of the motivation behind, FAVAR framework, factors selection with principal components, the specification and estimation of the model and also structural identification for structural impulse responses.

7.2.1 Structural FAVAR model

Recall the problem of identification in the unrestricted VAR model, and consequently, typical VAR models used for policy analysis include a small set of economic variables. In this case, this is suboptimal as the missing variables from the model due to a limit on the computation could lead to informational deficiency. The formation of the impulse responses and shocks computed would also be misled by the omitted variables. The relevance of a particular variable to the empirical model is also difficult to determine at times. Some concepts, such as 'economic output gap' and 'inflation', cannot be measured without error. Such concepts are themselves formed of highly aggregated information sets; therefore, if the goal is to understand policy shocks on a more granular level, then disaggregated data must be used to the extent that small unrestricted VAR models are no longer sufficient. This is particularly a problem as the number of regressors cannot exceed the number of observations.

During the following sections, we show how factor models can be used to condense the information from the vast datasets while retaining as much information as possible. It also shows how the estimated factors are incorporated into the FAVAR model for structural analysis.

7.2.2 Two equations approach

$$y_t = (F_t', z_t')' \tag{7.16}$$

$$x_t = \Lambda^F F_t + \Lambda^z Z_t + e_t \tag{7.17}$$

Observation equation - where x_t is a T by N panel data matrix containing large datasets of economic and relevant variables. Z_t is the variable of interest that we are trying to explain ('endogenous' variable and used for impulse response analysis), and it is linked to the sum of x_t contemporaneously (i.e. large datasets of economic and relevant variables). F_t is a T by K matrix of unobserved factors which summarise the important information in x_t. The Λ^F are the factor loadings.

$$B(L) \begin{bmatrix} F_t \\ z_t \end{bmatrix} = \omega_t \tag{7.18}$$

$$B_t = c + \sum_{p=1}^{P} \beta_p B_{t-p} + \omega_t \tag{7.19}$$

Essentially, the steps of estimating a FAVAR can be summarised in 5 steps below:

Step 1) Approximate F_t as K principal components of x_t where x_t is stationary and standardised

Step 2) Rotate the principal components to obtain $\hat{F}_t$

Step 3) Estimate a FAVAR using $\hat{F}_t$ and z_t and estimate the impulse response to a policy shock using a Cholesky decomposition.

Step 4) Calculate the impulse response of $\hat{F}_t$ and z_t to the policy shock.

Step 5) Calculate the impulse response standard errors using the bootstrap method.

7.2.3 Principle component analysis

Following Stock and Watson (2002), Bernanke et al. (2005) also used a two-stage procedure which used principal component analysis (PCA) to estimate the factors before estimating the VAR model. Principal component analysis (PCA) is a procedure that converts a set of observations x_t which are potentially correlated to Z_t into a set of factors (to be plugged into the FAVAR model) of linearly uncorrelated variables called principal components or PCs. When the transformation is completed, the first PC would have the largest possible variance, and the PCs after would contain the remaining variance in the data, which the PCs must be orthogonal to the preceding PCs.

$$\arg\min_{\hat{F}_t, \Lambda_i} \sum_{i=1}^{N}\sum_{t=1}^{T} (x_i - \Lambda_i F_t)^2 \tag{7.20}$$

Essentially, the PCA estimation above aims to find the minimum number of factors needed to explain the datasets, in which the distance between the factors is minimised and orthogonal to each other so that they are distinct variations. The eigenvector associated with the largest eigenvalue indicates the direction in which the data has the most variance. Similarly, the second largest eigenvalue in the associated eigenvector is orthogonal to the largest eigenvector, in which the data has the largest remaining variance. As PCA is sensitive to the scale of the data, the common practice is to convert the data into stationary and also standardisation, i.e:

$$Z_{ij} = \frac{X_{ij} - \bar{x}_j}{s_j} \tag{7.21}$$

Where X_{ij} from data for the variable j in the sample unit i, $\bar{x}_j$ for the sample mean for variable j, and s_j for sample standard deviation for variable j.

The PCs are then rotated so that they are orthogonal. The factors remain uncorrelated and variances are preserved. In terms of the number of PCs to be used in the models, common methods include looking at the scree plots of the PCAs (if available) visually or using formal statistics such as the information criteria in Bai and Ng (2002). However, very often it is simply an exercise depending on the output, such as the shocks on variables for impulse responses. For example, in Bernanke et al. (2005), the authors increased the number of PCs k until there is no change in impulse responses. They found that the first three principal components capture the information in the dataset sufficiently, and additional PCs did not contribute much.

7.2.4 Estimation of FAVAR and structural Identification

Now recall that the observation equation below, where $B_t = \hat{F}_t$, Z_t, from the estimation of the factors by the PCA, we should now have the factors so that the rest of the equation can be estimated.

$$B_t = c + \sum_{p=1}^{P} \beta_p B_{t-p} + \omega_t \tag{7.22}$$

In this case, ordinary least squares (OLS) can be used for the estimate equation above. In the example from Bernanke et al. (2005), for example, the authors used Cholesky decompilation with ordering $\hat{F}_t$ based on Z_t. For instance, the variable of interest was the federal fund rates, and the authors were interested in separately the economic variables into slow and fast-moving variables. The recursive ordering here implies that certain series such as equity prices and price index are likely to be affected first; therefore, they are ordered last and with slow variables ranking first, such as GDP.

Similarly, if we are interested in the sole effect from monetary policy only, to identify such effect, recursive ordering can be applied below such that:

$$(f_t^{s'}, z_t^{s'}, r_t, f_t^{f'}, z_t^{f'})' \tag{7.23}$$

Variables are grouped into slow and fast-moving groups (s for slow and f for fast), which implies that the factors are needed to be extracted separately from those two groups. When the variables above, e.g. $f_t^{s'}$ and $f_f^{f'}$ are ranked above or below the interest rate, the fast-moving factors can be instantaneously affected in a lower triangular recursive identification scheme. In this case, this restriction implies that the central bank, which has the control of r_t couldn't be affected by the fast-moving variables as they react to the change in r_t instantaneously (within the period t, so that cannot be observed). Further restrictions can also be applied for the identification schemes, such as sign restriction or imposing a zero factor loading so that the impulse responses would react accordingly (see chapter 16, Kilian and Lütkepohl 2017).

Similarly, impulse responses can be obtained akin to other VAR type models after estimating the FAVAR model. Bootstrapping is often then used for approximating the distribution of the impulse responses, although there is no formal criterion to the draws required.

7.3 DSGE model

7.3.1 Introduction

In this section, the focus is on the DSGE model. First, we demonstrate a simple, canonical DSGE model in detail, including the behavioural equations that form the model and its solution and shocks. We then compare DSGE models to VAR models in terms of their methodology. It is also possible to compare DSGE to VAR by transforming the DSGE model into a reduced VAR form. This is done via a state-space representation of the DSGE model into reduced VAR models. However, this process is complex and often hard to justify; therefore, it is not considered here (Giacomini, 2013). Instead, the focus is on the methodology behind the model and the possible output such as IRFs. As mentioned above, due to its differences to the VAR models in terms of the setup up and particularly the restrictions needed for the identification of shocks, it is difficult to compare the DSGE model to the GVAR model directly. As direct comparison is not available, we turn to comparison by means of impulse response analysis of shocks generated from the model. The actual experiment of comparing the DSGE with GVAR is demonstrated in the next chapter.

7.3.2 Canonical DSGE model

Since the birth of the real business cycle analysis in the 1980s, in response to Lucas's critique, countless DSGE have been published. Each has its own specification and reasoning for the chosen construction. To simplify the diversity and intricate details on such enormous numbers of papers published in this area, we focus on the canonical form of an example DSGE model that is constructed with two agents only, namely the households and firms. We then demonstrate the behavioural equations that are composed of in the model. Having established this basic equation model, we then demonstrate the solution to the general equilibrium state and the shocks used to study the dynamics within such a model. A simple model is used in this section, from the seminal paper by Kydland and Prescott (1982), with modified notations1.[1] The goal here is to examine the construction of the DSGE model from a comparison perspective which allows us to conduct the experiments in the following chapter. Extensions to the seminal model include many New Keynesian features such as different types of rigidities and more agents such as the government and other sectors are used in the literature and will be discussed further in the next chapter where the relevant models are being used for comparison with the estimated GVAR model.

Aside from the complexity that could be added into the model with other features, the basic, canonical DSGE model is relatively simple. As shown below, it consists of two representative agents in the economy, namely the households and the firms. More realistic features can also be added to the model, such as the government, the financial sector, etc., and such models will be considered when comparing with the GVAR model in the next chapter. The main selling point of the DSGE model was the fact that it was founded with a method based on micro and macro theories. The agents in this model behave like a perfectly logical economic agent such that it forward-looking and has rational expectations. It is obvious that this assumption cannot be realistic, but from a modelling approach, the goal is to construct agents that are representational to the whole population; therefore, such agents represent all consumers and firms. Another important assumption in this model is that the agents, i.e. firms and households, have infinite lives. This assumption is important for dynamic analysis, although the actual agents are themselves mortal new agents appear continuously throughout time, i.e. firms are created assuming that they will exist permanently and new generations of their off-springs represent households. When the representational agents are constructed, their decisions—guided by their behavioural equations founded on micro-foundations—will allow a general equilibrium that can be solved. The result is the interaction of the two agents that are based on the maximisation of their objective function. Shocks can then be applied to the system, and we can then trace out the possible reactions from the agents and, therefore, the changes in parameters that represent them.

7.3.3 Agents in the model

The Households

Households, which are families and consumers, consist of millions of individuals in the economy and make economic decisions that are slightly

---

[1] Discussion below is based on the studies on Kydland and Prescott (1982) with notations adapted from Chacon (2015). A more formal result can be seen in chapter 2 Canova (2007) or chapter 3 in De Jong and Dave (2011)

different. At the same time, we can also reasonably assume that, given rational expectation, people would choose leisure over work and wealth over poverty, which is universal values. In this case, we assume that an individual's happiness depends on two things, consumption, *C*, and leisure, *O*. The simple definitions are: consumption means the number of goods and services utilised by the representational consumer while leisure is the time not spent in working. The question of interest is how an individual maximises the utility function given the constraint of scare resources. In other words, we have:

$$U(C, O) \tag{7.24}$$

Where first derivatives are both positive for *C* and *O*, implying that extra consumption and leisure increases the utility for the individual. It also follows the law of diminishing return that the utility obtained by extra consumption and leisure will increase but at a lower rate given the same amount of *C* and *O* i.e. negative second derivative both negative, implying greater utility but at a decreasing rate, a concave function. A classic assumption is being used here in which the utility function is considered to be instantaneous, implying the consumer's utility over a period of time depends on consumption and leisure during this period. These are the so-called non-time-separable utility functions implicit in empirical studies such as Kydland and Prescott (1982), allowing the consumers to decide the best combination instantaneously to maximise the utility function. It is now clear that the consumer's goal is to maximise *C* and *O*, subject to a budget constraint.

$$\max_{(C_t, O_t)} E_t \sum_{t=0}^{\infty} \beta^t U(C_t, O_t) \tag{7.25}$$

subject to constraint:

$$C_t + S_t = W_t L_t + R_t K_t \tag{7.26}$$

The function above denotes the maximisation of *C* and *O* and subjects it to the budget constraint in the second equation. In the maximising function, the utility is also subject to an inter-temporal discount factor β^t which indicates how an individual value the future utility compared to the current utility; therefore, the higher the value of this parameter, the lower the consumer places future utility in relation to the instantaneous utility. Here we also have the budget constraint, which is defined by the consumer and saving at t. In this case, saving is also the same as investments, defined by money not consumed at time *t*. Therefore, the budget depends on the wage times hours spent on labour $W_t L_t$ and also the last term, $R_t K_t$, which is often referred to as the non-human rent such as income from capital (rent times capital). Therefore written in words, the goal of the consumer is to maximise its utility of consumption and leisure at time t at a rate, trade-off with future time $t + p$, based on the constraint of income, which is then defined as the income from labour and that of capital. If we also allow savings to accumulate through time so that the savings (investments) can boost future income, then we can also introduce the capital accumulation process:

$$K_{t+1} = (1 - \delta)K_t + I_t \tag{7.27}$$

This states that capital at $t + 1$ equals the capital at time t + savings (investments) I_t at time t. If we take this into account, then the budget constraint becomes:

$$C_t + K_{t+1} - (1 - \delta)K_t = W_t L_t + R_t K_t \tag{7.28}$$

Also, note that the capital depreciation rate δ could be estimated from empirical research or a calibrated value. For example, 6% was used in Kydland and Prescott (1982). This maximisation problem can now be solved by finding the Lagrangian parameter for L_t, C_t, K_t. Similar to solving a standard constrained optimisation with Lagrange multipliers, we first set the constraint equal to zero, then multiply it by the Lagrange multiplier L and adding the product to the original function.

The critical values of L_t, C_t, K_t can then be found by taking the partial derivates with respect to all these variables and setting them to zero. Therefore the first-order conditions (FOCs) for the three values in the utility function:

$$\frac{\partial \mathcal{L}}{\partial C} : \beta^t \left[\frac{\gamma}{Ct} - \lambda_t \right] = 0 \tag{7.29}$$

$$\frac{\partial \mathcal{L}}{\partial L} : \beta^t \left[\frac{1-\gamma}{1-L_t} - \lambda_t W_t \right] = 0 \tag{7.30}$$

$$\frac{\partial \mathcal{L}}{\partial K} : \beta^t \lambda_t [R_t + 1 - \delta] - \beta^t \lambda_{t-1} = 0 \tag{7.31}$$

If we solve this and substitute the first FOC into the second FOC, this leads to the equations that will go into the DSGE model:

$$\frac{(1-\gamma)}{\gamma} \frac{C_t}{1-L_t} = W_t \tag{7.32}$$

In which this represents a conditional that equates the marginal rate of substitution between consumption and leisure to the opportunity cost of an additional unit of leisure.

$$\frac{C_t}{C_{t-1}} = \beta[R_{t+1} + 1 - \delta]$$

(7.33)

From the third FOC, we find the equation above, which is the condition that equals the marginal rate of consumption with the marginal rate of investment. The equations above determine the individual decisions about savings/investments and also the constraint from labour, which the consumer will maximise its utility form. From the equations, we can see that there are four endogenous variables (C_t, L_t, W_t, R_t) that can be used as variables of interest for shocks. The response from these endogenous variables can then be traced out similarly to the impulse response analysis in VAR models.

The Firms

Another agent in this model is the firms representing entrepreneurs and the industry that produce goods and services consumed by the households. Therefore the firms create outputs by transforming capital and labour. During this section, we will demonstrate that the problem for the firm is to maximise the output, i.e. profit Π_t while lowering the wages to the labour $W_t L_t$ and cost of renting the capital $R_t K_t$. As seen in the above equations for the households, the budget was defined by $W_t L_t$ and $R_t K_t$. From the firm's perspective, this became the objects for minimisation. If we define the profit as the difference between revenue by selling output Y_t and the cost of production, i.e. $W_t L_t$ and $R_t K_t$ therefore we have:

$$\max \Pi_t = Y_t - W_t L_t - R_t K_t$$

(7.34)

which is subject to the constraint of capital and labour and also the technology that transforms those two factors:

$$Y_t = A_t F(K_t, L_t)$$

(7.35)

Here the term A_t stands for total factor productivity (TFP), which represents the state of the knowledge at time t that allows for utilising the factors.

If we also assume that the firm follows that Cobb-Douglas production function, we have the equation below and that α is the output elasticity.

$$A_t F(k_t, L_t) = A_t K_t^{\alpha} L_t^{1-\alpha}$$

(7.36)

Therefore if we substitute the Cobb - Douglas function into the maximisation problem, we have:

$$\max \Pi_t = A_t K_t^{\alpha} L_t^{1-\alpha} - W_t L_t - R_t K_t$$

(7.37)

Following a similar procedure from the example of the household, the Lagrange multiplier can also be used in this multivariate constrained optimisation problem. The actual derivation of the FOCs has been omitted here; for full derivation, see Chacon (2015). From this, we obtain the below equations representing the rent and also the wages in relation to productive factors.

$$R_t = \frac{\alpha A_t K_t^\alpha L_t^{1-\alpha}}{K_t} = \alpha \frac{Y_t}{K_t} \tag{7.38}$$

$$W_t = \frac{(1-\alpha)A_t K_t^\alpha L_t^{1-\alpha}}{L_t} = (1-\alpha)\frac{Y_t}{L_t} \tag{7.39}$$

7.3.4 Model Equations

So have we have described the behaviour of the two agents and to summarise, households maximise consumption and leisure and decide how much to save and work in order to obtain those needs. The firms maximise profits by producing goods selling to the households by maximising the profits such that the labour cost and capital rent will be minimised. From the equations above, we have now our model economy below:

$$\frac{(1-\gamma)}{\gamma}\frac{C_t}{1-L_t} = W_t \tag{7.40}$$

$$\frac{C_t + 1}{C_t} = \beta[R_{t+1} + 1 - \delta] \tag{7.41}$$

$$R_t = \frac{\alpha A_t K_t^\alpha L_t^{1-\alpha}}{K_t} = \alpha \frac{Y_t}{K_t} \tag{7.42}$$

$$W_t = \frac{(1-\alpha)A_t K_t^\alpha L_t^{1-\alpha}}{L_t} = (1-\alpha)\frac{Y_t}{L_t} \tag{7.43}$$

$$Y_t = A_t K_t^\alpha L_t^{1-\alpha} \tag{7.44}$$

If we also allow accumulation of physical capital over time and also the fact that final output is determined by C_t and I_t, then we also have:

$$K_{t+1} = (1-\delta)K_t + I_t \tag{7.45}$$

$$C_t + I_t = Y_t \tag{7.46}$$

Therefore we are now in a position to calculate the general equilibrium for the economy. If we assume a competitive economy that is the norm for most countries now, this will allow the agents to decide their objective functions. The competitive equilibrium is achieved when both agents are satisfied by their objective functions while no one is worse off, leading to a Pareto optimal solution. Again, this is also a constrained maximisation problem which is defined by the equation below and is also subject to the budget constraint.

$$\max_{(C_t, I_t, O_t)} \mathcal{L} \sum_{t=0}^{\infty} \beta^t [\gamma \log C_t + (1 - \gamma) \log(1 - L_t)] \tag{7.47}$$

$$C_t + I_t = W_t L_t + R_t K_t \tag{7.48}$$

$$I_t = K_{t+1} - (1 - \delta) K_t \tag{7.49}$$

From the equations above, we would be able to define the path of the model economy that is in equilibrium. Suppose we do not consider growth within this economy. In that case, we can also derive the steady states of the model, which can be used to obtain the stationary values for all seven endogenous variables: consumption, investment, capital, labour, rent, wages, and output. However, as these are non-linear differential equations that cannot be solved directly since there is no closed-form solution, they need to be approximated before being solved. Often, the non-linear models are first log-linearised first before approximated by a linear solution method. For example, Kydland and Prescott (1982) first used a quadratic approximation for the steady states. Later methods also emerged, such as Sims's method (2002) or Blanchard and Kahn's method (1980), which separate the non-linear equations into explosive and non-explosive components.[2] In particular, Sims's method and Klein's method (2002) are most relevant as the non-linear equations are converted into reduced form equations via VAR and state-space representation which directly link the two methods together. The relationship between DSGE and VAR will be discussed further in the last section of this chapter.

As can be seen from the above equations describing the agents' behaviour and their maximisation problem to solve for the general equilibrium, they will lead to a steady, deterministic state. However, this is only the case if there are no disturbances affecting the economy, which cannot be true; therefore, stochastic elements also need to be introduced into these equations. From the model equations above, we have seven endogenous variables. In this case, we can apply exogenous shocks such as productivity shock to our system and see how those variables react. Note that the shocks in the DSGE literature generally refer to an exogenous variable that is often assumed to be a stochastic first-order autoregressive AR(1) process.

---

[2] 2For further details on comparison of approximation methods see (p.65 -66 Canova, 2007)

7.3.5 Estimation

Once the approximation of the model has been done, and thus the general equilibrium conditions have been solved, we then need to parametrise the models. In the DSGE literature, there are, in general, two distinct methods to obtain the values for the parameters (such as discount factor β, capital depreciation rate δ). These are either obtained via calibration or estimation with econometric methods such as generalised methods of moments (GMM) or maximum likelihood (ML).[3] However, estimation of the DSGE models is often very difficult and problematic if we also involve stochastic elements in the model. For example, when there are fewer shocks than observables. Often there are ways to solve this problem but come with difficult trade-off decisions that will affect the final estimation of the result/inferences made from it. This could be amended, for example, by adding more shocks to the system, but shocks added to the DSGE model may lack a clear structural interpretation and increase the number of parameters for estimation. This would decrease the degrees of freedom available while simultaneously increase the chance of model misspecification (Ireland 2004). A more formal approach for calibration was used in Rotemberg and Woodford (1997), in which the parameters were chosen to match certain statistical moments of the data that match best with the monetary policy shocks. However, it still suffers from not using all information available from the data.

In light of these issues, many models often use calibrated values previously estimated in the literature. The actual implementation of calibration involves finding the value of the parameters in some methods, which may or may not be rigorous. An example is the calibrated value for capital depreciation rate \delta, which is assumed to be around 8-10% as it is often the case found in accounting. Therefore the benefit and drawback are easy to see that while this may seem arbitrary to assign a value that is not estimated rigorously, it does provide quick and feasible value to the actual data that may occur in the real world. From our example model above, five parameters need to be assigned values:

$$\Omega = \{\alpha, \beta, \delta, \gamma, \rho_A, \sigma_A\} \tag{7.50}$$

α = Technological parameter 0.50

From our equations in (2.46), (2.47) and (2.48), we can see that this parameter enters as part of the Cobb-Douglas production function. This is known as the technological parameter, which defines the productivity of capital. For example, it defines the capital that is actually being employed for the find output, minus the income paid to labour. Therefore this number is between 1

---

[3] For a full review of empirical methods of DSGE models see Part II, De Jong and Dave 2011.

and 0. From estimates in the literature, this is often between 30% ~ 50%, depending on the particular economy. In this case, we follow the values used in Kydland and Prescott (1982)[4], which is set to 0.5.

β = Discount factor 0.99

This discount factor appears in equation (2.45), which is simply how the agents value future utility over present utility. Therefore if the value is one, then the agent values the future the same as the present and does not discount it. Often the value used hovers between 0.97 to 0.99, and 0.99 is used in this example.

γ = Preference parameter 0.50

These parameters enter the equation (2.44), which is the household's preference regarding consumption against labour. Therefore this number would be less than one as the worker would choose the desired 'work-life' balance. The parameter is chosen to be 50% in Kydland and Prescott (1982), which is considered to be acceptable. For standard work hours now, if we assume the average person works 42.5 hours per week and also allows 1.5 hours for a daily commute and 1 hour for daily activities that are related to work (networking, professional qualification, homework, etc.), then work-related hours would amount to 55 hours out of 168 possible in 7 days = 33%. The 50% value is at the higher end, but it was more acceptable during the time of writing, as it was the norm where workers could work well up to 12 hours per day. In this case, we will retain the value for our example.

δ = Depreciation rate 0.1

This is the capital stock's physical depreciation rate, which appears in equation (2.49) and is assumed to be 10% per year. This slows down the accumulation process and, therefore, a lower rental gained from households who own the capital but also a lower rental paid by the firms.

ρ_A = TFP autoregressive parameter 0.95

σ_A = TFP standard deviation 0.02

$$\ln A_t = (1 - \rho_A) \ln \overline{A} + \rho_A \ln A_{t-1} + \varepsilon_t^A$$

(7.51)

---

[4] The parameters values here are adapter from (p.1363 Kydland and Prescott, 1982). The original paper was not precise on how it arrived at these numbers but gave a good reason behind most. More rigorous approach to calibration can also be seen in the literature and were also later expanded by Kydland and Prescott. For an overall review see (p.119 - 147 De Jong and Dave, 2011). Detailed technique discussion on comparing the pros and cons of different calibration and estimation methods can also be seen in Canova 2007, p.65-66.

There are two remaining parameters that need to be calibrated - ρ_A and σ_A, namely the TFP autoregressive parameter and standard deviation. So far, in the model, we have not included any shocks. However, if we are to include a productivity shock—for example, the total factor productivity A_t, which appears in the equations of (2.46), (2.47) and (2.48)—the common practice is to set it to an AR (1) process with residuals as seen from the equation above, although this can be changed. In this case, as the shock follows an AR(1) process similar to others, the autoregressive term $(1 - \rho_A)$ needs to be small; otherwise, it would be a non-stationary process. It is set to be 0.95 in this case. We also have $\bar{A}$ which denotes the steady values obtained during equilibrium. The residuals ε_t^A is also assumed to be normally distributed with zero mean and a standard deviation of σ_A^2. In this case, it is set to 0.02 (2% standard deviation shock) (p.1363 Kydland and Prescott, 1982). Like any other AR(1) process, these terms can be estimated with OLS or other econometric techniques, but as the actual TFP series cannot be observed, therefore this value can only be approximated or calibrated within economic reason.

7.3.6 Productivity Shock

We have now ready to solve for the general equilibrium and also the steady state values. TFP shock can also be applied to these variables, which will be reported in this section.

Given the calibrated values from the literature, our model has been solved as below, which shows the steady state values when in equilibrium. The initial value is also listed on the left column—assigned randomly—with plausible values that may occur in a real economy. For example, Y is set to 1, which has no intrinsic value in itself. Consumption was set to 0.8, slightly lower than the output, indicating the possible consumption ratio in an economy. The rest are also assigned in a similar fashion, which gives a stylised economy. However, importance should be placed on the steady state values, which are the values that have been solved for the general equilibrium, considering all behavioural equations and their maximisation problems. The Y has been reported as 2.17, which in itself does not signify much. However, as $Y = C + I$, the ratio of C and I compared to Y become meaningful. For example, from our DSGE model, we can see that out of all output, only 55% was consumed while 45% was saved as an investment for the next period. This is indicated by the discount factor β setting at 0.99, indicating the households discount very little regarding the future, i.e. willing to defer consumption until the next period. From the Kratio to output, we can see that it requires 4.5 times of capital stock per output. This is indicated by the accumulation process introduced in the model. As households would like to save for the future, therefore accumulate more capital in the process. As the firms are constrained to the wages of households and renting of the capital stock, more capital is required, and less rent can be extracted by households (given the abundance of the capital stock available).

Table 7.1: Endogenous variable values

Variable name	Initial value	Steady state value	Ratio to Y
Y	1	2.17105	100%
C	0.8	1.18512	55%
I	0.3	0.985931	45%
K	3.5	9.85931	454%
L	0.2	0.47807	
R	$\alpha\left(\frac{Y}{K}\right) = 0.142$	0.110101	
W	$(1-\alpha)\frac{Y}{L} = 2.5$	2.27064	
A	1	1	

Next, we consider the response from the seven endogenous variables. In this case, we assume that the shock for an AR(1) process and that we have set the shock to a 2% shock. Therefore, we are now checking the impulse responses and estimating what would happen if there is a positive 2% shock in Total factor productivity. From the graphs below, the red lines represent steady state values. As mentioned before, as the model itself is deterministic, the values will stay the same unless there is a perturbation from an outside force such as the exogenous TFP A.

From the results above, we can see that output quickly increases by more than 5% instantly, but this increase slowly decreases after the 10th period and gradually returns to the steady state, about 40+ periods later. The consumption also rises by more than 2% but at a slow rate before subduing. An interesting phenomenon here is that the investment, i.e. saving, increased sharply at near 4% before a sharp decrease in the later periods. Due to an increase in TFP, the time spent on working, i.e. labour in hours, also reduced although not as significantly. The wage also increased amid the increase before lowering later. We also see an increase in capital stock around 2% tops. However, the rent value from capital stock has decreased as an increase in capital lowers the rate.

The behavioural equations explain the results of these changes in the variables in the model. As we assume that the parameters do not change, i.e., they are deep parameters, akin to personalities and spending habits, the agents would dynamically adapt and re-optimise their objective functions given the new constraint in each period and re-maximise their solution. As can be seen, this model is a significantly simplified version of the modern economy where there are also the government, financial market and other agents. Therefore, by adding new agents and changing the agents' behaviour, we can also see that the complexity and the potential interactions from the newly added elements will significantly increase. From the above results, the outputs from the impulse response analysis can be compared to those produced by VAR class type of models. However, this is not straightforward, as the mechanisms behind those shocks differ significantly. The identification of shocks from the empirical and, therefore, the final results come from the specification, which is also hard to compare with a DSGE model.

Figure 7.1: Productivity shocks to endogenous variables

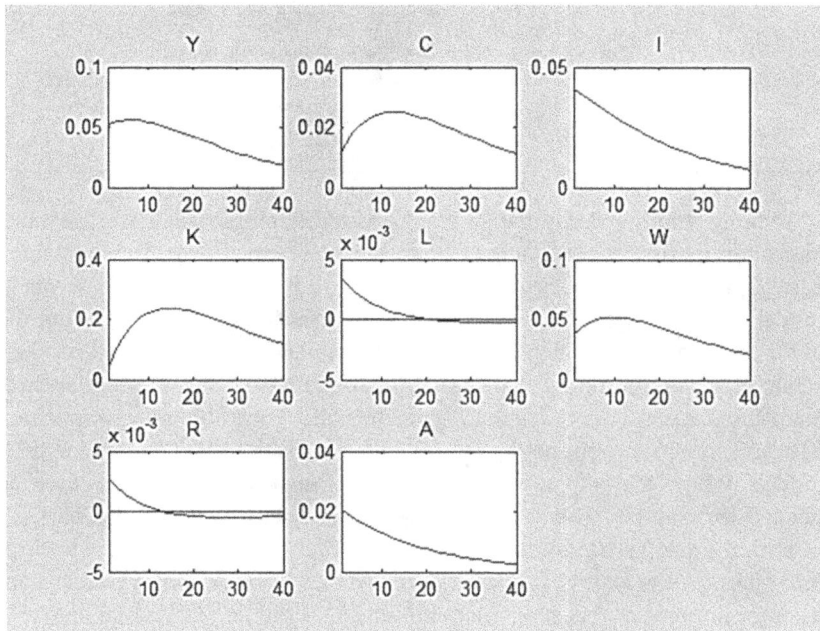

7.4 Summary of macroeconometric models

In conjunction with the first chapter, we have reviewed the history, rationale and methodologies of different macroeconometric models. This chapter's emphasis has been on the methodologies of the GVAR, FAVAR and DSGE models. To illustrate the workings of the DSGE model, a simple two-agents model has been calibrated and solved for the shocks. Extra attention has been paid to the peculiarities of the DSGE model as it is significantly different from the two other models, and it cannot be compared with them directly. In the next chapter, two experiments will be described that were made with the intention of comparing the two methods with the GVAR model. Much has been discussed on the technical details of different approaches, but an evaluation of the models is still needed for a conclusion.

Figure 7.2: Summary of models

Properties	SEM	VAR	SVAR	FAVAR	GVAR	DSGE
Number of variables	Very large	Few	Few	Many	Very large	Large
Number of countries	Many	Very few	Very few	Many	Many	Few
Number of shocks	Many	Few	Few	Many	Many	Few
Trend treatment	Implicit	Explicit	Explicit	N/A	Explicit	Explicit
Dynamic restrictions	Little.	No	Yes	N/A	Many	Few
Exogeneity restrictions	Many	No	No	No	Yes	Yes
Shock identification	Few	Few	Yes	Yes	Mixed	Explicit, AR(1)
Forecasting	Poor	Excellent	N/A	Excellent	Good	Good
Policy analysis	Poor	Poor	Good	Good	Good	Good
Diagnostic tests	Many	Many	Many	Few	Many	Many
Extensions	Few	Many	Many	Few	Few	Many
Computational resources	High	Very low	Medium	Low	Difficult	Very difficult

From the review and comparison made with different approaches, the table above summarises the evaluations made. If an economist wants to model for a certain purpose, say, policy analysis to simulate a monetary shock, then which model should be used? It is easy to have an impression that one model fits all, as this is often the case when certain camps of model followers deride the other schools for their promotion. However, from the extensive review in the last two chapters, it is now easy to see that, while there are many different approaches, with VAR and DSGE dominating most literature now, there is still room for SEM models, which are still served in a specialist area, when disaggregation is needed, for example, when a policymaker would like to forecast to the reaction in a local, regional economy (say, dominated by car industry and export to other parts of the world using local ports) from a foreign country increase on taxes for imports. In this case, the traditional SEM model or FAVAR models are both good choices as they allow a detailed description of the micro time series required for this question. The GVAR could also be a good choice for the modeller, as it allows regional interactions between different groups while allowing for common factors such as global oil price, metal price, etc., which would directly affect domestic and foreign countries.

For example, if the modeller indeed used all three methods (SEM, FAVAR and GVAR), what purpose do they serve and what is the one to use? Suppose the modeller is looking for microscopic interaction among different components of the local supply chain. In that case, the SEM is certainly the best for this, assuming that the modeller has no problem obtaining the data and has enough conviction in his own specification of the model. However, if such conviction is not available, we may rely on the data to tell a story, which the FAVAR models can be served best. The factors that will be estimated would significantly shrink the data without losing much information contained. This would allow econometric estimation of the VAR model with the factors. This would allow the most detailed iteration of shocks on all the variables in the model. By combining the impulse response graphs from shock with an increase of foreign import tax and variance decomposition, he would foresee the industry's reactions based on previous data. To ensure a meaningful interpretation of the shock, an identification strategy is also needed. This would be similar to the one in SVAR but for significantly more variables due to the extra variables being used. However, the main problem that he will face here is the fact that he would find very little guidance in terms of changes in structural parameters. Although the factors estimated summarises the data well, it does not give any economic interpretation to the modeller, and therefore there would not be enough information for him other than the forecasts and shock analysis. Lastly, if he has also used a GVAR model, he would have obtained a global model based on an intuitive domestic and foreign country setting. The data from both sides into each other's equation via the mean of the trade relationship. Intuitively, if the foreign country that the local industry is exporting cars to has a large trade volume, then the impact from an increase in import tax would very likely dampen the appeal of selling local cars. As seen in the literature, the identification of shocks mainly relies on the data's long-run restriction. Other restrictions are less developed for the GVAR approach. Therefore, in this case, the modeller would obtain a set of shocks that have been estimated based on a previously identified structure in the shocks.

From the brief example above, each approach has its own pros and cons, and that can be difficult to decide unless there are a clear purpose and structure to the question being asked. In general, the conclusion can be drawn that SEM models provide the best disaggregated, detailed information on future interactions based on the equations, but those equations could be misspecified, and the identification is inadequate for shocks. Logically, this leads to the DSGE model that models the representative agents and then solves them for their optimisation. Shocks are then applied to see how the steady states are being moved by perturbations. However, the difficulties in terms of estimation have made the models almost impossible to expand beyond a handful of countries. On the other hand, GVAR and FAVAR are very similar, although they are vastly different in terms of the setting and estimation procedure. However, it can be concluded that they both make use of the full information; while GVAR is stronger for economic intuition and interpretations of the estimated model for policy analysis, FAVAR is potentially better for forecasting and is also much quicker to run and evaluate. The older cousins of VAR and SVAR remain the workhorse models as both can be estimated and analysed very quickly, and they are, therefore, much better for a simple system. However, an actual comparison between the models is needed in order to properly evaluate them, which is the aim of the next chapter.

Chapter 8

GVAR Model Validation and Forecasting

8.1 Introduction

The purpose of this chapter is to further the comparison of GVAR with other models with empirical testing. During the last chapter, the various models have been illustrated with their specifications, and a comparison was made on the basis of their methodological similarities and differences. There is only so much that can be said about theoretical comparison, however. Therefore, to continue the comparison, empirical testing is needed to contrast the GVAR model's performance with others. In this comparison exercise, we have already covered the theoretical basis of the GVAR and other macroeconometric models; therefore, the previous chapters should already serve as a foundation to understand their similarities and differences. In the following pages, we first begin examining the model comparison strategy used in the literature, and empirical testing was made to apply forecasting and impulse response analysis. Discussion and conclusion come in the end.

To summarise, the GVAR model can be used for two types of applications, i.e. economic forecasting and scenario analysis. This is also akin to other macro models where they are also designed for such applications, and as such, GVAR models can be compared based on these two applications. In this chapter, we being by examining the forecasting power of the GVAR models. We begin by using a global data set and estimate two different GVAR models (the first one with a restriction on the interest rates and the second one with unrestricted interest rates) and forecast the data within the sample to have a benchmark on how well the forecasting power is. In the second step, we also compare the results from the forecasts of GVAR models to forecasts from the standard autoregressive model. Given the theoretical underpinning of the GVAR model and its emphasis on its ability to using the full information set available, it is our question to ask whether such extra information improve our forecasts. However, the conclusion from the empirical tests shows that GVAR ex-ante forecasts fare no better than simple AR models. Out of 30 AR estimated models, only 15 forecasts from the GVAR models won against the AR forecasts in terms of lower root mean square (RMSE) error. Although the forecasting results are no particularly good for the GVAR model, the verdict on its forecast ability is inconclusive. For example, GVAR was found to be very effective for a few variables, such as the exchange rates for a few countries. Further discussion in the latter part of this chapter.

The comparison of models based on scenario analysis is, however, less straightforward. The main difficulty is the absence of a 'true model' and also widely agreed objective measure. The logic behind forecast comparison is easy to grasp. The forecasting model with minimal distance between the forecasts and actual results is considered to be better. Although this is the sole factor, other factors can also increase the value of a forecasting tool, such as the usability and the economic reasoning behind it. The case for scenario analysis is more complex, however. By definition, scenario analysis is conditional forecasting, i.e. given that A happens, what will happen to B in time t+2, ceteris paribus. This is also not observable and cannot be compared directly in reality as the ceteris paribus cannot be fulfilled. Without such a true model that exists, we can only compare the relevant output, i.e. impulse response analysis from the GVAR and similar macro models.

As mentioned before, the comparison between DSGE type models and VAR models is often difficult and imprecise due to the peculiar setup of the DSGE models and the identification strategy used in the VAR models. On the other hand, if we have the same set of data, we can then compare the methods of GVAR with FAVAR since both are essentially VAR type models that are designed to handle large datasets. Therefore to aid the comparison of these models, an experiment was made for this chapter. Figure 9.11 shows the two sets of experiments that were carried out. The first experiment involved taking the datasets which were used for the estimation of a GVAR model in di Mauro and Smith (2013, chapter 1) and then approximating the results with a FAVAR model, using the same datasets but following the logical specification of a FAVAR model, which would allow us to compare the results coming from two models, in the form of impulse response functions from monetary shocks. As the DSGE model cannot be compared directly, in this case, we used four different multicountry DSGE models to estimate the effects of the monetary shocks on the US economy and compare the responses to those estimated with GVAR and FAVAR models. The significance of comparing IRFs from DSGE models to those of the GVAR datasets is to provide a second check and present the consensus of the DSGE models from the literature. From this exercise, we can see that even though the starting points are vastly different for the different methods, the conclusion can be comparable, although with the expected differences, particularly in the long-run dynamics.

In the following chapter, we first begin evaluating GVAR's forecasting ability. In the second part, we also examine and compare GVAR with alternative models with IRFs. Diagnostics tests and further details regarding the forecasts and tests are included in the appendix.

8.2 Evaluating the forecasting ability of the GVAR model

8.2.1 Comparing forecasts

Different users will have different forecasting needs. For example, an ordinary investor will probably be interested in understanding how the variables of interest, such as equity prices, are likely to be in order to adjust the portfolio. In this case, we can see that the forecast is served as a tool to illustrate what could happen in the future and so that the investor could adapt to it. On the other hand, central bankers and government economists setting for fiscal policies will likely use the forecast to act on it to alter the course of the future. In the first group, ordinary investors who are unlikely to yield the power to change the course of economic events will show adaptive behaviour, while the second group, i.e. central bankers and government economists who can set economic policies, are much more likely to affect the course of the economy, particularly in the near future. In this case, the second group shows a retroaction behaviour, implying that the forecast they made would react to such a forecast and change the action, therefore invalidating the forecast itself. Therefore, these two very different behaviours are two forms of forecasting, i.e. conditional and unconditional forecasts. Unconditional forecasts are much more familiar to what is generally known as forecast, i.e. a set of numbers forecasted about the future. It attempts to describe the most likely scenario, given the information we have now and the past. On the other hand, conditional forecasts are based on specific and possibly unrealistic assumptions on the economic agents/variables in order to see what would happen in the future, given such restrictions. For example, the central bankers would be interested in knowing what would happen to the world economy if interest rates are lowered.

Summarising from the economic forecasting literature—like Armstrong (2001), Carnot et al. (2011), Elliott and Timmermann (2013), and Granger and Newbold (2014)—we can see that the sole value of the forecast can only be understood in relation to and in the context of guiding decisions in areas of economics and finance. For example, Carnot et al. (2011, p.265-308) have summarised a widely used framework in evaluating economic forecasts. It first looks at some of the conceptual issues, i.e. how to compare forecasts (what is actually being compared), forecast accuracy, and measurement and potential errors. The variables being compared, for instance, are not necessarily the same, and there is a risk that comparison is being made with 'oranges and apples.' To mitigate this, the variables of interests must be defined clearly so that comparison can be made on the same basis. There is also model uncertainty in which the models that produce the forecasts are misspecified. In this case, the forecasts produced from such models would also be biased, either forecasting pressingly or vying in certain directions. To mitigate this, one can perform diagnostic tests on the estimated model itself to ensure that it is fit for forecasting purpose.

Accuracy is perhaps the most contentious issues with economic forecasts. This is also the value that is most attached to by their users and creators. Although far from straightforward, in general, we do have a 'true model' that a forecasting model can be used for comparison; therefore, the problem of assessing the accuracy of the forecasting model itself is not particularly hard. The problem is in how to define the measurement of accuracy. Another closely related is the concept is that of quality. Suppose we have two competing forecasting models, and both have the same equally good forecasts (as defined and measured for their accuracy); in that case, we have to consider the extra information that the model can convey. This depends heavily on the user's purpose, however. If the user is simply interested in knowing the forecast, i.e. possible outcome of the future, then a sophisticated model would not yield more value than a naïve approach which would also give forecast values, should it be more accurate than the sophisticated approach. During the rest of the paper, the focus is on the accuracy of the forecasts. The extra merits of employing GVAR, which give a larger information set than simply naïve forecasts, will be discussed in the end.

8.2.2 Forecasting accuracy

As shown above, not only are forecasts themselves inherently difficult to make, their accuracy is also difficult to assess. To make the comparison as fair as possible, a suite of techniques is often used to provide checks on the forecast accuracy so that the result does not solely depend on the comparison being made. Of the plethora of various comparison methods available, the following techniques would be used for this chapter to assess the accuracy of forecasts, in line with Carnot et al. (2011, p.270).

Summary statistics

This is an intuitive way to understand and characterise the size of the forecast errors. The goal here is simple, compare the forecasts and the actual values and summarise the difference. Often three different summary statistics are used in the literature, i.e. the mean error (ME), also known as the bias measure. It should be close to zero for a good forecast. It simply sums up the error (i.e. the difference between forecast values and actual values) and divided by the forecast horizons. A similar concept of mean absolute error (MAE) is also used, which measures the same thing but in absolute values; therefore, an overestimate of a forecast value, for example +3 points, will be treated the same as an underestimate of a forecasts value, e.g. -3 points. Both would be treated as a positive +3 points error, thus giving a penalty to both directions equally.

Another method of summarising the difference and treating both positive and negative errors equally is more squaring of the errors, thus yielding positive values. This is equal to $\sqrt{(\sum_1^T E_t^2/T)}$, root mean squared error (RMSE). However, it should be noted that the unit of RMSE is based directly on the forecasts it has measured. For example, say we have two sequences of forecasts in front, one GDP per capita of a country (forecast of $35000 and actual result of $36000) and another one for GDP annual growth rate (say a forecast of 1.2% and actual result of 1.5%), by definition, the RMSE would be larger for GDP per capita as the base unit of it uses is larger than that of percentage in growth rate. Therefore RMSEs cannot be used for direct comparison across models. If we wish to compare RMSE across different models with different values, we need to normalise the calculated RMSEs first. Similar to error differences, there are also several ways to normalise it. For the purpose of this chapter, RMSEs were divided by the mean of the sum squared difference from the forecast horizon. For instance, a forecast horizon is eight periods or two years (8 quarters), then we have n=8, the difference between forecast and actual would be squared. The RMSE would then be divided by this mean. Like other measures, the lower value, the better value for the forecasting model, and an exact forecast would give a perfect 0 value.

The table below shows the relationship between the two, where there are eight forecast results for two different sequences. The first forecasts show each period increase by 1% per period, reaching 1.07 after eight periods. The same increase is also applied to the second forecast sequence, which begins at 0.10 and with an increase of 1% per period also, reaching 0.11 after eight periods. As the base unit values they begin are different, the RMSE would be different for them.

Let's consider the two forecast sequences to be the squared difference between the forecast and actual values. We can see that the RMSE mean would punish the second sequence much more harshly than the first; this is due to the fact that, although both forecast errors grow by 1% each period, the 1% value increase is much bigger for the second sequence (since the base value is smaller). Although this is not ideal, it does allow comparison across forecast models while not distorted by the base values.

Figure 8.1: RMSE vs RMSE/mean

1	2	3	4	5	6	7	8	RMSE	RMSE_Std	RMSE_mean
1.000	1.010	1.020	1.030	1.041	1.051	1.062	1.072	1.018	40.317	0.983
0.100	0.101	0.102	0.103	0.104	0.105	0.106	0.107	0.322	127.495	3.107

Rank of RMSEs and Sum of RMSEs

We can then rank the ranks of RMSE, with the smallest being the best, the biggest the worst. The above result shows that even though the RMSE can be normalised by dividing the mean, it can still favour those that have larger base values to begin with. To mitigate this there are two ways. Instead of comparing RMSE or RMSE/mean across models, we can compare the sum of RMSEs of several models together. For example, say if we have two GVAR models, GVAR00 and GVAR01, both estimated with the same data, but with different specifications, instead of comparing the individual country model within the GVAR models, we can compare the sum of RMSEs or RMSE/mean of GVAR00 with GVAR01. Since both would have the same amount of country models within and the same variables, the sum of RMSEs for both models would not be distorted by the problems above. In this case, the comparison is much simpler than the model, with the smallest RMSE being better.

Theil's U Test

Another measure that is not distorted is using Theil's U Test. It is similar to the above concepts. The formula below shows the calculation where P equals the forecast value and A being the actual value. First finds the sum of squared difference then divided by the sum of squared actual values. This is an ideal indicator for judging the relative quality of a forecast that takes into consideration the values of the variables of interest i.e. A_i^2. In this case, a value of 0 would indicate a perfect forecast.

Figure 8.2: Directional test

	1	2	3	4	5	6	7	8	Diff 1&2	Diff 2&3	Diff 3&4	Diff 4&5	Diff 5&6	Diff 6&7	Diff 7&8	Pos	Neg	Pos diff	Neg diff
Forecast	5.15446	5.15396	5.15571	5.1576	5.15883	5.15992	5.16041	5.16151	-0.00049	0.00175	0.00188	0.00124	0.00109	0.00048	0.0011	6	1	4	-4
Actual	5.16994	5.19774	5.18922	5.18204	5.17559	5.15863	5.15178	5.16336	0.0278	-0.00852	-0.00718	-0.00645	-0.01696	-0.00685	0.01158	2	5		

$$U_t = \frac{\sqrt{\sum_{t=1}^{n} (P_i - A_i)^2}}{\sqrt{\sum_{t=1}^{n} A_i^2}}$$

(8.1)

Directional tests

Another measurement that can be made in the direction of the forecast. Often, if the user's only interest is in knowing whether a variable will go up or down, then the size of the forecast error is less important. In this case, all we need to measure in the direction of the forecast and the actual result. In a sequence of, say, forecasts for eight periods, any positive value would indicate a positive direction, whereas a negative value would point to a negative direction. By comparing the sum of directions, we can understand whether the model over or underestimate compares to the actual direction of the results. The example below shows a sequence of forecasts for eight periods and their actual values. Let's take the difference period nearby periods, i.e. difference between 1st and 2nd period, 2nd and 3rd etc. We can tell the direction of the sequence and contrast it to that of the forecasts. If the sum of the forecast's positive and negative directions equal the actual results, it would be perfect. The example below shows that there are six positive directions from the forecast, and only one is negative. However, the actual result was two positive and five negative; therefore, the trend is quite the opposite. It should also be noted that, by definition, the difference between positive and negative directions would equal as if one forecast is overestimated, then it must be underestimated from the actual result perspective. The summing of positive and negative directions provide a robustness check on the result to ensure that it was calculated correctly.

Comparison with naïve forecasts

Although the user will be able to compare different forecasts with the tools above, they often mean little in isolation and with no context to whether the forecast errors are due to the model or the nature of the variables being difficult for prediction. In this case, a relative comparison can be made with GVAR and other so-called naïve models. The purpose of using naïve models is to see if the additional features from GVAR models can add value to forecast accuracy. There are several popular naïve models that can be used; for example, one can simply generate random numbers given certain parameters that describe the distribution of the variables with Monte Carlo or a simple model that simply goes up or down by a certain percentage. Therefore it is expected that GVAR must at least beat randomly generated forecasts, as otherwise, it would prove the model useless. Similarly, a random walk model can also be used to compare whether the GVAR forecasts would be better. In this chapter, autoregressive models were estimated instead, as they tend to be more accurate and would be significantly more meaningful than randomly generated models. The forecasts of simple AR models solely rely on its lags; therefore, it should be the most simplistic and practical alternative to GVAR models instead of random walks. The equation below shows the AR(p). Similar to other time series models, the estimation of the models would also be subjected to diagnosis checks such as augmented dicky fuller test for unit root and AIC / BIC lag selection etc. Like the ordinary linear regression model, it is assumed that the error terms are independently distributed based on a normal distribution with zero mean and a constant variance and that the error terms are independent of the y values.

$$y_i = \varphi_0 + \varphi_1 y_{i-1} + \varphi_1 y_{i-2} + \dots + \varphi_1 y_{i-p} + \varepsilon_i \tag{8.2}$$

Comparing the RMSE of the AR model with the equivalent GVAR model would then allow us to gauge their performance. In the example below, we have two estimated GVAR models, GVAR0 and GVAR1, two AR models, one with ex-ante forecasts and the other with ex-post forecasts. In total, there are four forecasts made.[1] On the right-hand side of the table, it ranks the RMSE of the respective models, where the lowest is the best with the rank 1 and so forth. By taking the ratio of the RMSE of the GVAR and the AR model, we then get a percentage. If the percentage is less than 100%, i.e. the RMSE for GVAR is less than AR, this favours the GVAR model. On the other hand, AR would win if the percentage is higher with the GVAR RMSE. In the example below, the ratio is 57% and 58.13%, respectively, therefore both beating the AR model.

Further to the GVAR models, two types of AR forecasts were made, with both ex-post and ex-ante. As ex-post is estimated with the latest available data, it tends to be much better than ex-ante models. The purpose here is not to directly compare the AR (ex-post) to the GVAR model since such functionality is not currently available, but this allows us to see the potential room for improvement should we wish to conduct 'nowcasting' with the latest available data as input. Another purpose of estimating the ex-post forecast is that it shows how that particularly depends on the latest available data. Suppose the difference between ex-post and ex-ante is large, and the ex-post is much more accurate. In that case, it shows that the time series being forecast is much more reliable on its latest data point instead of historical data and the foreign variables (since it is produced from itself hence autoregressive).

Figure 8.3: Ranking forecasting models for Saudi Arabia, GDP quarterly growth, inverse of the natural log

		Model	2015Q1	2015Q2	2015Q3	2015Q4	2016Q1	2016Q2	2016Q3	2016Q4	Rank	won	
		GVAR1	5.356	5.361	5.364	5.368	5.373	5.377	5.382	5.387	2	57.00%	1
sarbia	y	AR (EX Post)	5.365	5.387	5.405	5.391	5.401	5.403	5.402	5.412	1		
		AR (Ex Ante)	5.365	5.383	5.401	5.417	5.432	5.446	5.460	5.474	4		
		GVAR	5.356	5.361	5.365	5.368	5.372	5.376	5.381	5.385	3	58.13%	1
		Actual	5.368	5.386	5.387	5.394	5.394	5.395	5.400	5.415			

8.3 Estimating the GVAR model

8.3.1 Estimating the model

The first step of the GVAR approach is the formulation of the individual VARX* (vector autoregressive with exogeneity) model for every country. This section presents the general methodology advanced in Dees et al. (2007) to model individual countries in the GVAR model applied to the model in this study. The

---

[1] It should be noted that ex-post forecast is currently not available with the GVAR toolbox therefore this is not featured.

approach assumes that there are N+1 countries in the global economy, indexed by $i = 0, 1, \ldots, N$, and the aim is to relate a set of country-specific variables, e.g. GDP, inflation, interest rates etc. that are of interest to the study. As the model contains a large number of variables, it is best to represent using linear algebra as per the standard convention in the literature. The vector of interest denoted as x_{it} collects the macroeconomic variables specific to the individual countries of interest indexed by i and over time, indexed by $t = 0, 1, \ldots, T$. Following the notation and definitions given in di Mauro and Pesaran (2013, p.14-17), the general individual country model VARX* (2, 2) is represented as x_{it} – is a vector with a dimension of $k_i \times 1$ of domestic macroeconomic variables indexed by individual country i and time as t; x_{it}^* – is a vector with a dimension of $k_i \times 1$ of foreign macroeconomic variables indexed by individual country i and time as t; u_{it} – is a serially uncorrelated and cross-sectionally weakly dependent process. The rest of the associated parameters are similar to those in a normal VAR, which are estimated to give context to economic interpretations of the model. It should be noted that x_{it}^*, as a vector that captures the foreign-specific macroeconomic variables related to domestic ones, is constructed via a weight matrix. Mathematically, this is defined as w_{ij}, where i is the domestic country and j is the foreign country; these are a set of weights that $w_{ij} = 0$, and when all the weights of i and j are combined, they will become 1. The scheme of the weight matrix can be designed to reflect the trade and/or financial linkages. For example, in our model, the weight of Britain (domestic) is expected to have a large trade with the EU countries such as Germany (foreign); therefore, it will have a larger weight than, for example, Malaysia. It should be noted that, similar to the framework of an unrestricted VAR, the VARX* model can also be written in its error-correction form VECMX*, which allows the differentiation of short and long-run effects. In particular, the long-run effects being treated as co-integrating. The individuals VECMX* models are estimated separately for each country i, based on reduced rank regression, thus identifying the long-run effects or I(1) relationships that exist within the domestic x_{it} and across x_{it} and also the foreign economies x_{it}^*. Thus, the total number of co-integrating relations and the speed of adjustment for each country can be derived and given economic meaning. The full derivation of the VECMX* can be seen in di Mauro and Pesaran (Ibid., p.15) and is not repeated here.

The GVAR approach is a two-stage process. The first was to estimate the VARX* model country by country, and the second is to stack all VARX* models together to be solved as a whole. We now examined the solution to solve the model as outlined in di Mauro and Pesaran (Ibid., p.16). Recall the generic VARX* (2,2) model:

$$x_{it} = a_{i0} + a_{i1}t + \varphi_{i1}x_{i,t-1} + \varphi_{i2}x_{i,t-2} + \Lambda_{i0} x_{it}^* + \Lambda_{i1}x_{it-1}^* + \Lambda_{i2}x_{it-2}^* + u_{it}$$

$$(8.3)$$

The definitions remain the same as defined before, and we now introduce a few terms to solve the model as a whole. To form the GVAR model, we first introduce a new term, z_{it}, and define it as:

$$z_{it} = (x'_{it}, x^*_{it})'$$ (8.4)

Therefore we have:

$$A_{i0} W_i x_t = a_{i0} + a_{i1} t + A_{i1} W_i x_{t-1} + A_{i2} W_i x_{t-2} + u_{it}$$ (8.5)

Also, recall that for i = 0, 1,. . ., N, which implies the equation above is individual and country-specific and requires stacking to solve for x_t, which links all individual models together. We now introduce a few more terms to tidy up the model:

$$G_0 = \begin{pmatrix} A_{00} \ W_0 \\ A_{10} \ W_1 \\ \vdots \\ A_{N0} W_N \end{pmatrix}, G_1 = \begin{pmatrix} A_{01} \ W_0 \\ A_{11} \ W_1 \\ \vdots \\ A_{N1} W_N \end{pmatrix}, G_1 = \begin{pmatrix} A_{02} \ W_0 \\ A_{12} \ W_1 \\ \vdots \\ A_{N2} W_N \end{pmatrix},$$

$$a_0 = \begin{pmatrix} a_{00} \\ a_{10} \\ \vdots \\ a_{N0} \end{pmatrix}, a_1 = \begin{pmatrix} a_{01} \\ a_{11} \\ \vdots \\ a_{N1} \end{pmatrix}, u_1 = \begin{pmatrix} u_{0t} \\ u_{1t} \\ \vdots \\ u_{Nt} \end{pmatrix}$$

Thus

$$G_0 x_t = a_0 + a_1 t + G_1 x_{t-1} + G_2 x_{t-2} + u_t$$ (8.6)

As the term G_0 is a known non-singular matrix (invertible matrix). G_0 is called non–singular if there exists an $n \times n$ matrix G_0^{-1} such that $G_0 G_0^{-1} = I_n = G_0^{-1} G_0$. Thus by multiplying its inverse G_0^{-1}, the term disappears, and we now obtain the GVAR (2) model with 2 lags as where

$$x_t = b_0 + b_1 t + F_1 x_{t-1} + F_2 x_{t-2} + \varepsilon_t$$ (8.7)

in which the new terms collect the inverse of G_0

$$F_1 = G_0^{-1} G1, \quad F1 = G_0^{-1} G2,$$

$$b_0 = G_0^{-1} a_0, b_0 = G_0^{-1} a_1 \quad \varepsilon t = G_0^{-1} u_t$$

The GVAR model above can be solved recursively (see Pesaran 2015). To summarise, as shown above, the GVAR model allows the interactions among the domestic and foreign economies through three diverse channels. The first is the contemporaneous and lagged dependence of domestic variables x_{it} on foreign variables x^*_{it}. In addition, it also allows the effect and dependence of domestic variables x it on global weakly exogenous variables such as oil and commodity prices. This can also be used as a simulation strategy that can reveal the contemporaneous effects of shocks from country i on j.

8.3.2 Data sources and variables

The current model contains 33 countries, of which eight eurozone countries are grouped into the Euro Area and treated as one country (in the sense of a separate VARX* model). This list of the countries in the model consists of the US, China, Japan, UK, the Euro Area (Germany, France, Italy, Spain, Netherlands, Belgium, Austria, Finland), Canada, Australia, New Zealand, Sweden, Switzerland, Norway, Korea, Indonesia, Thailand, Philippines, Malaysia, Singapore, India, South Africa, Turkey, Saudi Arabia, Brazil, Mexico, Argentina, Chile and Peru. As it stands, it contains the bulk of the world output at around 90% (di Mauro and Pesaran 2013, p.18). It is not surprising that due to data quality and availability, semi-emerging economies such as Russia, Nigeria, Pakistan, and Vietnam are not selected. It should also be noted that, due to the strict requirement of the data, unfortunately, most African countries are not included in the model. Relative young development of capital markets in emerging markets is also a big drawback for their exclusion. Therefore the current edition of the GVAR cannot yet accommodate them, but there are other models which could be useful, such as the SEMs, particularly those developed by earlier econometrics for soviet economies (see Shapiro, 1977) and developing countries (see Klein, 1965) which have a lot less requirement on the datasets.

8.3.3 GVAR model and Datasets

As noted in the chapter introduction, in the first experiment, we use a standard GVAR that was estimated by di Mauro and Smith (2013, chapter 1). The datasets that were used are currently available to be accessed with the GVAR toolbox[2]. In this section, we first describe the datasets and also the model estimated. The same estimated model would first be used for evaluating its forecasting ability. Then in the second part, it would be used for generating IRFs for shocks. We then proceed to illustrate the estimation of an approximated FAVAR model. In the end, we compare the results from the two models. In addition, 4 DSGE models were shocked to generate the IRFs for comparison with the GVAR and FAVAR. The last part of this section will discuss that.

---

[2] GVAR Toolbox-Global VAR Modelling. Retrieved from sites.google.com/site/gvar modelling/gvar-toolbox

The datasets contain a large selection of countries and their corresponding economic variables. Currently, the database contains 33 countries, spanning from 1979 to 2013. The model in this study describes the relationships between itself and across 33 countries from 1979q1–2016q4. Similarly to Dees et al. (Ibid.), the countries in the Eurozone are grouped and considered as 'Euro Area' in the model with its VARX* model. of which eight eurozone countries are grouped into Euro Area and treated as one country (in the sense of a separate VARX* model). This list of the countries in the model consists of the US, China, Japan, UK, the Euro area (Germany, France, Italy, Spain, Netherlands, Belgium, Austria, Finland), Canada, Australia, New Zealand, Sweden, Switzerland, Norway, Korea, Indonesia, Thailand, Philippines, Malaysia, Singapore, India, South Africa, Turkey, Saudi Arabia, Brazil, Mexico, Argentina, Chile and Peru. As it stands, it contains the bulk of the world output at around 90% (di Mauro and Pesaran 2013, p.18). Due to data quality and availability, semi-emerging economies such as Russia, Nigeria, Pakistan, and Vietnam are not included.

In terms of variables, there are real output (quarterly in the natural log, seasonally adjusted, with 2015 indexed at 100 for all countries), inflation (constructed from local CPI index, quarterly in the natural log), real exchange rate (constructed from local currency against USD, where USD is set as 1, also in the quarter and natural log), real equity price index (from the local largest stock market index, quarterly and in the natural log), short term interest rate (constructed from the local central bank using interest rate, deposit rates, T-bill rates and money market rates, quarterly averages, in natural log, long term interest rate, constructed with interest rates, government securities and bonds, in quarterly averages and natural log. The datasets also include three global variables, namely oil price, raw material and metal price. The oil price is constructed with the Brent crude index, also quarterly and in log. Both raw material and metal price are taken from primary commodity prices indices and also in quarterly and log.[3]

It is important to note that the compilation of the database has been kindly shared and allowed for academic usages. However, there is some missing data in the database, making it difficult to account for some variables' effects. For example, the real equity price index is not available to China and a few other countries. Also, for the long term interest rate, only a handful of countries publish the data; therefore, only advanced economies are included. As such, rather than having all 33 countries and the six variables plus three global variables = $(33*6)+3 = 201$ time series, we have only 178 series, with 23 series missing (201-178). As can see from the figure, the only complete time series are available for real output and inflation, therefore in the second part for

---

[3] The full description can be found on page 169 in Smith and Galesi (2017).

comparing IRFs, only these are the variables that would be used for model comparison. However, for the model estimation exercise, we would include all variables in two models.

Figure 8.4: GVAR data series

Real output	33
Inflation	33
Equity price	26
Exchange rate	33
Short interest	32
Long interest	18
Oil Price	1
Material price	1
Metal price	1

8.3.4 Lag orders of individual VARX* models

Recall that a generic VARX* (p,q) model has lag orders p for both domestic lag orders q for foreign variables. The exact lag orders to be selected are similar to those employed in time series literature with the Akaike information criterion (AIC) or the Schwarz Bayesian criterion (SBC). This is embedded in the GVAR toolbox, and the largest values from AIC or SBC is selected for the lag orders.

The table above shows the lag orders selected by either AIC or SBC, whichever value is the highest. It should be noted that it does not matter whether the lag orders of p and q are equal. However, also due to data limitation, an upper limit of two lags is imposed for the test as higher lags would consume too much degree of freedom. This means during the test, the order of (0, 0), (1, 0), (0, 1), (1, 1) tested for all countries. As the table shows, all countries either have the lag order of (2, 1) or (1, 1).

8.3.5 Unit root test

A big advantage of the GVAR approach is the indifference to the stationarity / non-stationarity of the variables. However, unit root tests are still useful in the sense that it allows the identification of short-run and long-run relations (as cointegrating). Like many other papers in the literature, the Augmented Dickey-Fuller test is used instead of the older standard Dickey-Fuller test. The ADF test was carried out at 95%, implying if the test statistic for the variable is more negative than the critical values, then it will be rejected as there is no unit root. The test was carried out on level, differenced, twice differenced, with trend and without trend on all variables, namely real output (y), inflation (price level, p), equity price (eq), exchange rate (ep), short-term interest rate (rs), long-term interest rate (lr). The output of the original test on all variables (domestic and foreign) is carried out in MATLAB, and the results are displayed in appendix C, with the notation N meaning the null hypothesis of non-stationarity is not rejected, and Rej for rejected. It can be summarised that the results from the test indicate most variables have either I(0) or I(1) characteristic, which is ideal for the GVAR approach.

Figure 8.5: VARX order

	p	q
ARGENTINA	2	1
AUSTRALIA	1	1
BRAZIL	2	1
CANADA	2	1
CHINA	2	1
CHILE	2	1
EURO	2	1
INDIA	2	1
INDONESIA	2	1
JAPAN	2	1
KOREA	2	1
MALAYSIA	1	1
MEXICO	1	1
NORWAY	2	1
NEW ZEALAND	2	1
PERU	2	1
PHILIPPINES	2	1
SOUTH AFRICA	2	1
SAUDI ARABIA	2	1
SINGAPORE	2	1
SWEDEN	2	1
SWITZERLAND	1	1
THAILAND	2	1
TURKEY	2	1
UNITED KINGDOM	1	1
USA	2	1

8.3.6 Testing for Cointegrating relationships

Once the unit root has been tested, the corresponding cointegrating VARX* models are estimated as VECMX*. The next step is the identification of the cointegrating relationships within the individual models. The rank of cointegrating relationships for each model is then computed using Johansen's trace and maximal eigenvalue statistics (see Pesaran et al. 2000). The summary of output from both tests is displayed above. The number of cointegrating relationships found is somewhat different from the result in Dees et al. (2007); however, this is expected as it is mostly due to newly revised data. Japan has the biggest difference between this estimation to those in Dees et al. (Ibid., 17), with only two found here, but four before while the rest remain similar to ± 1.

8.3.7 Testing for weak exogeneity

As mentioned before, the main assumption in the GVAR approach is the weak exogeneity of the foreign variables x_{it}^* concerning the respective VARX* model. As described in Pesaran et al. (2004), this assumption is compatible with a certain degree of weak dependence across u_{it} (the residuals). Following the work on weak exogeneity testing by Johansen (1992) and Granger and Lin (1995), the weak exogeneity assumption implies no long-run feedback from x_{it} to x_{it}^*, suggesting that x_{it}^* error correction terms of the individual country VECMX* models do not enter in the marginal model of x_{it}^* (Smith and Galesi, 2014). This implies we can consistently estimate the VARX* models individually and later combing together to form the GVAR. The proof of weak exogeneity implication on x* it can be seen in Pesaran (2015, ch.23, p.569). The test is a regression model described in Johansen (1992) and Harbo et al. (1998). The test employed by Dees et al. (2007) is as follow:

$$\Delta x_{it\ell}^* = a_{ij} + \sum_{j=1}^{r_i} \delta_{ij\ell} ECM_{ij,t-1} + \sum_{k=1}^{s_i} \Phi'_{ikj} \Delta x_{i,t-k} + \sum_{m=1}^{n_i} \Psi'_{im\ell ikj} \Delta \tilde{x}_{i,\ell-m} + \eta_{it\ell}$$

$$(8.8)$$

where ECMij,t1, j = 1,2,. . .,ri are the estimated error-correction terms corresponding to the cointegrating terms found as shown in previous section. It also should be noted that $\Delta x_{it\ell}^*$ is the differenced vector collection of the foreign variables. This is a F-test for the significance of ij, = 0, j = 1,2,. . .,ri above. While the lag orders of p and q were determined earlier via AIC.

The regression was run on the foreign variables in the VARX* models real output (y), inflation (price level, Dp), equity price (eq), short-term interest rate (rs), long-term interest rate (lr), as well as the global variables such as price of metal (pmetal), oil (poil) and raw material (pmat) with 5% significance level. The table on the next page shows the result of 208 regressions run and their F-statistics. Also reported is whether they are rejected or not. The cell of orange indicates it has surpassed the critical value at 5% (defined by their degree of freedom, shown in the second column), which means the assumption of weak exogeneity is not met. Based on all 208 regressions run, only nine variables (4.3%) are unable to meet the assumption. This result is a slight increase from

Pesaran (2004) and Dees et al. (2007). Therefore, for example, the foreign long-term interest rate would not enter Australia, Brazil and Turkey VARX* models. Similarly, this applies to other rejected variables.

8.3.8 Testing for structural breaks

Having considered the rather harmless integrated series in the previous section and also the possible violations of weak exogeneity and its treatment, we now turn to one of the most fundamental problems in econometric modelling. So far, we have shown that the problems mentioned above can be mitigated but unfortunately, similarly to other time-series/econometric models, the GVAR is also susceptible to structural breaks. The core concept of structural breaks is straightforward; it refers to the unexpected sudden shift of the time-series. Consider a daily stock price time series where a sudden shift is very common due to stock split, unexpected announcements, overnight trading, oversea stock exchange performance etc. This renders the original time-series model unreliable as the time-series have shifted unexpectedly and are therefore not within the range of the forecast; this also implies forecast errors would be greater. The problem of structural breaks has been discussed extensively in the literature since the 1960s by Quandt (1958, 1960), who proposed the Sup F test that calculates the likelihood ratio test for a change in model parameters and identifies the break date. The Sup F test was quite adaptable but only worked on univariate regression; nevertheless, it became the basis for future research. In the GVAR literature—mainly those in Pesaran et al. (2004), Pesaran and Smith (2006), Dees et al. (2007), Pesaran et al. (2009), di Mauro and Pesaran (2013), Chudik and Pesaran (2014)—there has been an extensive discussion of the problem. The GVAR Handbook by di Mauro and Pesaran (2013) surveyed the existing strategy that the GVAR literature employed. These include several test statistics to assess the structural stability of the estimated coefficients and error variances of the individual VARX* / VECMX* models. Specifically, the survey indicated the methods used are (p.21): the maximal OLS cumulative sum (CUSUM) statistic, and its mean square variant by Ploberger and Krämer (1992); a test for parameter constancy against non-stationary alternatives by Nyblom (1989); as well as sequential Wald type tests "of a one-time structural change at an unknown change point specifically"; also the QLR statistic by Quandt (1960), the MW statistic (Hansen, 1992), and the APW statistic (Andrews and Ploberger, 1994).' Compare to the results in Dees et al. (2007), we have two extra years and also two global variables included in the model. Therefore, it is expected that the increased sample period would increase the chance of structural. This prediction is confirmed from the tests described above. All tests begin with their standard version, with their robust version carried out in arrears. Details of the structural break tests can be seen in the appendix. Although structural breaks occur more in the current model, overall, it is similar to those described in the literature. It is fair to conclude that the robust versions of the tests are performed much better. As Dees et al. (2007) concluded, despite the evidence for some structural breaks, they are mostly from the error variances that would not impact the application with impulse responses based on the bootstrap method for median and confidence boundaries rather than just point estimates. The tables below show the percentage of variables found to have breaks and the breaks' estimated dates. It is not surprising to find that the dates are mostly related to episodes of financial distresses as it is where volatility dominates.

8.3.9 Forecasting

Similar to most econometric models, one of the main outputs of the GVAR model is the forecasts of the economic variables. Recall that the GVAR is constructed by stacking multiple VARX* models. In our case, we have estimated 33 individual VARX* (p,q) models with variable lags and stacked together and became a GVAR (2) model. We now show that forecasts can be made from the generic GVAR (p) and applied the method to our study. Recall that the individual VARX* (2,2), i.e. two lags for both domestic and foreign variables:

$$x_{it} = a_{i0} + a_{i1}t + \varphi_{i1}x_{i,t-1} + \varphi_{i2}x_{i,t-2} + \Lambda_{i0}x_{it}^* + \Lambda_{i1}x_{it-1}^* + \Lambda_{i2}x_{it-2}^* + u_{it}$$

(8.9)

Where x it is a vector with a dimension of ki × 1 of domestic macroeconomic variables indexed by individual country (i) and time as t; x_{it}^* is a vector with a dimension of ki × 1 of foreign macroeconomic variables indexed by individual country (i) and time as t, and $u_i t$ is a serially uncorrelated and cross-sectionally weakly dependent process. This can be re-written into:

$$A_i(L, P)W_i x_t = \phi_{it}$$

(8.10)

Where $\phi_i t$ equals x_{it}, L as the lag operator; p as the domestic variable lag orders; W as weight matrix and x_t as the domestic variables denoted in t and i denotes the country. In other words, it is simply a re-statement of the VARX* model as a function of domestic variables with lag orders multiplied by their corresponding weights. Also, recall that, once the VARX* models have been estimated individually, the next step is to stack the models together to form the GVAR model.

Again, using the notations in Dees et al. (2007), by stacking the individual VARX* models (written as ϕ_{it}), we obtain the GVAR (p) model as

$$G(L, p)x_t = \phi_t$$

(8.11)

where

$$G(L,p) = \begin{pmatrix} A_0(L,p)W_0 \\ A_1(L,p)W_1 \\ \vdots \\ A_N(L,p)W_N \end{pmatrix}, \varphi_t = \begin{pmatrix} \varphi_{0t} \\ \varphi_{1t} \\ \vdots \\ \varphi_{Nt} \end{pmatrix} \qquad (8.12)$$

The GVAR ex-ante forecast model has now formed and can be solved via recursive method at any horizons N.

Chapter 9

Testing Forecasting Ability of GVAR Model

9.0.1 GVAR ex-ante forecasts

We now turn to the results produced by the estimated GVAR model. As mentioned before, there are 33 countries in total, with 8 Euro countries which will be estimated as one—; therefore, there are 26 country models. Each has its combination of lag orders up to a maximum of 2 as determined by AIC/ BIC. It should be noted not all VARX* models have equivalent lag orders nor the same set of domestic and foreign variables due to the specification tests of lag order and weak exogeneity in the last section. In the end, after removing the variables which did not meet the weak exogeneity assumption, we have 271 variables estimated placed in 26 VARX models and one auxiliary model for global variables such as oil price, metal and raw material price for eight quarters, i.e. two years. This means 2184 point estimates were created for all variables. For the original output, see the appendix.

9.0.2 GVAR (conditional forecast) and GVAR1 (unconditional forecast)

As mentioned previously, forecasts can either be conditional or unconditional. In this case, we estimate two sets of forecasts from the same estimated GVAR model. Summary statistics like RMSEs were calculated to see which model is more accurate and whether the restrictions imposed improved the forecast accuracy. If there is a strong conviction or that the future values are already known for a variable in advance, then there is a case to impose such restrictions, fixing the values and letting other values be estimated in light of these restrictions. In this case, restrictions were placed on US short and long interest rates setting both at 1% for short and 2% for long. The GVAR forecasts (also denoted in GVAR0 for easy differentiation) with the restriction is simply shown as GVAR below, while the one without restriction is displayed as GVAR1.

9.0.3 Forecasting models comparison

As there are too many forecasts produced and due to space limit, below shows only a small selection of the forecasts produced. Looking at the forecasts produced in figures 3.6 below for US interest rate, for example, it is easy to see that the GVAR1 forecast was off by a big margin as it was calculated based on previous data, culminating in a negative interest rate is lower each quarter. This is clearly not the case in reality; thus, the GVAR0 forecasts, with the predetermined restrictions, fared better than the GVAR1 forecasts. Compare the GVAR1 forecast to the AR (ex-ante), and we can see that the AR model is of no use in forecasting the interest rate movement. In this case, a more naive approach proved to be more useful than forecasts based on time series alone. In general, AR ex-ante forecasts and also unrestricted GVAR ex-ante forecasts are useless for forecasting interest rates. This is because interest rates are often decided in advance in light of possible future scenarios; therefore, it is retroaction based. Past influence is likely to be less useful. If we consider AR ex-post forecasts, then we can see that it is much better in its performance. In this case, we can conclude that if we wish to improve the forecast on the interest rate, we can employ the latest figure; thus, it would be much closer to a nowcasting exercise.

Now consider other forecasts in figure 3.5. Let's take oil price, material and metal price, for example. These prices are constantly changing on a daily basis; therefore, there is not enough information reflected if we take them quarterly. The actual values for oil price fluctuated a lot from 4.0 (about $54 USD if we inverse the natural log) to 3.5 ($33) and back to near 4. None of the four forecast models provided a similar description of this trend as historical prices matter very little in this case. Similar summaries can also be drawn about material and metal prices. However, the AR ex-post forecasts were much closer to actual results in these two prices, while it was also incorrect for the oil price. If we turn to Argentina's equity index, we can see that the performances are better with the GVAR forecasts. Both GVAR forecasts were indicating a downward trend, while AR ex-ante was indicating no inaccurate trend. In the example for both Brazil's GDP and UK's equity index, both GVAR forecasts and AR ex-ante are no better than random guesses. In this case, it proves that the time series data itself did not provide much information, and unless the latest actual data is considered like in the AR ex-post case, it shows that there are little values in terms of accuracy. In the example of the Chinese inflation rate, it was fluctuating by a large amount which was not captured by the forecasts. However, the GVAR forecasts provided a middle course and are the best compared to the AR ex-ante. We can see that GVAR is often better than AR models in other interest rates forecasts, whether conditional or unconditional. This is possibly due to the extra information conveyed from the past and the interrelationships between international central banks. If one decides to decrease rates, it could trigger other central banks to follow. This element could not be captured by the AR models; therefore, the GVAR forecasts are much better.

Since there are too many forecasts to compare with, it is more efficient to compare at a macro level. In this case, RMSEs were calculated for each individual, of which there are 271 in total. It has been mentioned previously that individual RMSEs should not be used for comparing across models. However, by summing up the totals, we can then use it to compare two GVAR forecasts and decide which is more accurate. Figures 3.7 to 3.10 show two GVAR0 and GVAR1 and their variable respective average RMSE/ mean, arranged by country and variables. We can see that the RMSEs for emerging markets tend to be more accurate than developed markets in both cases. If we rank the RMSEs, where the best has the value of 1, and the worst has 271, then we would have a sum of 9453 ranks in total (1+2+3...+271). The table below shows, for example, in the GVAR0 model, that the combined ranks for the Brazil forecasts are the best of all countries with a rank of only 148, while the USA has a much larger combined rank of 485. Looking at figure 3.8. we then see that the same is true for Brazil, where the combined ranks are now 92, and Switzerland became the worst at 525. This shows that setting restrictions on the interest rates helped some countries but worsened the forecasts for others. If we compare the two models, we find that GVAR0 has a sum of RMSE/mean of 43234 and GVAR1 of 32003. Therefore the RMSE/mean is much smaller for the GVAR1 model, where the interest rates are left to be estimated by the time series. Now a paradox has appeared. Although setting restrictions on interest rates increased accuracy for country interest rates, on the whole, it has failed to improve the overall accuracy.

The table below summarises the RMSE/mean difference between GVAR and GVAR1 model $\Delta Gvar0$, $Gvar1 = Gvar0 - Gvar1$. Except for the case of the long interest rates (lr), all variables performed better for GVAR0 forecasts, as the RMSEs are much smaller. Again, this proves the same conclusion from the previous paragraph.

If we now compare the AR (ex-ante) to GVAR models, we can now see that AR models forecast better in general as they all have smaller values. It is easy to conclude that GVAR forecasts are no better than AR models. However, as mentioned before, this could be distorted by the initial values it started; therefore, Theil's U statistics were also calculated using the equation defined earlier. From this measurement, we can see that the AR ex-post performed the best—as expected—with a sum of 7.76. However GVAR0 model now performs much better than GVAR1, with a sum of 11.07 over 19.56. In this case, GVAR0 was also better than AR ex-ante, therefore proving that GVAR forecasts are actually better than a simplistic AR model if restrictions are not set.

Figure 9.1: Forecasts comparison

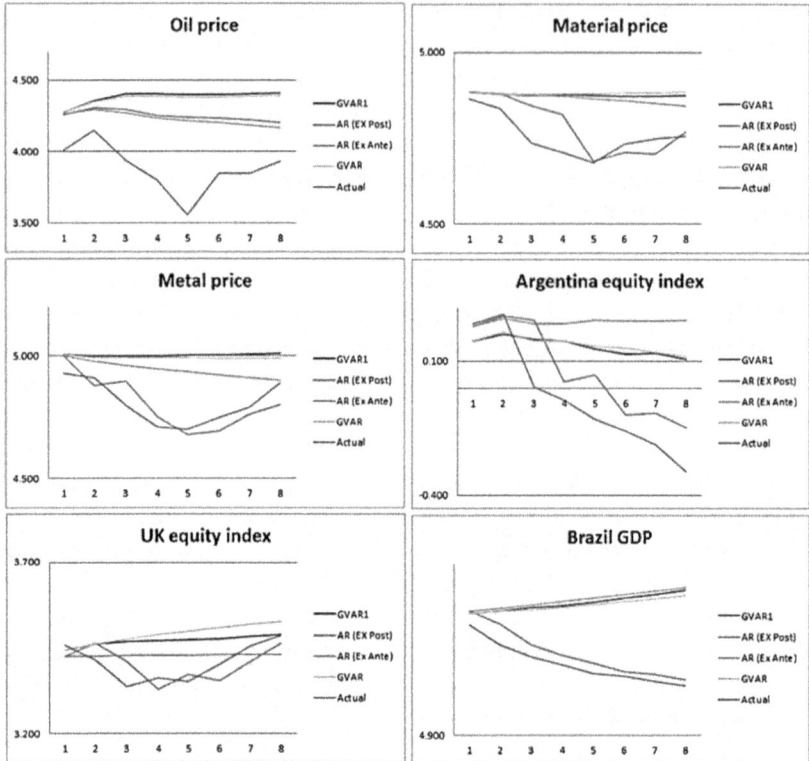

Figure 9.2: Forecasts comparison

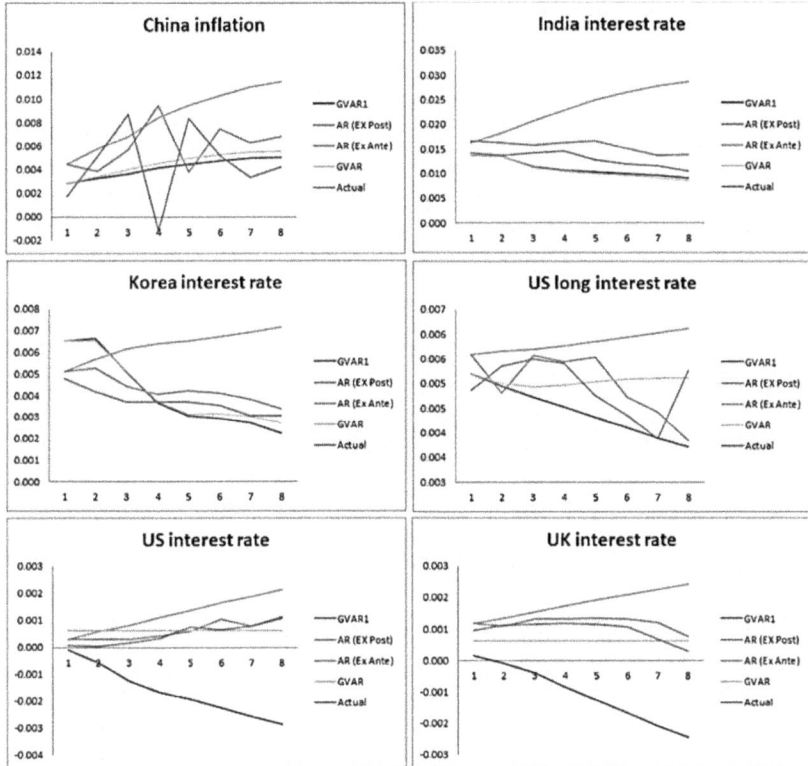

Figure 9.3: GVAR country ranks

Country	Data Sum of Rank	Sum of RMSE_mean	Average of RMSE_mean
du_model	29	14.3	4.77
bra	148	75.1	18.77
per	165	90.5	22.62
arg	199	108.9	21.77
sarbia	204	230.5	76.83
chl	248	351.1	70.22
turk	219	446.6	111.65
mex	253	492.2	123.05
phlp	326	572.6	114.51
indns	323	785.1	196.28
thai	358	808.4	161.69
india	432	1037.2	172.87
nzld	429	1147.4	191.24
switz	485	1508.4	251.40
nor	402	1667.3	277.88
mal	313	1792.4	358.49
swe	432	1842.0	307.01
austlia	454	1996.5	332.75
china	340	2011.7	502.93
sing	349	2294.6	458.92
safrc	459	2331.2	388.53
euro	473	2577.7	429.62
kor	448	2825.4	470.89
can	481	3587.5	597.92
japan	496	3841.6	640.26
uk	503	4081.3	680.22
usa	485	4716.4	943.28
Grand Total	**9453**	**43234.0**	**315.58**

Figure 9.4: GVAR- variable ranks

Variable	Data Sum of Rank	Sum of RMSE_mean	Average of RMSE_mean
poil	1	1.9	1.95
pmetal	8	5.0	5.01
pmat	20	7.4	7.36
eq	434	169.0	8.90
ep	730	359.1	14.36
lr	1594	14415.3	1108.87
y	1764	2293.1	88.20
Dp	2245	5714.2	219.78
r	2657	20268.8	810.75
Grand Total	**9453**	**43234.0**	**315.58**

Figure 9.5: GVAR 1 country ranks

Country	Data Sum of Rank	Sum of RMSE_mean	Average of RMSE_mean
du_model	31	12.76166921	4.253889737
bra	92	29.16544716	7.291361791
arg	178	69.23511708	13.84702342
per	186	80.98285726	20.24571432
sarbia	215	201.1677103	67.05590344
turk	234	457.1112637	114.2778159
chl	247	258.36996	51.67399201
mex	271	515.7965162	128.949129
phlp	293	277.9633973	55.59267946
thai	320	551.310971	110.2621942
mal	324	1698.011169	339.6022338
indns	337	760.8596665	190.2149166
sing	341	1042.03751	208.4075019
china	357	1788.455377	447.1138441
nor	421	1709.587074	284.931179
india	423	634.1435858	105.6905976
usa	446	1439.597501	287.9195003
nzld	447	997.8389228	166.3064871
kor	448	1556.865097	259.4775161
swe	450	3015.005359	502.5008931
safrc	455	1543.850439	257.3084065
austlia	455	1633.845196	272.3075326
can	466	1944.267464	324.0445773
uk	496	1776.007803	296.0013006
euro	497	2559.35763	426.5596051
japan	498	3309.130892	551.5218153
switz	525	2141.131881	356.8553135
Grand Total	9453	32003.85748	233.6047991

Figure 9.6: GVAR 1- Variable ranks

	Data		
Variable ⌄	Sum of Rank	Sum of RMSE_mean	Average of RMSE_mean
poil	1	1.65	1.65
pmetal	9	4.32	4.32
pmat	21	6.79	6.79
eq	509	151.72	7.99
ep	714	277.59	11.10
lr	1627	12997.62	999.82
y	1810	2005.14	77.12
Dp	2210	4255.78	163.68
r	2552	12303.25	492.13
Grand Total	9453	32003.86	233.60

Figure 9.7: Difference between GVAR and GVAR1

Variable	Count of RMSE_mean	Sum of RMSE_mean	Average of RMSE_mean	Max of RMSE_mean	Min of RMSE_mean	StdDevp of RMSE_mean
Dp	0.0	-1458.5	-56.1	-37.1	-6.5	-22.4
ep	0.0	-81.5	-3.3	-21.8	-0.5	-4.5
eq	0.0	-17.3	-0.9	-6.1	-1.2	-0.9
lr	0.0	-1417.7	-109.1	872.3	-62.5	145.1
pmat	0.0	-0.6	-0.6	-0.6	-0.6	0.0
pmetal	0.0	-0.7	-0.7	-0.7	-0.7	0.0
poil	0.0	-0.3	-0.3	-0.3	-0.3	0.0
r	0.0	-7965.6	-318.6	-819.9	-6.1	-288.4
y	0.0	-288.0	-11.1	61.9	-4.2	16.3
Grand Total	0.0	-11230.1	-500.6	47.7	-82.5	-154.8
Average	0.0	-1247.8	-55.6	5.3	-9.2	-17.2

Figure 9.8: Forecast evaluation with RMSE

Model	Count of RMSE	Count of Rank	Average of RMSE	Average of Rank	StdDevp of RMSE	Max of RMSE	Min of RMSE
AR (Ex Ante)	30	30	0.057	2.733	0.095	0.373	0.001
AR (EX Post)	30	30	0.043	1.600	0.096	0.394	0.000
GVAR	30	30	0.080	2.867	0.133	0.513	0.000
GVAR1	30	30	0.082	2.800	0.135	0.529	0.000
Grand Total	120	120	0.066	2.500	0.118	0.529	0.000

9.0.4 Directional test

Using the method mentioned earlier, the directional test was used to check whether GVAR forecasts can anticipate direction change, whether the forecasts are going up or down.

Out of 931 forecasts points made from the GVAR0 model (unrestricted model), there are 48% indicting a positive change and a 52% negative change, no variable stayed the same course.

This contrasts with 56% up and 44% down for the actual results, where no variable stayed in the same course for eight quarters (2 years). This implies 8% of GVAR forecasts were overestimated and that 8% were underestimated. In other words, there were 77 incorrect calls by the GVAR model, indicating that it is correct for 92% of the time.

Figure 9.9: Theil's U statistics

Model	Data Count of Theil's U	Sum of Theil's U2	Max of Theil's U2	Average of Theil's U2	Min of Theil's U2
AR (EX Post)	30	7.76	1.797	0.259	0.000369
GVAR	30	11.07	1.857	0.369	0.000799
AR (Ex Ante)	30	14.34	1.752	0.478	0.000539
GVAR1	30	19.56	4.407	0.652	0.000473
Grand Total	120	52.73	4.407	0.439	0.000369

Figure 9.10: Directional test

Forecast	Positive	446	931		48%		-8%
	Negative	485			52%		8%
Actual	Positive	523	931		56%		
	Negative	408			44%		

9.0.5 Summary and conclusion

In this section, we have examined the ability of GVAR for producing forecasts. When compared to simple AR models, the forecast accuracy is no better with RMSE/mean measures. Although Theil's U statistics show a different answer, indicating that GVAR0 is actually better than AR and GVAR1 by a significant margin. The discrepancy between the two is possibly due to the fact that RMSE/mean would punish errors when the magnitude is relatively big while Theil's U does not, as it treats errors equally by the actual unit it is comparing it to. In this case, it would be more robust to consider that Theil's U is more appropriate; although RMSE/mean is helpful in selecting GVAR0 over GVAR01, it is not too helpful when it comes to assessing accuracy across different models. This is also backed up by the directional test, which indicates that GVAR is 92% accurate for forecasting directions.

Overall, it shows a mixed but positive picture for GVAR forecasts. Recall the earlier discussion that forecasts should not be judged solely on their accuracy, as the extra information conveyed could also be important. In this case, we have found evidence that GVAR forecasts are better than AR ex-ante forecasts. It also provides a much richer background in terms of linking different economic variables together, thus allowing a more detailed understanding for the user.

9.1 Impulse response analysis

9.1.1 Introduction

During the last section, the GVAR model was evaluated in terms of its forecasting ability. The basis for IRFs and their theoretical comparisons have been thoroughly explored in the previous chapter. The aim of this section is to complement the previous one and to further illustrate this comparison exercise by means of empirical testing with IRFs.

Figure 9.11: Experiment 1

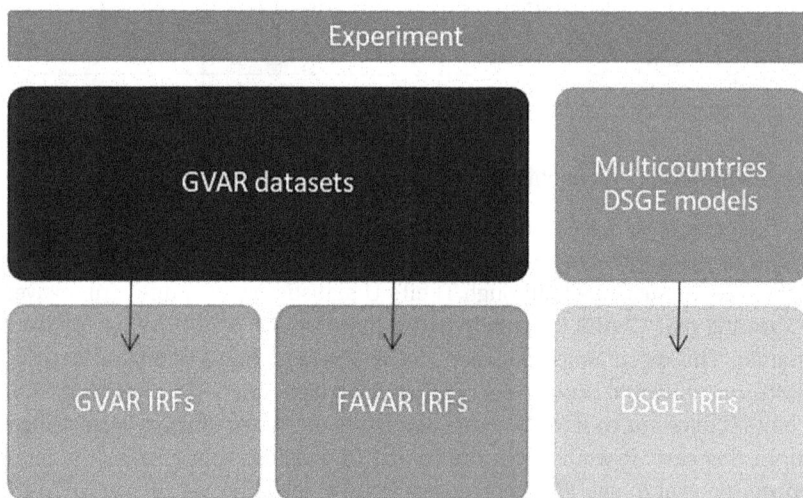

As mentioned before, the comparison between DSGE type models and VAR models is often difficult and imprecise due to the peculiar setup of the DSGE models and the identification strategy used in the VAR models. On the other hand, if we have the same set of data, we can then compare the methods of GVAR with FAVAR since both are essentially VAR type models that are designed to handle large datasets. Therefore to aid the comparison of these models, an experiment was made for this chapter. Figure 9.11 shows the two sets of experiments that were carried out. The first experiment involved taking the datasets which were used for the estimation of a GVAR model in di Mauro and Smith (2013, chapter 1) and then approximated the results with a FAVAR model, using the same datasets but following the logical specification of a FAVAR model; this would allow us to compare the results coming from two models, in the form of impulse response functions from monetary shocks. As the DSGE model cannot be compared directly, in this case, we used four different multicountry DSGE models to estimate the effects of the monetary shocks on the US economy and compare the responses to those estimated with GVAR and FAVAR models. The significance of comparing IRFs from DSGE models to those of the GVAR datasets is to provide a second check and present the consensus of the DSGE models from the literature. From this exercise, we can see that even though the starting points are vastly different for the different methods, the conclusion can be comparable, although with the expected differences, particularly in the long-run dynamics.

Recall from chapter 2 that the first step is to estimate the individual model. In this case, we have 33 individual VARX* (p,q) models. There are two lags for the individual VARX* model: p lags for domestic variables and q lags for foreign variables. The exact lag orders to be selected are similar to those employed in time series literature with the Akaike information criterion (AIC) or the Schwarz Bayesian criterion (SBC). From the estimation, we can see that the lag structures for most countries are either 1 or 2 lags maximum for domestic variables but only 1 lag for all foreign variables. Unit root tests were also run for identification. Like many other papers in the literature, the Augmented Dickey-Fuller test is used instead of the older standard Dickey-Fuller test. The ADF test was carried out at 95%, implying if the test statistic for the variable is more negative than the critical values, then it will be rejected as there is no unit root. The test was carried out on the level, differenced, twice differenced, with the trend and without trend on all variables, namely real output (y), inflation (price level, p), equity price (eq), the exchange rate (ep), short-term interest rate (rs), long-term interest rate (LR). Once unit-roots had been found, corresponding VARX* models were estimated as VECMX*. The next step is the identification of the cointegrating relationships within the individual models. The rank of cointegrating relationships for each model is then computed using Johansen's trace and maximal eigenvalue statistics.

Another important assumption is the weak exogeneity of the foreign variables with respect to the domestic variables. Following the work on weak exogeneity testing by Johansen (1992) and Granger and Lin (1995), the weak exogeneity assumption implies no long-run feedback from x it to x* it, suggesting that x* it error correction terms of the individual country VECMX* models do not enter in the marginal model of x* (Smith and Galesi, 2014). This implies we can consistently estimate the VARX* models individually and later combing together to form the GVAR. The regression was run on the foreign variables in the VARX* models real output, inflation, equity price, short-term interest rate, long-term interest rate, as well as the global variables such as the price of the metal, oil and raw material with 5% significance level. Based on all 178 regressions run, only 9 variables (5%) are unable to meet the assumption. Therefore, the foreign long-term interest rate would not enter Australia, Brazil and Turkey VARX* models. Similarly, this applies to other rejected variables.

As described in the last chapter, impulse response functions can be used to estimate the shocks from an increase or decrease. In this case, the use of GIRF is preferred over OIRF as it does not depend on the ordering of the variables. In this case, we specify a shock of 1 positive standard error to the US interest rate and see what would happen to the rest of the 33 (including the US) economies. As the shock was applied to all variables and models, there are 178 GIRFs estimated for the horizon of 40 quarters, equivalent to 8 years. As there are too many IRFs run, therefore only a handful of samples are demonstrated here. For comparison, Argentina, Brazil, China, Malaysia, Mexico, Peru, the UK, and the USA were used for their respective real GDP and inflation variables. The IRFs used for comparison are listed in fig 9.12, 9.14 and also 9.13.

9.1.2 FAVAR model estimation

A two-stage process was used for the estimation of a FAVAR model from the GVAR datasets. First, PCA was used to estimate the numbers needed to represent the data, and the data then augmented into the VAR model for estimation, and the IRFs are then created. The impulse response functions were then calculated from the model variables. Before estimating the model, the data were first normalised. In this case, we would like to know the effect of a monetary shock of 1 standard error from the US on the rest of the economies. Therefore the nominal interest rate of the US was used as the endogenous variable. Recall that there are 178 time series from the datasets, as the US is itself a time series; thus, this is taken out from the total datasets for PCA estimation, i.e. there are 177 time series for PCA. Then PCA was run, and 3 factors were found to be the best fit for the data. From the output of the model, 4 factors were also used but did not increase the significance of the IRFs; therefore, only 3 factors were used.

Regarding the identification of the shocks, the main method is to separate the variables into either slow- or fast-moving. In the case of fast-moving variables such as interest rate and equity prices, the effect from any shock would have already been reflected in them before the next succession of data at t+1, i.e. if there is an increase in US interest rate, it would have been reflected well into the real equity data before the next quarter data is updated. Therefore these series are assumed to be affected by the increase contemptuously. This restriction is also applied in this estimation, similar to the one used in Bernanke et al. (2005), where GDP and inflation are set as slow, while the rest of the data—oil price, material price, metal price, exchange rate, real equity price, interest rates (long and short)—are set to be fast. IRFs are then produced, with a 1 positive standard error to the US short term interest rate to the model variables, also with 40 periods. In terms of model lag, different tests were used to run the model from 1 to 16 lags (4 years). In the end, the lags of 7 periods were found to be the most significant with the ADF test, as additional lags did not add more to the results. The results are reproduced below for comparison with the GVAR model estimation.

Figure 9.12: GVAR-FAVAR policy shocks

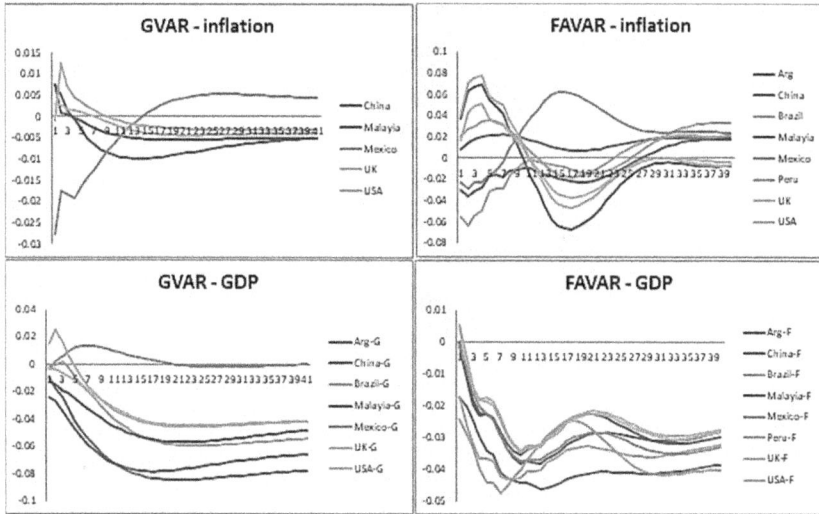

9.2 Comparison of GVAR, FAVAR and DSGE

The IRFs produced are listed in The IRFs used for comparison are listed in fig 9.12, 9.14 and also9.13. The first figure, 9.12, summarises how GDP and inflation from the countries reacted to the increase in the short-term US interest rate. Looking at the graphs for GVAR-GDP and FAVAR GDP, we can see that there is a consensus regarding the general direction of the shock. From the FAVAR estimation, we can see that all countries suffer from the shock and decrease as much as the 0.04 per cent point for most countries. We can see that South and Latin American countries are particularly affected. For example, Brazil, Peru, Mexico fared worst. This is possible considering the strong trade links between the US and these countries.

However, the particular effect on these countries is not that prominent, considering that other countries also suffer a similar decrease of around 0.03%. From these examples, we can see that all FAVAR IRFs for GDP are negative (for individual comparison, see fig 9.13). If we compare this to the GVAR results, the results are also similar, and we can see that most countries also trend downward. This is also true for most of the 33 countries in the model, although they are not reported here due to space limitation. However, there is also the

case for Mexico and Peru which appear very differently from the GVAR model.
In both cases, the increase of the US interest rate causes an increase of the US
dollars against the respective local currencies. Therefore, the strong exports
from these countries toward the US actually contributed to their economies
compared to the FAVAR model. The trade weights were explicitly included in
the GVAR, illustrating the possible scenarios for these countries, particularly
prominent for those influenced by the US.

Figure 9.13: GVAR-FAVAR - Real GDP

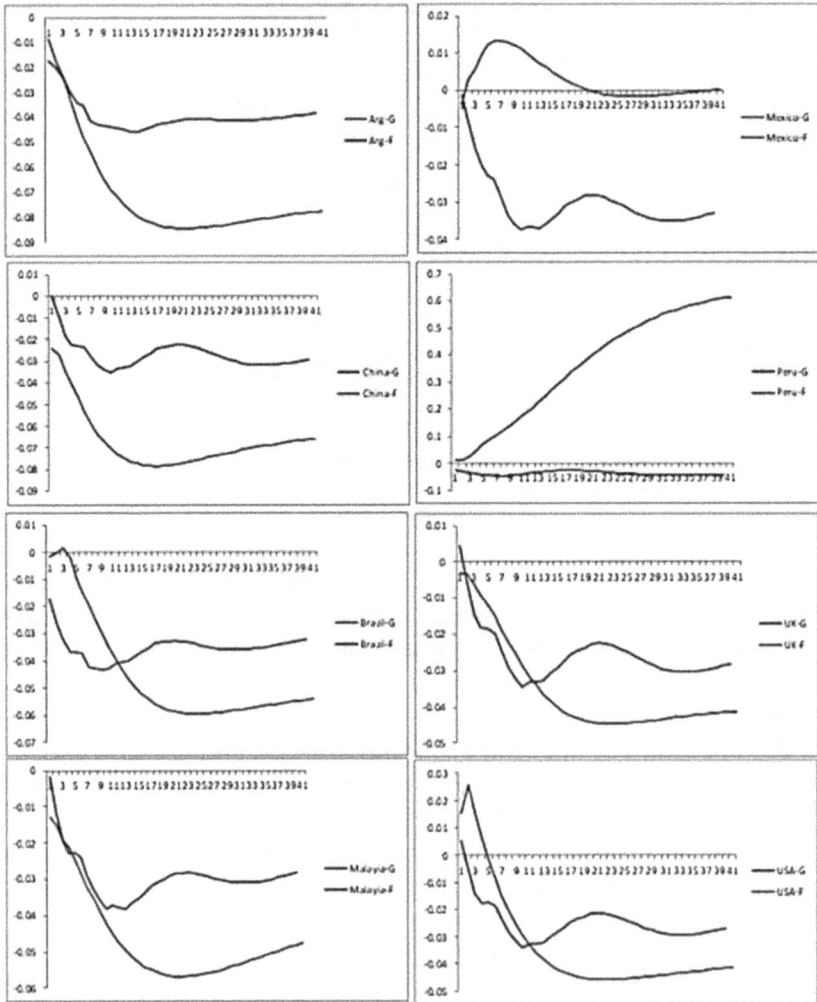

Figure 9.14: GVAR-FAVAR - Inflation

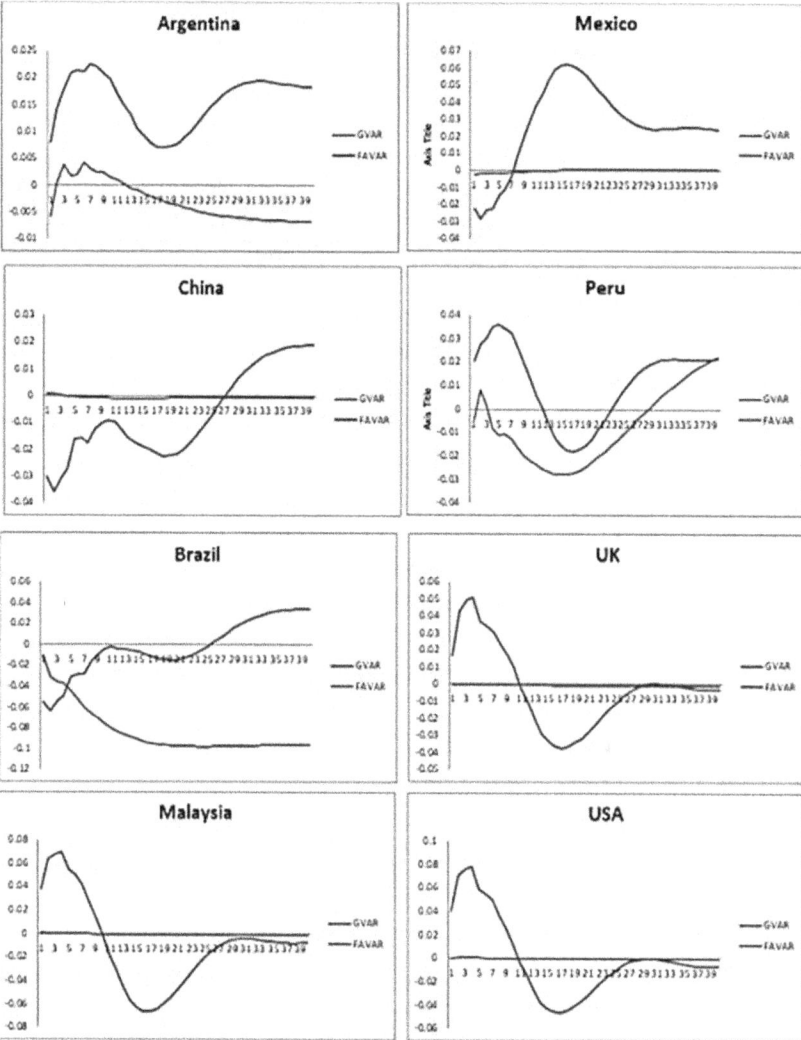

While both models produced a similar outlook for GDP, the shock to inflation was much more complicated. In the case of the GVAR model, most economies inflation IRF did not respond much to an increase in the US interest rate, with most countries hovering around 0 impacts, except the case of Mexico, Argentina, Brazil and Peru. In particular, with Peru, both IRFs behave very similarly, with the inflation peaking at 0.02 per cent and a similar trajectory, growing positively before running negative and later picking up again. An interesting example is the so-called inflation puzzle produced in the US IRF. In this case, we can see that the inflation shot up by a small amount of 0.01 % before dropping down again. This puzzle was originally found in Sims (1992) and was solved by adding commodity price. However, in this case, the inflation puzzle remains even though there are much more data used in this GVAR model so that any transmission channel of interest shock should have been identified. However, it is worth noting that the effect is very insignificant at 0.01% and sharply turning into negative. For example, Dees et al. (2007)—see fig 9.15—also found a similar phenomenon that could not be explained away by the data. The authors found that changing the order of the variables had an effect on the IRFs, as documented from using OIRFs (see chapter 2). However, in this case, the IRFs were produced with GIRFs; therefore, the underlying variable order should not matter. In the case of the FAVAR inflation, it is much strong, with the price puzzle presenting in many countries, which could be affected due to the ordering of the slow/fast category of variables.[1]

Another observation from this comparison is that the IRF values from the FAVAR models are higher than those in the GVAR model, and the values are also more even. This could be due to the fact that the shock is affecting all countries equally under the current identification scheme, in which no particular country is more prone to the effects. In the case of the GVAR model, due to the trade weights used to define the domestic and foreign economies, we can see that the effects on each country are more specific and individual, whereas the ones from FAVARs are more spread out. In this case, we can conclude that the GVAR model allows a much stronger transmission of shocks among countries, specifically assigned by their respective trade weights. From this perspective, the FAVAR model appears to be much less nuanced.

To further look into the responses of the shock on output and inflation, a short experiment was also run on 4 different multicountry DSGE models. In this experiment, 4 models were chosen as they have the US as the core plus a range of foreign countries as auxiliaries. In this case, the estimation was carried out in MMB, with the application extension of Dynare.[2] This tool, MMB (Macroeconomic Model Database), contained a range of estimated and calibrated models taken from the DSGE literature and allowed simple operations of applying policy shocks on a range of DSGE models. As mentioned in the previous chapter, the DSGE model often has a range of behavioural equation models representing the agents in the said countries of a unit with the

[1] At the moment, there is no tool developed for using GIRFs with FAVAR models, therefore this could be further investigated
[2] 2MMB: https://www.macromodelbase.com/ which requires installation of Dynare on Matlab first. https://www.dynare.org/ Also see (Wieland et al., 2012).

parameters estimated either by calibration or Bayesian method. In this case, the simulation exercise is done by taking the calibrated values for the parameters and applying them to the respective equation models. In this case, four models that were widely used in the DSGE literature and contained foreign countries were chosen, although they are very different from each other and, therefore, to the GVAR / FAVAR models above. It is a good idea to compare the DSGE literature to the model perspective to check if the responses are similar.

In this exercise, four models were selected, namely US_FRB08 (Levin et al. 2003), G7_TAY93 (Taylor 1993), G3_CW03 (Wieland et al. 2012), and GPM6_IMF13 (Carabenciov et al. 2013) run, and were shocked with 1 positive standard error of the US interest rate. As mentioned before, it would be very difficult to compare DSGE models directly to GVAR models. Therefore, in this example, the models above were chosen with the intention to find a reasonable similarity to the GVAR and FAVAR models estimated above. The goal here is to find out if there are similar results from the DSGE literature, i.e. if the signs from shocks are the same. Starting from US_FRB08 (Levin et al. 2003), these models were developed at the FED in the US, which contained a relatively detailed representation of the US economy and augmented with 12 other developed foreign countries. Another classic DSGE model used was the Taylor model constructed in 1993 and containing the G7 countries. The G3_CW03 model was developed at the ECB, with the US, Euro area, and Japan, created in 2003. The model's actual setup is very similar to the G7_TAY93 model but was calibrated with newer data. Last, we have GPM6_IMF13, created at the IMF, containing 6 regions: the US, the Euro area, Japan, emerging Asia, and Latin America, with 13 countries in total. In fact, this is currently the only large scale global model that could be compared to the GVAR model directly, as this one also includes the financial sector as it was built after the financial crisis in 2013. Financial spillovers are allowed across countries. However, the equations for each country are considerably smaller, given the enlarged size and various linkages in the economy.[3]

A positive 1 standard error shock was applied to all those four models, and the impulse responses are listed below for the IRFs of the US on inflation and output (see fig. 9.16). In this case, although the models were all calibrated from different periods of data and had vastly different details on the economy (disaggregation vs countries lumped together as a group), we can see that there is consensus that an increase in US interest could reduce the output in the short-run, even if it makes the impact after a few periods (e.g. circa 6 quarters)

---

[3] A list of available models from the MMB is available on its website. Actual equations contained in each model can also be downloaded from the website, therefore they are not repeated here.

insignificant. These results are very similar to those found with GVAR and FAVAR models, due to which we could conclude that there is a consensus that positive monetary shock would decrease the output. However, the difference between models comes from the period to the time needed for the economies to recover. In this case of DSGE models, the period is short, typicality between 6–8 periods before the effect cancelled out and return to the steady states. In the case of GVAR / FAVAR models, we can see that the effects are much more prolonged, lasting many years and do not return to 0% until much later, although it should be noted that the effects are also small in the long-run.

On the other hand, however, the effect on inflation is much murkier for GVAR / FAVAR models, where we can see that the results are much affected by trade weights. In the examples from DSGE models, we can see that the results are also not as uniform, with the FED model implying an increase in inflation rather than a decrease. The other three models point to a decrease, though. These different models contained a wide variety of believes on the economy and the effect it may have from inflation; therefore, the behavioural equations are different, hence the shocks are also affected differently.

Figure 9.15: US Inflation puzzle

**US
Inflation**

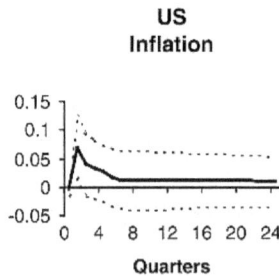

Quarters

Figure 9.16: DSGE models - US output / inflation

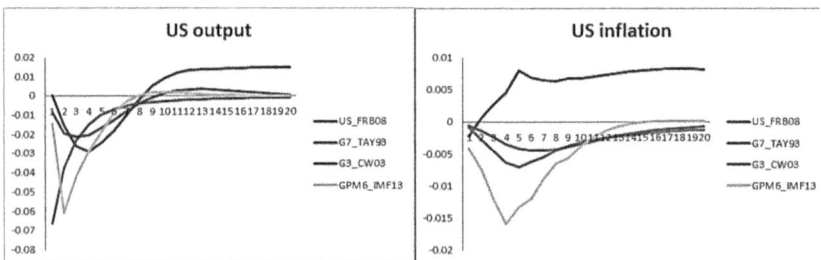

9.3 Summary

So far, we have compared the difference between different models and their IRFs. It is easy to see that certain properties are similar among different models, such as the long-run appear to be unaffected by a monetary shock or that the GDP is negatively affected by it. However, there are also many discrepancies in the short-run, particularly in the first 4 quarters. From this, we can conclude that the GVAR model fares best because it explicitly allows error correction mechanisms among country models; this is reflected by the dynamic responses from each economy. On the other hand, the FAVAR results look more uniform in their values and shape. The comparison was also made with DSGE IRFs, and it showed that there is a certain consensus among theory-driven versus data-driven models. As noted before, the results from DSGE IRFs cannot be compared directly with other results due to the specific setups. At this stage, this leads us to a further question, which is whether the IRFs can actually be evaluated at all. In a paper on the evaluation of global models (Granger and Jeon 2007), the authors pointed out that, in contrast with forecasting, the scenario analysis provided IRFs cannot be evaluated against real-world events. For example, if we have two forecasting models (F_1, F_2) in front, and both are adapted to forecast the US's next quarter GDP $(\hat{Y})$, and given the same datasets and the publishing of the latest actual value of the US GDP Y, we can then measure the distance between the estimated forecasts $(\hat{Y} - Y)$ and the forecast model with the lowest distance would be deemed as the best-fit model. However, in the case of IRFs, there is no 'true' model to speak of to compare with the true values in the forecasting application. Consequently, the IRFs inform us more about the underlying methodology and assumption of the models themselves than can actually be used to evaluate their accuracies.

As there are no robust evaluations for scenario analysis, we could only evaluate global models in terms of their purpose for the application. One way to improve the comparison made here is to include the confidence intervals of the IRFs. Accordingly, pooling different results from a range of models could potentially increase accuracy. This approach, which takes in multiple models rather than relying on a single model, is also known as thick modelling in the literature (Granger and Jeon 2004). The final application of the models is pooled together to reduce the extremes of model outputs.

From this comparison exercise in terms of this chapter, we can conclude that the GVAR model is quite adaptable in allowing the data to dictate the short-run and relying on more theory-led identification for the long-run. Naturally, the policymakers or users of this model would be more interested in the short-run as these are often the forces behind any economic policies changes or investment decisions. The rich dynamics allowed in the GVAR model is superior compare to the other two approaches. It appears that it would also be useful to combine the outputs from theory led DSGE models to evaluate the directions of the IRFs coming from the GVAR model.

9.4 Conclusion

The main contribution here is letting GVAR compete with other models with different benchmarks and tests, which is not done in the literature. This chapter has assessed and evaluated GVAR's ability to forecasting with a benchmark model with various tests. Impulse response functions were also used to compare with alternative models.

Judging from the analysis above, it certainly shows that GVAR is capable of forecasting data, and the extra information could potentially help. However, this is far from conclusive since its forecasting ability is not much better—if not the same—as a simple AR model. The emphasis on the value of the GVAR model then comes in its ability to include much available data coherently while also providing an adequate forecasting ability. The evaluation from impulse responses provides an extra check on the model itself and can be used to compare with alternative models. In this case, the IRFs show that certain properties are similar among different models, such as the long-run appear to be unaffected by a monetary shock or that the GDP is negatively affected by it. However, there are also many discrepancies in the short-run, particularly in the first 4 quarters. From this, we can conclude that the GVAR model fares best in that it explicitly allows error correction mechanisms among country models; this is reflected by the dynamic responses from each economy.

9.5 Appendix

Figure 9.17: ADF test 1

Domestic Variables	y (with trend)	y (no trend)	Dy	DDy	Dp (with trend)	Dp (no trend)	DDp	DDDp	eq (with trend)	eq (no trend)	Deq	DDeq
Argentina	N	N	Rej	Rej	Rej	N	Rej	Rej	Rej	Rej	Rej	Rej
Australia	Rej	Rej	Rej	Rej	Rej	Rej	N	N	Rej	N	N	Rej
Brazil	N	N	Rej	N	N	N	N	N	N	N	N	N
Canada	N	N	N	N	N	N	N	N	N	N	N	Rej
China	Rej	Rej	Rej	Rej	Rej	Rej	Rej	Rej	Rej	Rej	Rej	N
Chile	N	Rej	N	N	Rej	Rej	N	N	N	Rej	N	Rej
Euro	Rej	Rej	Rej	N	N	N	Rej	Rej	Rej	Rej	Rej	N
India	Rej	N	N	N	Rej	Rej	N	N	N	N	N	Rej
Indonesia	Rej	Rej	Rej	Rej	Rej	Rej	Rej	Rej	Rej	Rej	N	N
Japan	N	Rej	N	Rej	N	N	N	N	Rej	N	N	N
Korea	N	N	Rej	N	Rej	Rej	Rej	Rej	Rej	Rej	Rej	Rej
Malaysia	Rej	N	Rej	Rej	Rej	Rej	N	N	Rej	N	N	N
Mexico	Rej	N	Rej	N	N	N	Rej	Rej	N	N	Rej	Rej
Norway	N	Rej	N	Rej	N	N	N	N	N	N	N	N
New Zealand	Rej	N	Rej	N	Rej	Rej	Rej	Rej	Rej	Rej	N	Rej
Peru	N	N	N	Rej	N	N	N	N	N	N	N	N
Philippines	Rej	N	Rej	Rej	Rej	Rej	Rej	Rej	Rej	Rej	Rej	Rej
South Africa	N	Rej	N	N	N	N	N	N	Rej	N	Rej	N
Saudi Arabia	N	N	Rej	Rej	Rej	Rej	Rej	Rej	N	N	N	N
Singapore	Rej	Rej	N	N	N	Rej	Rej	N	Rej	Rej	Rej	Rej
Sweden	Rej	N	N	Rej	Rej	Rej	N	Rej	N	N	N	Rej
Switzerland	N	Rej	Rej	Rej	N	N	Rej	N	N	Rej	N	N
Thailand	N	N	N	N	Rej	Rej	N	Rej	N	N	N	Rej
Turkey	Rej	Rej	Rej	N	N	N	Rej	N	Rej	Rej	Rej	N
UK	N	Rej	N	Rej	Rej	Rej	N	Rej	N	N	N	Rej
USA	N	N	Rej	Rej	N	N	Rej	N	Rej	N	N	Rej

Figure 9.18: ADF test2

Domestic Variables	ep (with trend)	ep (no trend)	Dep	DDep	r (with trend)	r (no trend)	Dr	DDr	lr (with trend)	lr (no trend)	Dlr	DDlr
Argentina	N	N	Rej	Rej	N	N	Rej	Rej	N	N	N	N
Australia	Rej	N	N	Rej	Rej	N	N	N	Rej	Rej	Rej	Rej
Brazil	N	Rej	Rej	N	N	Rej	Rej	Rej	Rej	N	N	N
Canada	N	Rej	Rej	Rej	N	N	N	N	N	Rej	Rej	N
China	N	N	N	Rej	N	N	N	N	N	N	N	N
Chile	Rej	Rej	Rej	Rej	Rej	Rej	Rej	Rej	Rej	Rej	Rej	Rej
Euro	Rej	Rej	Rej	N	N	N	N	Rej	Rej	Rej	Rej	Rej
India	N	N	N	Rej	Rej	Rej	Rej	Rej	N	N	N	N
Indonesia	Rej	Rej	Rej	Rej	Rej	Rej	Rej	Rej	Rej	Rej	Rej	Rej
Japan	N	Rej	N	N	N	N	Rej	N	Rej	Rej	Rej	Rej
Korea	Rej	N	Rej	N	N	Rej	N	N	Rej	Rej	Rej	Rej
Malaysia	N	N	Rej	Rej	N	N	N	N	N	N	N	N
Mexico	Rej	Rej	Rej	Rej	Rej	N	Rej	Rej	Rej	Rej	Rej	Rej
Norway	N	N	Rej	N	N	N	Rej	Rej	Rej	Rej	Rej	Rej
New Zealand	N	N	N	N	Rej	Rej	N	N	N	Rej	N	Rej
Peru	N	Rej	Rej	Rej	Rej	Rej	N	N	N	N	N	N
Philippines	N	N	N	Rej	Rej	N	Rej	Rej	Rej	Rej	Rej	Rej
South Africa	Rej	Rej	N	Rej	N	Rej	Rej	Rej	Rej	Rej	Rej	Rej
Saudi Arabia	N	N	N	N	Rej	N	N	N	N	N	N	N
Singapore	Rej	Rej	Rej	Rej	Rej	Rej	Rej	Rej	Rej	Rej	Rej	Rej
Sweden	Rej	Rej	Rej	N	N	N	N	N	Rej	Rej	Rej	Rej
Switzerland	Rej	N	Rej	N	Rej	Rej	N	N	N	Rej	N	N
Thailand	N	Rej	N	Rej	N	Rej	Rej	Rej	N	N	N	N
Turkey	Rej	N	Rej	Rej	Rej	N	Rej	Rej	Rej	Rej	Rej	Rej
UK	Rej	Rej	Rej	N	Rej	N	N	N	Rej	Rej	Rej	Rej
USA	N	N	N	N	Rej	Rej	N	N	N	N	N	N

Figure 9.19: Exogeneity test 1

Foreign Variables	ys (with trend)	ys (no trend)	Dys	DDy	Dps (with trend)	Dps (no trend)	DDps	DDDp	eqs (with trend)	eqs (no trend)	eqs (no trend)	Deqs	DDeq
Argentina	Rej	N	Rej	Rej	N	N	Rej	Rej	N	N	N	Rej	Rej
Australia	N	Rej	N	Rej	Rej	Rej	Rej	Rej	Rej	Rej	Rej	Rej	N
Brazil	Rej	N	Rej	N	Rej	Rej	Rej	Rej	Rej	N	N	N	Rej
Canada	N	Rej	Rej	N	N	N	N	Rej	N	N	N	Rej	Rej
China	N	Rej	N	Rej	Rej	N	N	N	Rej	Rej	Rej	Rej	N
Chile	Rej	N	Rej	Rej	N	N	N	N	Rej	Rej	Rej	Rej	Rej
Euro	Rej	Rej	Rej	N	Rej	Rej	Rej	Rej	N	N	N	N	N
India	N	N	Rej	Rej	Rej	N	N	N	Rej	Rej	Rej	Rej	Rej
Indonesia	N	Rej	N	Rej	N	N	Rej	Rej	Rej	Rej	Rej	N	N
Japan	Rej	N	Rej	Rej	N	Rej	N	Rej	N	N	N	N	Rej
Korea	Rej	N	Rej	N	Rej	Rej	Rej	N	N	N	N	N	Rej
Malaysia	N	Rej	Rej	Rej	Rej	Rej	Rej	Rej	Rej	Rej	Rej	Rej	N
Mexico	N	N	N	N	N	N	N	N	N	N	N	N	Rej
Norway	Rej	N	Rej	Rej	Rej	Rej	Rej	Rej	Rej	Rej	Rej	Rej	N
New Zealand	Rej	N	Rej	Rej	Rej	N	N	Rej	Rej	N	N	Rej	Rej
Peru	Rej	N	N	N	N	N	N	N	N	N	N	N	N
Philippines	N	Rej	Rej	Rej	Rej	Rej	N	Rej	Rej	Rej	Rej	Rej	Rej
South Africa	Rej	N	N	N	N	N	N	N	N	N	N	Rej	N
Saudi Arabia	N	Rej	Rej	Rej	Rej	N	Rej	Rej	Rej	Rej	Rej	N	N
Singapore	Rej	N	Rej	N	N	Rej	N	Rej	Rej	Rej	Rej	Rej	N
Sweden	N	Rej	N	Rej	Rej	N	Rej	Rej	Rej	Rej	Rej	N	Rej
Switzerland	N	Rej	N	N	N	N	N	N	N	N	N	N	Rej
Thailand	Rej	N	Rej	Rej	Rej	Rej	Rej	Rej	Rej	Rej	Rej	Rej	N
Turkey	N	Rej	Rej	Rej	N	N	N	Rej	N	N	N	Rej	Rej
United Kingdom	N	Rej	N	N	Rej	N	N	N	Rej	N	N	Rej	N
USA	Rej	N	Rej	N	N	N	N	N	Rej	Rej	Rej	Rej	N

Figure 9.20: Exogeneity test 2

Foreign Variables	eps (with trend)	eps (no trend)	Deps	DDep	rs (with trend)	rs (no trend)	Drs	DDr	lrs (with trend)	lrs (no trend)	Dlrs	DDlr
Argentina	N	N	Rej	Rej	N	N	Rej	Rej	N	N	Rej	Rej
Australia	Rej	N	Rej	N	N	N	N	Rej	N	Rej	Rej	Rej
Brazil	Rej	Rej	Rej	Rej	N	Rej	N	N	Rej	N	N	N
Canada	Rej	N	Rej	N	Rej	N	N	N	Rej	Rej	N	N
China	N	Rej	N	Rej	N	Rej	Rej	Rej	N	Rej	Rej	Rej
Chile	Rej	N	Rej	Rej	Rej	Rej	N	N	N	Rej	N	N
Euro	Rej	Rej	N	N	N	N	Rej	Rej	Rej	N	N	Rej
India	N	Rej	Rej	N	Rej	Rej	N	N	N	Rej	Rej	N
Indonesia	N	N	N	N	N	N	N	N	N	Rej	N	Rej
Japan	N	N	N	N	N	N	N	N	N	N	Rej	N
Korea	Rej	Rej	Rej	Rej	Rej	Rej	Rej	Rej	Rej	Rej	N	Rej
Malaysia	Rej	Rej	N	Rej	Rej	Rej	Rej	Rej	Rej	N	Rej	N
Mexico	Rej	N	Rej	Rej	Rej	Rej	N	N	N	N	N	N
Norway	Rej	Rej	Rej	Rej	N	N	Rej	Rej	N	N	N	Rej
New Zealand	N	N	N	N	Rej	Rej	N	N	Rej	Rej	Rej	N
Peru	N	N	N	N	N	Rej	Rej	N	Rej	N	N	Rej
Philippines	N	Rej	Rej	Rej	Rej	N	N	Rej	N	Rej	Rej	N
South Africa	Rej	N	Rej	Rej	N	N	N	N	N	N	Rej	N
Saudi Arabia	N	Rej	N	N	N	N	N	N	N	N	Rej	Rej
Singapore	N	N	N	N	Rej	Rej	Rej	Rej	Rej	N	Rej	N
Sweden	Rej	Rej	Rej	Rej	N	N	Rej	Rej	N	Rej	N	N
Switzerland	N	N	N	N	Rej	Rej	Rej	N	N	N	N	N
Thailand	N	Rej	N	Rej	N	Rej	Rej	N	Rej	Rej	Rej	Rej
Turkey	Rej	Rej	Rej	N	Rej	N	N	Rej	Rej	N	Rej	N
United Kingdom	N	N	N	N	N	N	N	Rej	Rej	N	N	N
USA	N	N	Rej	N	N	Rej	Rej	Rej	Rej	Rej	N	Rej

Figure 9.21: Structural breaks test (Robust Nyblom)

Robust Nyblom	y	Dp	eq	ep	r	lr
Argentina	2.953541	3.146841	1.999663	1.909101	3.463778	
Australia	1.764284	1.931707	3.786889	3.221922	2.66649	2.687704
Brazil	1.800249	1.848536		3.164303	1.723004	
Canada	3.552406	2.731728	4.660976	4.279611	3.355533	2.941285
China	1.653787	0.947639		2.91935	1.223273	
Chile	1.970049	2.499115	2.876095	4.164153	2.697642	
Euro	2.558133	2.883485	3.018835	4.052198	2.93141	4.73403
India	2.582658	2.956216	3.428548	3.524114	2.550534	
Indonesia	2.919634	2.277946		2.774119	2.203778	
Japan	3.081098	2.990741	3.12708	2.037467	3.274721	3.145031
Korea	3.813137	2.900511	3.118479	2.758992	2.586311	3.887373
Malaysia	1.474512	1.981961	1.760533	1.401647	1.423196	
Mexico	1.333248	2.556819		1.912992	1.943911	
Norway	2.388377	3.744269	2.804295	3.683783	3.829636	3.704679
New Zealand	3.095192	2.941996	2.600281	4.309031	2.344703	4.07466
Peru	3.83071	2.711688		3.997139	1.435369	
Philippines	2.853757	2.783364	1.94271	3.42901	3.464143	
South Africa	2.282471	2.708302	4.070636	4.322448	3.715288	2.864857
Saudi Arabia	2.044661	1.77247		1.56551		
Singapore	2.731067	2.762536	3.434762	2.406843	2.860341	
Sweden	2.188007	3.318184	2.983002	2.814973	3.256422	3.454819
Switzerland	1.888119	3.106003	2.963398	2.321531	2.874641	1.928848
Thailand	3.067645	2.771301	2.936038	3.580469	2.53138	
Turkey	2.764314	2.275538		2.434123	1.674392	
United Kingdom	2.945494	2.473127	1.92572	2.401595	1.73586	2.777053
Usa	2.244617	3.137891	2.376479		3.215694	4.294044

Figure 9.22: GVAR - Variable RMSEs

Variable	Count of RMSE_mean	Sum of RMSE_mean	Average of RMSE_mean	Max of RMSE_mean	Min of RMSE_mean	StdDevp of RMSE_mean
Dp	26	5714.24	219.78	488.37	15.01	139.31
ep	25	359.12	14.36	69.51	3.37	14.79
eq	19	169.03	8.90	18.81	3.78	3.83
lr	13	14415.30	1108.87	1803.26	336.78	453.12
pmat	1	7.36	7.36	7.36	7.36	0.00
pmetal	1	5.01	5.01	5.01	5.01	0.00
poil	1	1.95	1.95	1.95	1.95	0.00
r	25	20268.83	810.75	2576.31	13.81	748.10
y	26	2293.12	88.20	242.54	13.63	63.98
Grand Total	137	43233.95	315.58	2576.31	1.95	523.30

Figure 9.23: GVAR - Country RMSEs

Country	Count of RMSE_mean	Sum of RMSE_mean	Average of RMSE_mean	Max of RMSE_mean	Min of RMSE_mean	StdDevp of RMSE_mean
arg	5	108.86	21.77	43.45	3.78	13.93
austlia	6	1996.49	332.75	1004.87	5.98	350.45
bra	4	75.08	18.77	33.11	3.37	11.26
can	6	3587.50	597.92	1920.54	6.17	714.31
china	4	2011.71	502.93	1612.93	17.72	651.59
chl	5	351.09	70.22	189.87	4.86	72.90
du_model	3	14.31	4.77	7.36	1.95	2.21
euro	6	2577.75	429.62	1597.05	11.26	561.42
india	6	1037.24	172.87	544.89	6.10	182.17
indns	4	785.12	196.28	401.59	18.12	151.08
japan	6	3841.57	640.26	1715.86	9.66	756.29
kor	6	2825.36	470.89	1803.26	5.86	664.30
mal	5	1792.43	358.49	1562.23	5.63	603.67
mex	4	492.19	123.05	213.40	3.97	82.07
nor	6	1667.29	277.88	749.29	5.04	331.05
nzld	6	1147.43	191.24	443.42	8.60	166.49
per	4	90.48	22.62	55.33	6.33	19.18
phlp	5	572.56	114.51	318.73	12.90	122.45
safrc	6	2331.16	388.53	1135.74	4.56	447.79
sarbia	3	230.49	76.83	138.00	44.64	43.27
sing	5	2294.58	458.92	1787.77	6.38	687.10
swe	6	1842.05	307.01	901.54	5.36	332.01
switz	6	1508.38	251.40	651.28	7.83	223.27
thai	5	808.45	161.69	395.29	11.78	145.37
turk	4	446.61	111.65	374.48	4.55	152.36
uk	6	4081.34	680.22	2264.82	6.99	816.52
usa	5	4716.42	943.28	2576.31	11.47	1003.52
Grand Total	137	43233.95	315.58	2576.31	1.95	523.30

Figure 9.24: GVAR 1 - Variable RMSEs

Variable	Count of RMSE_mean	Sum of RMSE_mean	Average of RMSE_mean	Max of RMSE_mean	Min of RMSE_mean	StdDevp of RMSE_mean
Dp	26	4255.78	163.68	451.30	8.48	116.86
ep	25	277.59	11.10	47.72	2.92	10.31
eq	19	151.72	7.99	12.71	2.60	2.94
lr	13	12997.62	999.82	2675.53	274.24	598.18
pmat	1	6.79	6.79	6.79	6.79	0.00
pmetal	1	4.32	4.32	4.32	4.32	0.00
poil	1	1.65	1.65	1.65	1.65	0.00
r	25	12303.25	492.13	1756.42	7.76	459.74
y	26	2005.14	77.12	304.40	9.42	80.32
Grand Total	137	32003.86	233.60	2675.53	1.65	408.76

Figure 9.25: GVAR 1 - Country RMSEs

Conutry	Count of RMSE_mean	Sum of RMSE_mean	Average of RMSE_mean	Max of RMSE_mean	Min of RMSE_mean	StdDevp of RMSE_mean
arg	5	69.24	13.85	35.25	2.60	11.19
austlia	6	1633.85	272.31	879.84	5.49	313.22
bra	4	29.17	7.29	9.42	3.51	2.26
can	6	1944.27	324.04	1277.38	5.15	442.83
china	4	1788.46	447.11	1422.21	21.79	575.48
chl	5	258.37	51.67	162.16	3.87	60.00
du_model	3	12.76	4.25	6.79	1.65	2.10
euro	6	2559.36	426.56	1670.51	7.36	591.63
india	6	634.14	105.69	298.04	6.56	102.74
indns	4	760.86	190.21	412.39	14.86	159.29
japan	6	3309.13	551.52	2675.53	9.54	961.12
kor	6	1556.87	259.48	771.03	5.84	323.07
mal	5	1698.01	339.60	1507.72	4.44	585.65
mex	4	515.80	128.95	267.33	2.92	100.51
nor	6	1709.59	284.93	853.87	5.49	353.42
nzld	6	997.84	166.31	400.37	8.23	148.80
per	4	80.98	20.25	37.07	5.52	11.20
phlp	5	277.96	55.59	121.90	8.41	52.35
safrc	6	1543.85	257.31	900.99	4.27	321.28
sarbia	3	201.17	67.06	126.20	36.76	41.83
sing	5	1042.04	208.41	650.21	6.34	258.89
swe	6	3015.01	502.50	1756.42	5.50	677.73
switz	6	2141.13	356.86	832.12	8.69	318.44
thai	5	551.31	110.26	304.40	5.00	110.02
turk	4	457.11	114.28	398.55	3.55	164.48
uk	6	1776.01	296.00	854.28	3.69	283.53
usa	5	1439.60	287.92	898.10	10.86	317.02
Grand Total	137	32003.86	233.60	2675.53	1.65	408.76

Figure 9.26: GVAR 00 and 01- top ten ranks

Country	Variable	Country	Variable	Rank
GVAR		GVAR1		
du_model	poil	du_model	poil	1
bra	ep	arg	eq	2
arg	eq	mex	ep	3
mex	ep	bra	ep	4
turk	ep	turk	ep	5
safrc	ep	uk	ep	6
chl	eq	chl	eq	7
du_model	pmetal	safrc	ep	8
nor	eq	du_model	pmetal	9
swe	eq	mal	ep	10
mal	ep	thai	eq	11
kor	eq	can	ep	12
austlia	eq	austlia	eq	13
india	eq	nor	eq	14
can	ep	swe	eq	15
nor	ep	per	ep	16
per	ep	nor	ep	17
sing	eq	kor	eq	18
uk	ep	sing	eq	19
du_model	pmat	india	eq	20
mal	eq	du_model	pmat	21
switz	eq	swe	ep	22
nzld	ep	euro	ep	23
austlia	ep	bra	r	24
chl	ep	chl	ep	25
can	eq	mal	eq	26
japan	eq	nzld	ep	27
swe	ep	phlp	ep	28
uk	eq	bra	Dp	29
nzld	eq	austlia	ep	30

Figure 9.27: GVAR 00 and 01- bottom ten ranks

GVAR		GVAR1		
Country	Variable	Country	Variable	Rank
can	Dp	switz	Dp	108
switz	Dp	can	Dp	109
indns	r	china	Dp	110
nzld	r	uk	r	111
sing	Dp	sing	Dp	112
austlia	Dp	turk	r	113
swe	r	nzld	r	114
india	lr	indns	r	115
euro	r	safrc	r	116
switz	lr	japan	r	117
nor	lr	austlia	Dp	118
nor	r	euro	r	119
kor	r	sing	r	120
safrc	r	kor	lr	121
swe	lr	nor	lr	122
austlia	lr	switz	r	123
safrc	lr	kor	r	124
can	lr	switz	lr	125
uk	lr	nor	r	126
mal	r	uk	lr	127
euro	lr	austlia	lr	128
china	r	usa	lr	129
usa	lr	safrc	lr	130
japan	lr	swe	lr	131
japan	r	can	lr	132
sing	r	china	r	133
kor	lr	mal	r	134
can	r	euro	lr	135
uk	r	swe	r	136
usa	r	japan	lr	137

Figure 9.28: Model comparison 1

GVAR1 Rank	GVAR0 Rank	Model	2015Q1	2015Q2	2015Q3	2015Q4	2016Q1	2016Q2	2016Q3	2016Q4	Rank	won	Remarks
1	1 du_model poll	GVAR1	4.278	4.356	4.406	4.403	4.398	4.401	4.405	4.410	4	1.42%	0
		AR (EX Post)	4.260	4.310	4.297	4.252	4.239	4.237	4.223	4.207	2		
		AR (Ex Ante)	4.266	4.295	4.274	4.236	4.218	4.205	4.136	4.168	1	1.37%	0
		GVAR	4.278	4.349	4.386	4.385	4.380	4.382	4.387	4.391	3		
		Actual	4.069	4.151	3.537	3.799	3.561	3.850	3.850	3.933			
21	20 du_model pmat	GVAR1	4.885	4.877	4.875	4.876	4.874	4.873	4.873	4.874	3	1.08%	0
		AR (EX Post)	4.885	4.879	4.844	4.813	4.883	4.707	4.702	4.758	1		
		AR (Ex Ante)	4.885	4.879	4.876	4.872	4.865	4.858	4.851	4.845	2	1.12%	0
		GVAR	4.885	4.877	4.877	4.878	4.880	4.882	4.883	4.834	4		
		Actual	4.864	4.836	4.736	4.709	4.678	4.733	4.750	4.756			
9	8 du_model pmetal	GVAR1	5.005	5.000	4.599	5.001	5.004	5.004	5.006	5.009	4	1.36%	0
		AR (EX Post)	5.000	4.880	4.898	4.752	4.577	4.692	4.765	4.802	1		
		AR (Ex Ante)	5.000	4.978	4.952	4.948	4.935	4.923	4.911	4.900	2	1.29%	0
		GVAR	5.005	4.994	4.592	4.992	4.991	4.990	4.988	4.988	3		
		Actual	4.927	4.910	4.890	4.711	4.659	4.750	4.792	4.890			
3	3 arg eq	GVAR1	0.176	0.202	0.180	0.175	0.145	0.127	0.129	0.108	4	1.42%	0 Best eq
		AR (EX Post)	0.231	0.267	0.254	0.022	0.047	-0.099	-0.094	-0.147	2		
		AR (Ex Ante)	0.231	0.258	0.241	0.241	0.251	0.250	0.249	0.253	1	1.37%	0
		GVAR	0.176	0.209	0.175	0.176	0.156	0.150	0.133	0.115	3		
		Actual	0.241	0.275	0.003	-0.045	-0.116	-0.161	-0.213	-0.311			
44	29 uk eq	GVAR1	3.444	3.450	3.469	3.472	3.473	3.477	3.483	3.490	3	1.48%	0
		AR (EX Post)	3.425	3.462	3.411	3.330	3.373	3.356	3.412	3.463	1		
		AR (Ex Ante)	3.425	3.426	3.428	3.428	3.429	3.430	3.431	3.431	2	1.79%	0
		GVAR	3.444	3.461	3.477	3.488	3.499	3.510	3.519	3.526	4		
		Actual	3.457	3.416	3.337	3.364	3.353	3.404	3.457	3.485			
35	39 bra y	GVAR1	5.041	5.045	5.049	5.051	5.055	5.060	5.054	5.069	3	0.95%	1 Best y
		AR (EX Post)	5.044	5.030	5.006	4.993	4.984	4.974	4.971	4.965	1		
		AR (Ex Ante)	5.044	5.048	5.052	5.056	5.060	5.064	5.068	5.072	4		
		GVAR	5.041	5.044	5.046	5.049	5.052	5.055	5.059	5.063	2	0.91%	1
		Actual	5.029	5.005	4.992	4.983	4.973	4.969	4.963	4.958			
51	49 sing y	GVAR1	5.289	5.302	5.314	5.326	5.337	5.349	5.362	5.375	3	1.42%	0
		AR (EX Post)	5.286	5.281	5.282	5.295	5.293	5.302	5.302	5.306	1		
		AR (Ex Ante)	5.286	5.296	5.305	5.315	5.325	5.334	5.344	5.353	4		
		GVAR	5.289	5.302	5.313	5.326	5.338	5.350	5.363	5.376	2	1.43%	0
		Actual	5.273	5.274	5.286	5.286	5.293	5.295	5.298	5.315			
65	60 serbia y	GVAR1	5.356	5.361	5.364	5.368	5.373	5.377	5.382	5.387	2	0.57%	1
		AR (EX Post)	5.365	5.387	5.405	5.391	5.401	5.403	5.402	5.412	1		
		AR (Ex Ante)	5.365	5.383	5.401	5.417	5.432	5.446	5.460	5.474	4		
		GVAR	5.356	5.361	5.365	5.368	5.372	5.376	5.381	5.385	3	0.58%	1

Figure 9.29: Model comparison 2

#	Group	Var	Model									Count	%	Flag
73	70 indns	y	GVAR1	5.366	5.382	5.392	5.400	5.410	5.420	5.430	5.440	3		
			AR (Ex Post)	5.370	5.380	5.392	5.405	5.420	5.423	5.442	5.454	1	2.18%	0
			AR (Ex Ante)	5.370	5.382	5.393	5.404	5.415	5.426	5.437	5.448	2	2.55%	0
			GVAR	5.366	5.382	5.391	5.399	5.408	5.418	5.427	5.437	4		
			Actual	5.369	5.381	5.394	5.409	5.417	5.431	5.442	5.457			
86	80 mal	Dp	GVAR1	0.005	0.005	0.006	0.006	0.006	0.006	0.006	0.006	1		
			AR (Ex Post)	0.008	0.002	0.009	0.009	0.006	0.005	0.006	0.006	4	0.96%	1
			AR (Ex Ante)	0.008	0.007	0.007	0.007	0.007	0.007	0.007	0.007	3	0.97%	1
			GVAR	0.005	0.005	0.005	0.005	0.006	0.006	0.006	0.006	2		
			Actual	-0.010	0.019	0.011	0.005	-0.001	0.004	0.005	0.009			
103	91 uk	y	GVAR1	4.829	4.832	4.835	4.839	4.844	4.848	4.852	4.857	2		
			AR (Ex Post)	4.832	4.834	4.838	4.839	4.846	4.848	4.855	4.860	1	0.39%	1
			AR (Ex Ante)	4.832	4.838	4.843	4.848	4.853	4.857	4.861	4.865	4	0.71%	1
			GVAR	4.829	4.832	4.835	4.838	4.842	4.846	4.850	4.853	3		
			Actual	4.829	4.833	4.836	4.842	4.845	4.850	4.856	4.861			
110	100 china	Dp	GVAR1	0.003	0.003	0.004	0.004	0.004	0.005	0.005	0.005	2		
			AR (Ex Post)	0.004	0.004	0.006	0.009	0.004	0.007	0.006	0.007	3	0.56%	1
			AR (Ex Ante)	0.003	0.006	0.007	0.008	0.009	0.010	0.011	0.011	4	0.56%	1
			GVAR	0.003	0.003	0.004	0.005	0.005	0.005	0.005	0.006	1		
			Actual	0.002	0.005	0.009	-0.001	0.008	0.005	0.003	0.004			
115	110 indns	r	GVAR1	0.014	0.014	0.011	0.011	0.010	0.010	0.010	0.009	1		
			AR (Ex Post)	0.017	0.016	0.016	0.016	0.017	0.015	0.014	0.014	3	0.19%	1
			AR (Ex Ante)	0.016	0.018	0.021	0.023	0.025	0.027	0.028	0.029	4	0.21%	1
			GVAR	0.014	0.013	0.011	0.010	0.010	0.010	0.009	0.009	2		
			Actual	0.014	0.014	0.014	0.015	0.013	0.012	0.012	0.011			
124	120 kor	r	GVAR1	0.007	0.007	0.005	0.004	0.003	0.003	0.003	0.002	3		
			AR (Ex Post)	0.005	0.005	0.004	0.004	0.004	0.004	0.004	0.003	1	0.44%	1
			AR (Ex Ante)	0.005	0.006	0.006	0.005	0.007	0.007	0.007	0.007	4	0.41%	1
			GVAR	0.007	0.007	0.005	0.004	0.003	0.003	0.003	0.003	2		
			Actual	0.005	0.004	0.004	0.004	0.004	0.004	0.003	0.003			
129	130 usa	lr	GVAR1	0.005	0.005	0.005	0.005	0.004	0.004	0.004	0.004	3		
			AR (Ex Post)	0.006	0.005	0.006	0.005	0.006	0.005	0.004	0.004	2	0.66%	0
			AR (Ex Ante)	0.006	0.006	0.006	0.005	0.005	0.006	0.006	0.006	4	0.55%	1
			GVAR	0.005	0.005	0.005	0.005	0.005	0.005	0.005	0.005	1		
			Actual	0.005	0.005	0.005	0.005	0.004	0.004	0.005	0.005			
110	136 uk	r	GVAR1	0.000	0.001	0.000	-0.001	-0.001	-0.002	-0.002	-0.002	4		
			AR (Ex Post)	0.001	0.001	0.001	0.001	0.001	0.001	0.001	0.001	1	2.01%	0
			AR (Ex Ante)	0.001	0.001	0.002	0.002	0.002	0.002	0.002	0.002	3	0.41%	1
			GVAR	0.001	0.001	0.001	0.001	0.001	0.001	0.001	0.001	2		
			Actual	0.001	0.001	0.001	0.001	0.001	0.001	0.000	0.000			

Figure 9.30: Model comparison 3

#	Country	Var	Model	c1	c2	c3	c4	c5	c6	c7	c8	%	Rank	Flag
102	137 usa	r	GVAR1	0.000	-0.001	-0.001	-0.002	-0.002	-0.002	-0.003	-0.003	3.12%	4	0
			AR (Ex Post)	0.000	0.000	0.000	0.000	0.001	0.001	0.001	0.001		1	
			AR (Ex Ante)	0.001	0.001	0.001	0.001	0.001	0.002	0.002	0.002	0.49%	3	1
			GVAR	0.001	0.001	0.001	0.001	0.001	0.001	0.001	0.002		2	
			Actual	0.000	0.000	0.000	0.000	0.001	0.001	0.001	0.001			
4	3 mex	ep	GVAR1	-2.596	-2.609	-2.624	-2.634	-2.642	-2.651	-2.661	-2.670	1.56%	3	0 Best ep
			AR (Ex Post)	-2.594	-2.513	-2.500	-2.429	-2.429	-2.347	-2.371	-2.333		1	
			AR (Ex Ante)	-2.596	-2.585	-2.572	-2.563	-2.554	-2.545	-2.537	-2.529	1.62%	2	0
			GVAR	-2.596	-2.609	-2.625	-2.638	-2.651	-2.664	-2.676	-2.687		4	
			Actual	-2.531	-2.513	-2.451	-2.437	-2.367	-2.373	-2.346	-2.301			
57	68 india	ep	GVAR1	-1.449	-1.453	-1.458	-1.465	-1.471	-1.476	-1.482	-1.487	1.62%	4	0 Worst ep
			AR (Ex Post)	-1.454	-1.474	-1.463	-1.445	-1.446	-1.443	-1.477	-1.472		3	
			AR (Ex Ante)	-1.454	-1.455	-1.458	-1.461	-1.463	-1.466	-1.469	-1.471	1.38%	1	0
			GVAR	-1.449	-1.452	-1.457	-1.463	-1.468	-1.473	-1.477	-1.481		2	
			Actual	-1.470	-1.462	-1.448	-1.458	-1.444	-1.469	-1.469	-1.462			
51	29 bra	Dp	GVAR1	-0.016	-0.047	-0.056	-0.071	-0.089	-0.092	-0.096	-0.101	7.04%	4	0 Best DP
			AR (Ex Post)	0.027	0.039	0.048	0.053	0.057	0.063	0.070	0.076		2	
			AR (Ex Ante)	0.027	0.038	0.034	0.033	0.035	0.035	0.027	0.033	2.97%	1	0
			GVAR	-0.016	-0.002	-0.014	-0.022	-0.020	-0.026	-0.019	-0.032		3	
			Actual	0.026	0.025	0.024	0.024	0.024	0.016	0.020	0.008			
113	118 austlia	Dp	GVAR1	0.004	0.005	0.005	0.005	0.005	0.005	0.004	0.004	0.87%	2	1 Worst dp
			AR (Ex Post)	0.005	0.004	0.005	0.005	0.005	0.004	0.004	0.005		3	
			AR (Ex Ante)	0.004	0.005	0.005	0.005	0.006	0.006	0.006	0.006	0.86%	4	1
			GVAR	0.004	0.007	0.002	0.004	0.003	0.003	0.005	0.006		1	
			Actual											
15	10 swe	eq	GVAR1	3.478	3.507	3.523	3.536	3.549	3.563	3.581	3.599	2.43%	3	0 SWE Eq
			AR (Ex Post)	3.423	3.590	3.423	3.372	3.418	3.321	3.319	3.427		2	
			AR (Ex Ante)	3.423	3.417	3.413	3.408	3.401	3.393	3.386	3.378	2.55%	1	0
			GVAR	3.478	3.503	3.530	3.556	3.584	3.611	3.635	3.658		4	
			Actual	3.551	3.470	3.384	3.412	3.357	3.325	3.405	3.448			
40	22 switz	eq	GVAR1	2.250	2.255	2.258	2.261	2.267	2.274	2.283		1.06%	3	0 worst eq
			AR (Ex Post)	2.254	2.277	2.221	2.200	2.113	2.172	2.183			1	
			AR (Ex Ante)	2.254	2.257	2.260	2.261	2.263	2.264	2.265		1.78%	2	0
			GVAR	2.250	2.266	2.284	2.302	2.336	2.350	2.361			4	
			Actual	2.269	2.230	2.204	2.250	2.162	2.181	2.191				
101	104 ntld	lr	GVAR1	0.009	0.009	0.009	0.009	0.009	0.009	0.009	0.009	0.83%	2	1 best lr
			AR (Ex Post)	0.009	0.009	0.008	0.008	0.009	0.007	0.006	0.006		1	
			AR (Ex Ante)	0.009	0.009	0.009	0.009	0.010	0.010	0.009	0.010	0.94%	4	1
			GVAR	0.009	0.009	0.009	0.009	0.009	0.009	0.009	0.010		3	
			Actual	0.008	0.008	0.007	0.007	0.006	0.005	0.005	0.006			

Figure 9.31: Model comparison 4

													Rank	%	Note
131	137 japan	lr	GVAR1	0.001	0.001	0.001	0.001	0.001	0.000	0.000	0.000	1	0.38%	1 worst lr
			AR (EX Post)	0.001	0.001	0.001	0.001	0.001	0.000	0.000	0.000	2		
			AR (Ex Ante)	0.001	0.001	0.001	0.001	0.001	0.001	0.001	0.001	4	0.69%	1
			GVAR	0.001	0.001	0.001	0.001	0.001	0.001	0.001	0.001	3		
			Actual	0.001	0.001	0.001	0.001	0.000	0.000	0.000	0.000			
56	24 bra	r	GVAR1	-0.029	-0.046	-0.050	-0.073	-0.085	-0.084	-0.090	-0.092	4	1.96%	0 best r
			AR (EX Post)	0.046	0.048	0.049	0.051	0.051	0.052	0.052	0.052	1		
			AR (Ex Ante)	0.046	0.061	0.070	0.078	0.087	0.095	0.103	0.110	3		
			GVAR	0.001	0.015	0.001	0.001	0.001	0.001	0.001	0.001	2	0.57%	1
			Actual	0.029	0.031	0.033	0.033	0.033	0.033	0.033	0.032			
114	136 swe	r	GVAR1	-0.001	-0.001	-0.001	-0.001	-0.001	-0.002	-0.002	-0.002	2	0.30%	1 worst r
			AR (EX Post)	0.000	0.000	-0.001	-0.001	-0.001	-0.001	-0.001	-0.002	1		
			AR (Ex Ante)	0.000	0.000	0.001	0.001	0.001	0.001	0.001	0.001	3		
			GVAR	0.001	0.001	0.000	0.001	0.001	0.001	0.001	0.001	4	1.01%	0
			Actual	0.000	-0.001	-0.001	-0.001	-0.001	-0.002	-0.002	-0.002			
92	107 thai	y	GVAR1	5.131	5.138	5.145	5.153	5.161	5.169	5.178	5.187	2	0.76%	1 worst y
			AR (EX Post)	5.136	5.140	5.145	5.154	5.161	5.171	5.182	5.186	1		
			AR (Ex Ante)	5.136	5.143	5.149	5.155	5.162	5.168	5.174	5.180	3		
			GVAR	5.131	5.138	5.145	5.152	5.160	5.167	5.174	5.181	4	1.03%	0
			Actual	5.133	5.139	5.148	5.154	5.165	5.175	5.179	5.184			
42	41 safrc	eq	GVAR1	4.873	4.873	4.864	4.856	4.851	4.853	4.860	4.868	2	0.85%	1
			AR (EX Post)	4.882	4.944	4.887	4.796	4.810	4.861	4.825	4.814	1		
			AR (Ex Ante)	4.882	4.878	4.876	4.877	4.878	4.879	4.880	4.880	4		
			GVAR	4.873	4.873	4.869	4.868	4.870	4.874	4.877	4.878	3	0.97%	1
			Actual	4.937	4.906	4.809	4.794	4.847	4.836	4.815	4.745			
53	53 phlp	y	GVAR1	5.326	5.337	5.346	5.355	5.364	5.374	5.384	5.394	3	12.19%	0
			AR (EX Post)	5.335	5.346	5.367	5.381	5.401	5.415	5.436	5.451	2		
			AR (Ex Ante)	5.335	5.351	5.366	5.382	5.398	5.414	5.431	5.447	1		
			GVAR	5.326	5.337	5.346	5.356	5.365	5.374	5.384	5.393	4	12.25%	0
			Actual	5.331	5.351	5.365	5.385	5.399	5.419	5.434	5.448			

Part III:
Portfolio Management and Backtesting

Chapter 10

Portfolio Management:
Forecasts, Risk and Position Size

10.1 Introduction

During the last two parts of the book, I have covered a lot of ground on different aspects of financial theories and macroeconometric models. In particular, the last part has discussed and shown how macroeconometric models can be estimated for producing forecasts. The ultimate question for any reader attempting to apply the models would be - how are we supposed to apply them to my portfolio?

To answer this question, this part is going to demonstrate how the forecasting models can be integrated into portfolio management and, in the end, how to translate the forecasts into tradable quantities by the investors. This part contains 4 chapters. The first chapter will be explaining how the forecasts from macroeconometric models can be integrated into portfolio management practices, in light of the risk and reward preferences of the investor, risk management and related topics such as portfolio diversification and, in the end, how are we to put these together. The next chapter will put all these tools together into a BlackBox, a sort of laboratory that allows us to experiment with different financial instruments, price data, portfolio criteria and goals and most importantly, the returns. A million questions here from the investor would be simple - is it profitable? To answer this question, this chapter will cover the details of how to assess a trading/investing strategy and demonstrate how to run through the tests within the excel workbook that is available on the book's website. In the end, there are two chapters covering a simple case of a single-position long-short trading strategy and another on how to backtest a strategy that includes multiple positions and incorporates portfolio management tools. While reading this chapter, it is recommended that the reader also has downloaded the excel workbook from the website as it will be much clearer to look at the example there and with the explanations in these chapters.

10.2 The need to integrate forecasts into portfolio management

Most readers are probably familiar with some forecasting tools if they have trained during degree level economics/finance courses or during their career. A typical econometric course is likely to cover the basic of univariate/multivariate regressions, VAR models and sometimes time series and panel data models. The learning outcome from these courses is to equip the students with knowledge of these models' intricacies and that they will be able to interpret and run these models by themselves. The trouble, however, often comes after the course as the students then ask: so, what do we do with the forecasts for my portfolio? If the daily and weekly forecasts for the oil price is up for the coming days and two weeks, then that means I should be buying related securities such as oil futures or oil-producing company shares. However, the question remains—how much, exactly, should I pay for the said securities? Furthermore, how do I take into account my personal risk and reward preferences? If I am an investor that seeks only a stable income while only requiring a modest increase in a capital increase in the long-run—surely this will be different from a day trader's objectives? The answer to this question—which is practical but fairly tricky—would not be found in a degree course. However, this is perhaps the single most important question that needs answering as it is exactly what the practitioners are tackling.

The answers to the above question are largely confined to the practical realm of portfolio management which is essentially the art and science of selecting and overseeing a group of investment while taking account of the long/short term financial goals and risk-reward preferences of the investor. While the book has covered the issues of financial theories in Part I, the emphasis here is on translating the forecasts into actionable trades while taking into account the criteria and investor preferences.

10.3 Investor preferences - Risk and Reward

The first thing that needs to be determined is the size of the trading capital. This can be defined as the amount of capital that the investor is willing to risk, should all the investments have failed and result in a 100% loss. Inherently, investments can be quite risky, but the good news is, similar to many things in life, this can be managed quite effectively. After setting the initial trading capital, for example £50,000, the investor is then required to state the risk and reward expected from this capital. The investor's risk and reward preference will then be used as a guide to set up the rest of the portfolio and trading positions. In this case, we will assume the investor has £50k free cash ready to take on the risk and potential rewards that it may provide. Based on the historical returns on the share market, which is around 7% annually, the investor decided that it is not enough; therefore, he would like to trade into the oil futures market, which is much more volatile, thus increasing both the potential risk and reward.

10.4 Risk management

The statement above means that the investor is ready to set aside a bigger pile of capital to gain an extra return from the market. This then requires extra risk management to plan and control the potential risks. This function of stating the risk that an investor is willing to risk during trades, not the entire capital, is the goal of volatility targeting. This function will require the investor to answer how much can be lost from the portfolio? How much risk can the investor cope with? And can the instrument he picked actually return the required returns? For example, it would be very difficult to make an annual return of 15% if the investor only invests in high-grade government bonds since the return is much lower, around 1-2% annually.

In this example, the investor is willing to lose up to 20% annually of the initial £50k capital, i.e. £10k. This figure was chosen as it is a relatively high figure that suits a higher volatility instrument such as commodity futures. As things stand, this threshold is also suitable for oil futures as it has a quick reaction to economic and geopolitical information; therefore, daily volatility of up to 10% is not uncommon. Setting a reasonably benign threshold would allow the trade to still in the market before being automatically closed due to hitting the target by natural fluctuation in the price. Furthermore, this is also a good figure that would not allow trades entering into a permanent loss amount such as -50%, where a 100% gain is required to break even. The reader can put in the desirable capital and that percentage of the volatility they are willing to accept in the excel work in the "Multiple positions" tab. This figure dictates all other subsequent formulae and calculations on the final positions for trading. To find the daily volatility target, given the annual target, the investor will need to divide the annual figure of £10k by 16; this is because there are normally 256 working days in a year, and the daily figure is derived by taking the square root of time, i.e. SQRT (256) = 16. This is the maximum daily target volatility the investor is willing to meet.

Next, we need to consider the actual price of the instrument and its related price volatility. Price volatility can vary greatly throughout the year. This was particularly true in early 2020 as the COVID19 pandemic broke out, wiping out global oil demand. The volatility during normal is around +/- 5% per day but could become more than 20% during stressed periods. There are many ways to calculate and estimate future volatility; GARCH, as described in an earlier chapter, is one example. In the example of the workbook, it is simply assumed +/- 5% per day. This figure can be changed by re-estimating, such as finding the previous volatility but calculating the standard deviation from the open, high, low and closing price. The most distinguishing feature of this figure is that volatility is a penalty on the trading position. It is designed in this way to ensure that the trader would not exceed the daily volatility. The daily volatility was approaching 20% during early 2020, and this high figure would automatically reduce the tradable position for the trader.

From the example in the workbook, the oil price was £53.14 in 2017, and that the minimum trade size is 5 contracts; therefore, the minimum trade position would be £265.7. Assuming a normal 5% daily volatility, this translates to about £13.28 volatility per block of trade. Under this scenario, we would require to trade at least 47 contracts, i.e. £12.487.90 of net position, to fully achieve the 20% daily volatility target. Therefore this will only be triggered when there is a very strong forecast, i.e. 1 or above. The details on how to fine-tune the backtest based on risk and other changes will be discussed in the next chapter.

The investor can also try to implement diversification of different assets in order to spread the risk. A portfolio will have a lower standard deviation of returns, i.e. the volatility, than the individual security that comprises it. The rationale behind this method is that a portfolio constructed of various kinds of uncorrelated assets will, on average, yield higher long-term returns and lower risk. This is based on the correlation of the asset returns and that those assets should have a low correlation with each other. The example given in this workbook does not take diversification into account as it assumes that the trader is trading one instrument only and that the trade will be bought and cleared on each trading day.

10.5 Translating forecasts into tradable quantity

From the exposition above, the reader can see that the final trading position is directly related to the instrument's expected volatility. The example given here is set to 5% and kept constant. While keeping it the same thorough the period, the investor will see how the final position is determined, based on other changing quantities such as forecasts and changing trading capital. Suppose the investor has lost money and the trading capital is down to £48,538. In that case, the daily volatility target will also be lower at £607 as the portfolio has now become smaller, but the 20% is capped at the same level. This automatically ensures that the investor is sticking to the initial volatility target initially to make no excessive losses, despite lower or higher capital.

The most important factor that determines the final trade position is the forecast. The example here has been constructed with the mind of standardising the final position according to the risk level. Given the constant 5% risk, a forecast of +1 will allow the investor to trade 47 contacts at £53.14 for the oil price. This is because 5% of these 47 contracts equal £12,487.90, of which 5% hit the daily volatility target of £625.00. In order words, this gives the investor a multiple of 47 in order to fully achieve this target. If, however, during the height of a market meltdown, a volatility of 30% is expected, a multiple of

7.84 is allowed, which is rounded up to 8 contracts only, given the exact +1 forecast. The examples in the final two chapters will demonstrate how the forecasts were created from the macroeconometric models and then applied to the backtesting tool.

10.6 Conclusion

This chapter has shown the necessary building blocks in order to maintain a disciplined approach to portfolio management. Particular emphasis is on risk management in which the final trading position is determined not by forecasts alone but also the expected risk of the underlying instrument. The trading capital is also highly important and the annal volatility level desired by the investor. The next chapter will discuss the methods to backtesting a trading strategy and how it can be used to determine whether a strategy is profitable. The last two chapters will illustrate the details of how the backtest and portfolio management tools can be used together along with the forecasts.

Chapter 11

Trading Rules and Backtesting

11.1 Introduction

Once the investor has set out the portfolio's goal, they are now required to determine a trading rule or strategy. The most common adage—buy low sell high—in itself is not a very useful strategy since it clearly does not describe nor define what low or high is. This is particularly misleading when a company's shares have decreased 95% prior to entering into administration, or the company is on the verge of a liquidity crisis. This adage, however, has a glimpse of truth as it certainly applies to healthy companies with excellent balance sheets but fell due to temporary economic or political reasons. The above example is a trading idea. Although it is simple and not quite precise, it is indeed the core of many trading strategies which elaborate on the details. From this simple idea, we can then build into a more elaborated trading strategy. This chapter discusses some common strategies and further resources on how to develop them.

The next question would then be - is it profitable? This can be answered in several ways. Any attempts to answer this ultimate question will have to answer the following sub-questions: 1) how profitable is the overall strategy? 2) how risky is it? 3) how to implement this strategy? The last chapter has covered aspects of the second question on how to define and control risk. This chapter answers the first and third question. The emphasis is on determining the profitability of the strategy. This is achieved by adopting a procedure called backtesting that has been used very prominently in the industry. In essence, a backtest is just a historical simulation of what investment performance and result would have been given the financial securities' historical data. In the next two chapters, examples of how to backtest a strategy will be shown for single-position and multiple-positions trading.

11.2 Trading ideas and trading rules

A note on nomenclature: 'trading rule' is used here instead of investment rule or investment strategy. However, there is no strict demarcation between trading and investing; they are essentially different sides of the same coin. The common usage and understanding among the industry are that trading is reserved for short-term profit-seeking actions, while investment often has a long-term connotation. If we follow this definition, then what may be counted as forecasting, creating buying/selling signal and the act of backtesting a strategy certainly fall within the realm of trading, albeit trading falls within the larger circle of portfolio management and investing. Another aspect is that, very often, long-term investment goals are sometimes difficult to define as tradable orders. Investment goals such as 'buying the company that produces the best product from the sector' are notably successful but difficult to turn into a systematic trading rule. This is simply due to the fact that best can have many meanings and is too subjective to the investor. On the other hand, the trading idea of 'buy S&P500 ETFs when it has dropped below 52 weeks average' is much more applicable.

Some resources in the literature summarise the state of finding the best trading rules and the methods to discover them particularly well. The best overview of this subject matter is perhaps Kaufman (2013) 1200 pages volume which outlined and demonstrated most trading ideas out there. As mentioned above, essentially, trading rules fall within the trading hemisphere, which is much more concrete and has more actionable commands than long-term investment goals, which are vaguer, and it is necessary to have a larger view for the future. Due to this affinity with the concept of trading, it is therefore not surprising to see that many trading rules are formed based on technical analysis.

The discipline of technical analysis was developed to evaluate investments and identify trading opportunities by analysing statistical trends gathered from trading activity, such as price movement and volume. While the validity of technical analysis is debatable, its philosophy is deeply incorporated into the professional proprietary trading, active and quantitative asset management industry. This transition from technical analysis into systematic trading based on trading rules and forecasts is necessary if the investors would like to remain as emotionally detached as possible when putting on or closing a trade. This emphasis on technical analysis is, however, not to discount fundamental analysis. When compared to technical analysis, fundamental analysis avoids observing the price patterns individually and seeks to analyse the performance by evaluating business results such as sales and earnings. Prior to determining a trading rule for an instrument, the investor is required to confirm the assets they would like to have in the portfolio. This problem, required for asset allocation, is better served by fundamental analysis than technical analysis. Technical analysis is then used to generate trading signals from various metrics or trading rules.

Regarding fundamental analysis, ultimately and particularly in the long-run, the market is indeed driven by fundamentals. Economic metrics such as unemployment ratio, GDP growth, inflation, consumer confidence, supply and demand or even geopolitical factors - such as the recent US-China trade war will ultimately shape the long-run performance of investments. However, if we recall the chapters in part I, efficient markets always take this latest news into the price; therefore, the price would have been updated to the latest information by the time a market reopens. By the time a quarterly GDP figure or consumer confidence has been reported for the public, the price would have changed, thus cancelling the trading opportunity. And this is precisely the rationale that forecasting is needed in order to participate in this change of movement.

It should not be surprising that at any moment, there are plenty—if not thousands—of trading ideas available in the public domain. A quick browse on the internet and forums, and you will find plenty of ideas that may or may not be profitable. If one turns to academic papers and books, there are also plenty of technical papers that require a lot of deep and complicated setup. However, it is often difficult to ascertain whether they work or not.

The logical question would then be if such profitable ideas or rules have been successful then, why would anyone publish them for the public, which would erode their profitability? The answer is somehow benign as most ideas or rules out there taken at the vanilla version seldom work immediately. The rules often require tweaking, such as changing the applicable instruments like using small-cap instead of big-cap stocks or lowering the holding period. The only possible way to find out if they work is to carry out a backtest. However, before doing the backtest, the investor will need to identify the trading ideas and form them into rules. The difference between a trading idea and a trading rule here is simple. A trading idea is any idea that can potentially lead to a profit resulting from the trade. The trading rule is simply expressing the trading idea into a tradable command that is actionable, such as 'sell oil futures contracts when oil WTI price is above 52-week level and buy when it is lowest in the past 52 weeks.'

11.3 Common trading rule

A trading rule is just a trade idea but translated into an actionable rule. For practical purpose, it should also be systematic and consistent. This means that the rule itself should not be too complex to be easily toppled when unexpected events happen. In a typical portfolio, there can be as many trading rules as desirable, but again, it should only be kept to the necessary level based on the risk and reward preference of the investor. This rule will allow the system to predict whether an instrument's price will go up or down and the magnitude. If there are multiple trading rules simultaneously, such as a carry rule and a momentum rule, the portfolio return will be determined by these two rules. It should be noted that those rules should not conflict with each other as they will give the wrong signal to the buy/sell orders. For example, when the price is above the 10 days, which has a price of £1 per share, a rule of buy should not have another rule in the system that states sell when the share price is £1.

However, these two rules can coexist if the underlying instruments are different.

Any good trading rule should have a good, balanced risk/reward ratio. This can be measured with a metric called the Sharpe ratio. A Sharpe ratio is a measure of how profitable a trading strategy is when the return is adjusted for risk. Mathematically, the mean return over the backtest period is divided by the standard deviation of returns over the same period. Therefore the higher the volatility, the lower the ratio is. Say that the average annual return for S&P500 is around 8%, but the standard deviation of return is around 20%, including all the peaks and troughs, then the Sharpe ratio would be 0.4. If, however, a strategy can deliver the same return of 8% but at much lower volatility, for example 10% only, then the Sharpe ratio will be 0.8, double to that of the first strategy, thus winning the contest. A good trading rule will have a good Sharpe ratio.

Below a common strategy that trend followers often adopt is described.

Long Short Moving Average Crossover

This strategy is perhaps the most common and applicable trading rule available. It is simple in its design but needs a lot of calibration for each instrument in order to be profitable. The reason to use a moving average is self-explanatory. The daily price change of an instrument can appear to be random, as indicated by EMH. However, this is often not the case when we consider market trends in the long-run. For example, most equities show unrelenting growth, despite experiencing major global wars and macroeconomic crises. This gives the first idea that at least some part of the trend can be forecasted and be taken advantage of. Calculating a moving average, for instance 5 days, would capture the average price of an instrument of the previous 5-day averages while not being disturbed by daily movements. This, of course, does not indicate any future movements as it has almost no predictability on its own. A moving average of 5 previous days or MA(5) is just a historical mirror looking at the trends as they were revealed. If, however, we use another, slower MA—for example 25 days, which represents a whole working month—this line also captures trends and effects that have been developing but at a slower speed. This combination of a fast and a slow trend line is the basic principle behind many rules.

The economic rationale behind this is that some information is more digested quicker by than financial market while some are less so. Recall the chapter on the FAVAR model, which is exactly the same reason behind the slow/fast factors differentiation. Overnight currency exchange rate movement, for example, would immediately be priced in for the underlying instruments. For example, HSBC share listed on the London Stock Exchange is priced in GBP.

The same company is also listed on the Hong Kong Stock Exchange, which is priced in Hong Kong dollars, pegged to the US dollars. Consider a sudden announcement of a decrease in interest rate by the FED in the US, and this depreciated the value of US dollars. As a result, the share in HK would follow suit, all else being equal, would decrease the value slightly. Assuming that the GBP has stayed the same overnight and that the LSE is opened later—at 8 am UK time—, by the time HSBC begins trading, the LSE would have increased the share price since GBP now is worth more. This change would then bring two shares into the same value again as they are shares of the same company; therefore, they must have the same price. Any discrepancy between the two would have been arbitraged away by traders, providing a free lunch.

While events like currency movement would be reflected almost immediately by the financial market, some are less obvious. Examples include the aforementioned interest rate change. Although interest rate change surprise often accompanies a sudden change in share price, for example, it also has a lingering effect that may last a longer period until other companies/industries price in this information. This is particularly obvious for events like a sudden event that has not been anticipated. Take the most recent coronavirus, which was first reported in January 2020. Its effects were already known by February 2020, but there was no significant drop until March, which saw most markets dropping below 30% or more. Oil futures also crashed to sub-zero price for the first time in history. This is a case of showing that different information travels at a different speed; therefore, there are at least more than one trend happening at any one moment. To identify the most recent, quicker changes/trends, a short, quick-moving average of 5 days would be sufficient. However, if we are to capture trends that are long terms such as a policy shock or pandemic progress, then a longer monthly trend may be required. Naturally, this raises the question, how many days exactly gives the best overall indication of trends? This is indeed the millionaire question that needs to be answered by the investor, perhaps with backtesting.

The answer to the problem of identifying a slow and fast trend is often solved by plotting two MA lines on the chart. Whenever a fast-moving average is now above the slow moving average, then this signals a buy. The opposite of the fast MA dropping below the slow line would then signal a sell as it now enters a decreasing trend. This, of course, isn't a guarantee to profit, but there is indeed a reasonable economic rationale behind for it to work; therefore, it is worth investigating.

If we are to express this particular rule into pseudo codes that can be input into a programme, then it would be as below:

- If the previous day, the fast SMA was below the slow SMA and the current trade day, there is a change where the fast SMA is now above the slow SMA, then signals to Buy.
- However, if the previous day, the fast SMA was above the slow SMA, and in the current trade day, the fast SMA is now below the slow SMA, then signals to Sell.
- If none of the conditions met, then do nothing.

The example in the next chapter shows how this rule was tested with oil futures with the excel workbook.

11.4 Resources on trading ideas, trading rules, forecasting tools and backtesting platforms

This challenge of identifying working/profitable trading ideas have gathered a lot of attention from industry and academia. Since then, countless efforts have been made to identify market abnormalities such as those mentioned in part I. Below is a list of the most useful sources where ideas and rules can be found. A list of backtesting platforms is also included. I have also included a list of forecasting tools that can help the users create the forecasts. Due to the complexity, some of these models can be quite difficult to use on their own.

Academic journals/Industry journals

Most trading strategies would have been originated from academic or industry journals. This is particularly true among finance field journals. The only problem is that it will take a considerable effort in order to unearth all the relevant and profitable results. This sphere of research is also highly sought after by industry practitioners; therefore, whatever may have worked when published may no longer work. Due to popularity, any edge may have been arbitraged away. Also, that academic journals often require a university membership to access as most journals have to paywalls.

Quantpedia[1]

This is a more expensive premium resource. However, it provides wide coverage of analysis and backtesting results of academic papers publishers in journals. A quick search on quantpedia, and there are currently more than 500 strategies based on academic studies. All these strategies were assessed, including the period of rebalancing, applicable markets and, most importantly, the risk and

---

[1] https://quantpedia.com/

reward expected. One of the strategies is titled "Asset Class Trend-Following", which was based on an academic/industry paper published in the Journal of Wealth Management.[2] This strategy aims to take advantage of periods where returns from some asset classes are below average, and volatility is much higher, similar to that of a momentum strategy widely accepted in the academic world and practices by professionals.[3] From the various backtest results, this shows a compounding annual return of 5.9% with a very low annual standard deviation of 0.1. This strategy's shape ratio was calculated at 0.545, which is a respectable ratio for a good return but with a low volatility strategy.

Social Science Research Network[4]

You can find many academic papers, working papers, and policy reports written by academics and practitioners. Many users can access this site for academic papers, as most of the papers can be downloaded for free.

Books:

Quantitative Trading - Ernie Chan (2008)

This is perhaps the best introduction to quantitative trading if the reader is interested in fully incorporating quantitative tools into portfolio management. It describes the whole process, from selecting ideas and turning them into rules to backtesting. It provides a very initiative way to explain the pros and cons of trading with this type of method. However, this book does not provide workable templates on its own. Although the author's website provides regular updates and has other books on offer for anyone interested to pursue further.

Quantitative Equity Portfolio Management - Chincarini and Kim (2006)

This book was written by two academics focusing on defining investment approach and strategy into quantifiable rules and uses them to construct the portfolio. Its focus is on how to use factor investing to beat the index. The steps described in this book are the blueprint for many passive and smart-beta funds such as the famous Vanguard Global Momentum Factor and the low PE ratio

---

[2] https://quantpedia.com/strategies/asset-class-trend-following/. The paper: https://papers.ssrn.com/sol3/pa-pers.cfm?abstract_id=962461

[3] For example Global Momentum Factor UCITS ETF (VMOM) - https://www.vanguard investor.co.uk/invest-ments/vanguard-global-momentum-factor-ucits-etf-usd-accumulating

[4] https://www.ssrn.com/index.cfm/en/

Vanguard Value Index Fund ETF. The main drawback of this book is the lack of macro contents and codes, for example.

Trading Systems and Methods 6th Ed- Perry Kaufman (2019)

This is perhaps the most comprehensive book in the market on trading rules and methods. It has an exhaustive list detailing the different types of methods. The book is heavily based on technical analysis and contains strategies that are rather difficult to backtest, such as event-driven trades. It also has chapters that deal with portfolio management aspects such as risk management and system testing.

Systematic Trading - Robert Carver (2015)

This book is written by a very popular quantitative hedge fund manager, which uses a systematic way to trade the market. The framework outlined in this book is a common systematic trading framework for quantitative traders and investors. It discusses from a portfolio management perspective how trading rules can be formed and how to implement them. However, it does not detail how to create a forecast and incorporate it into the portfolio. It should be noted that the author also had two chapters for forecasting asset returns and prices but do not go into details since this is proprietary and sensitive information for the traders.

Backtesting platforms:

Quantopian[5]

Quantopian is a platform that allows freelance quantitative analysts to exchange trade strategies. It has a backtesting platform that can test different strategies. Some historical data are also available to be used. Some programming skill is needed, such as Python which is used for coding the strategy.

QSTrader[6]

This is an open-source platform built by Quantstart. It is very customisable but requires the most programming skills as it is also catered for institutional clients, which may have more complicated requirements.

---

[5] https://www.quantopian.com/
[6] https://www.quantstart.com/qstrader/

TradeStation[7]

TradeStation itself is a broker but also provides a backtesting platform for its clients.

MATLAB / Python / R / Excel

Most readers who already have some kind of technical background would be familiar with these tools above. The most efficient way to backtest would probably be a mixture of database and software that can process the backtesting criteria and goals. MATLAB is particularly good as it is a matrix-based language that is great for dealing with the correlation and different combinations of assets in a portfolio. It can also connect very well with other software and has a large community online, offering more modifications. The main disadvantage is probably that it is rather expensive and can be slow compared to the most fundamental programs that do not have an interface. Python is perhaps the next best alternative as it essentially free and open source. Lots of code libraries are available for users to use and modify. It can also be used with other OS systems such as Linex. R is also widely used in the industry as it is also free. R's main advantage is that it offers a very comprehensive library of statistics and mathematical commands as it was initially designed for such purposes.

Forecasting model tools and books:

EconMod Network - Network for economic modelling academics and practitioners[8]

GVAR modelling - tools and forum [9]

Dynare - DSGE modelling and network[10]

The GVAR Handbook: Structure and Applications of a Macro Model of the Global Economy for Policy Analysis (Oxford Press, 2013).

Edited by Dr Filippo di Mauro (ECB & Fed), Dr M. Hashem Pesaran (Cambridge and USC). This book is a comprehensive treatment of the applications of the GVAR. Most examples are relevant to central banks and financial institutions.

---

[7] https://www.tradestation.com/
[8] https://ecomod.net
[9] https://sites.google.com/site/gvarmodelling/home
[10] https://www.dynare.org/

Global and National Macroeconometric Modelling: A Long-Run Structural Approach (Oxford Press, 2012). Authored by Anthony Garratt, Kevin Lee, M. Hashem Pesaran and Yongcheol Shin. This book describes the „long-run structural approach, which is the basis for VARX* (VECMX*) before later being incorporated into the GVAR framework. It also has two chapters on comparing GVAR with other macro models.

Global and National Macroeconometric Modelling: A Long-Run Structural Approach (Oxford Press, 2012).

Authored by Anthony Garratt, Kevin Lee, M. Hashem Pesaran and Yongcheol Shin. This book describes the long-run structural approach, which is the basis for VARX* (VECMX*) before later being incorporated into the GVAR framework. It also has two chapters on comparing GVAR with other macro models.

Introduction to Dynamic Macroeconomic General Equilibrium (Vernon Press, 2015).

Authored by Jose L. Torres. In my opinion, this book is the best for introducing DSGE models as it contains coding and free access for Dynare. All models presented are available on Vernon's website. I have recommended this book for the librarian and macro classes.

Economic Forecasting and Policy (Palgrave Macmillan, 2011).

Authored by Nicolas Carnot, Vincent Koen and Bruno Tissot. This book looks at economic forecasting from a central bank/public organisation perspective and dissects the types of forecasting models and how they are used for decision-making.

Chapter 12

Backtesting with the Excel Workbook

12.1 Introduction

To illustrate how backtesting can be used and, in particular, how forecasts from the macroeconometric model can be applied to this framework, I have provided an excel workbook that would allow the user to input daily price data, forecasts from models and a long short moving average cross-over trading rule. This trading rule would then determine whether the investor should buy or sell or do nothing at all. The price data depicts oil WTI futures from the beginning of 2017 until the most recent available data. By the end of this time period, the trading rule would have triggered 40 orders with 20 buys and 20 sells. In the end, the user can then see the overall performance of the trading rule. Sharpe ratio, highest/lowest returns, and a host of other performance metrics are also readily available to be used for assessing the performance. It should be noted that two different trading scenarios are demonstrated here.

12.2 Single position, long short moving average cross over

The first is a single position trading only. This is a simplified version where when the trading rule has triggered, and it will buy or sell one contract only. It is assumed that one contract is the same price as the closing price. This is a simplified version of reality as the actual cost is likely to be different from the closing price if the trade was executed some other time. However, this does not distract the point the backtest is trying to show here, which tests whether the trading rule is profitable. However, it would be possible to develop a more nuanced model with an exact transaction cost and commission. This would not be suitable with excel as excel is not ideally designed for this purpose. Its cellular, grid-based design is great for copying and extending commands to several columns, etc. It is poorly equipped to run more complex commands such as recording exact transaction cost when buying/selling in different blocks intra-day or across the week. The calculation of the profit and loss would become a problem as it needs a precise way to automatically determine exact buying/selling points throughout the day and then recording them.

Once the trading rule criteria has been hit, it will trigger an either buy or sell signal. This allows the trader to hold one position at any time, either buying or shorting. Therefore the trader's net position can either be short (-1), no holding (0) or long (+1). For example, the first trigger was a sell signal; therefore, the investor will sell 1 contract, holding a negative one position -1. The next signal will then be a buy signal when the rule has triggered. By buying back the 1 contract, the investor now has a null net position, i.e. 0 contracts, thus realising profit or loss from this trade. As a result, the total trades would be even-numbered in the end, with the alternation of one buy and one sell, etc., flip-flopping until the test finishes. To be precise, the trading rule has been inscribed in the command line per below:

= IF (AND (*SMA*, 5_t>*SMA*, 25_t, *SMA*, 5_{t-1}<*SMA*, 25_{t-1}), "BUY",IF (AND (*SMA*, 5_t<*SMA*, 25_t, *SMA*, 5_{t-1}>*SMA*, 25_{t-1}), "SELL",""))

This trading rule is the same as described in the last chapter; therefore, it will not be repeated here.

A host of performance metrics are also calculated automatically. For example, the user will be able to determine which case is the best with Sharpe ratio across different cases and also the highest and lowest returns,

Currently, there are also three forecast options associated with these trading scenarios. The first is a no forecast scenario. This is essentially trading according to the latest available information, i.e. only trade at the end of the day when the market closes. For example, on 07/03/2017 the trading rule has decided to execute a sell order; the trade would then purchase the oil futures at the closing price of 08/03/2017; thus waiting until the end of the day. However, this is not ideal in reality as the trader is most likely to have traded before the close due to liquidity or other concerns. Thus this no forecast case requires the user to rely on perfect information, i.e. when the end of the day has arrived, the investor has complete information to calculate the moving averages. The second and third case is to use forecasting models. The workbook presents two forecasts created with FAVAR and GVAR model, which were covered in earlier chapters. The FAVAR and GVAR forecasts are then placed onto the workbook. The trading rules now rely on these values to determine whether a trade would be triggered. Compared to the no forecast scenario, this is more realistic as it reflects how actual traders behave: they always forecast, albeit with different models or purely on gut feelings. Incorporating the forecasts element from the models in this book is the biggest contribution of this workbook as most other applications do not allow such additions. Again it is possible to include forecasting elements to determine the trading rules trigger points, but currently available templates do not accommodate this, and it is a case of requiring the investor on a customisable programming project. It is expected that the no forecast/perfect information case will provide the best return as it has full information. Therefore the closer the forecast result, the better it will be.

12.3 Multiple position long short moving average cross over with portfolio management

The second trading scenario is a more complex one as it allows more than one position to be transacted and held by the investor at each trade and at any time. This increase from single position introduces a few challenges to the modeller. First and perhaps most importantly, how should the investor now allocate his risk and reward preference? During the single scenario, it did not really matter because the investor can hold only one position at any time; therefore, there is no need to introduce any trading capital requirement nor risk target as the investor will be exposed to exactly one contract equivalent of risk and reward, no matter the action is. The only way to avoid this risk and reward problem in holding a single position is to not trade altogether. Therefore portfolio management principles or tools are not really applicable for that scenario since there is only one position.

Now that we have introduced multiple positions, the investor can now purchase more than one contact at any given buy/sell triggered by the rule, depending on the investor's conviction of the forecasts and the trading rule. From this, I have calculated a buy/sell strength indicator. The higher the indicator, the bigger the investor is going to purchase or sell. This exact size of trade for transact entirely depends on the forecasts. As mentioned in an earlier chapter, the forecasts are also standardised by volatility before being translated into actual positions. This ensures that the trader adheres to the principles and volatility target set up in the beginning. Another assumption here, which was explained in the previous chapter, is that the price volatility has been assumed to be 5% here. By holding the volatility to a fixed level, we can determine whether other parts of the strategy can still be profitable. In practice, however, this assumption is likely to be invalidated and will need updating.

A very important implication here is that, when a forecast has been made correctly and the forecast strength has also been calculated correctly, there is a much bigger room for profits and losses. This is because the investor may no longer be restricted by one position only. For example, consider that the forecast from GVAR asks the trader to purchase 10 contracts while the no forecast case is only asking for 3, whatever the profit and loss prompted by the forecast will be much bigger than that of the no forecast case.

Another important implication with holding multiple positions here is that the returns and risks are much smoother now. This is simply due to the diversification of positions. In the single position scenario, the trader will profit and lose solely on the trade's correct direction; therefore, if he wins, he wins big and vice versa. This, however, does not apply to the multiple holdings because if the trader was prompted to sell, for example, 5 contracts on the first trade—

which results in a net position of -5 contracts—but the forecast has prompted a buy signal of +12, the investor would first buy back the first 5 contracts he had shorted at the new trade price and then buy a further of 7 contracts at the same price. Therefore by the end of this trading day, the investor now holds +7 in his net position. The mixing of clearing one's position from the previous trade plus adding new contracts according to the signal has resulted in smoothing the returns and risk. This is evidence by the highest, lowest returns in the excel example. The no forecast case in the single position strategy has the highest return of 50.5% and the lowest of -12.3% for a single trade. In contrast, the no forecast approach's multiple positions have the highest return of 16.8% and lowest of -2.2% only. This, of course, was also a result of setting the maximum annual volatility of 20%; therefore, the final return and risk would have also decreased as a result.

12.4 Conclusion

This chapter has shown that the overall design and implications of testing single and multiple positions. This is an important distinction as portfolio management is much more important in the multiple scenarios as the single position has virtually no need for its tools at all. This also shows that the final calculated Sharpe ratio is not the only implicated in picking a trading strategy. While the first scenario clearly shows whether a strategy could have been profitable, the second scenario is much more realistic as it incorporates portfolio management tools to control the risk and reward, not solely based on the strength of the forecasts. As we know, forecasts can only be as best as the input we feed them. Despite best diligence has been taken to ensure that the input, estimation and forecasts are as valid as possible, there could still be unexpected errors since the future is always uncertain; therefore, we must include a risk and reward structure to manage the unforeseeable risk. I have also shown how a forecast produced from the models can now be used in this backtest as part of portfolio management, not as a stand-alone number or reference point. The next two chapters will show and analyse the backtest results.

Chapter 13

Example 1 - Backtesting Strategy
- Single Position Long-Short

13.1 Introduction

Having laid out the groundwork for the backtest rationale and methods in previous chapters, this chapter proceeds to show how the backtest was carried out. The first example here is for the single position with the long-short moving average cross over the trading rule. The financial instrument chosen for this example was crude oil West Texas intermediate (WTI).

Figure 13.1: Crude oil WTI price 2017-2020

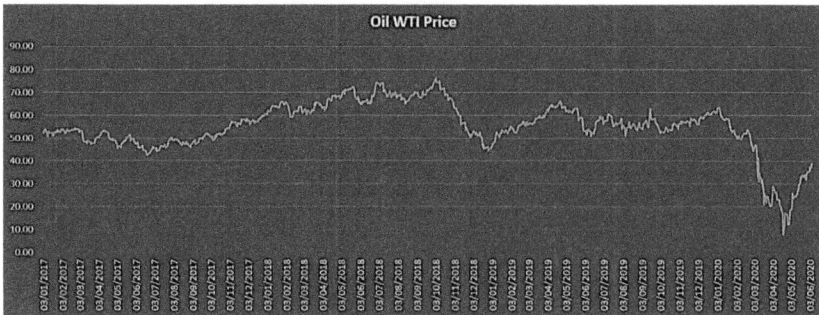

In theory, any financial instrument can be chosen for this backtest as long as there are historical data and that the trading rule can be applied. The reason to choose oil price, though, is not entirely arbitrary. The oil price has seen beginning from its collection has always seen a wide range of intraday and long term movements. It is very common to see oil price riding a very long continuous uptrend or downtrend. The longest uptrend of oil price beginning from the end of 1998 at $12 per barrel to a peak of $140 in August 2008 before crashing down to $34 at the end of 2009. The recent coronavirus outbreak also saw the price of reaching a subzero first time in history. An investor who has purchased a barrel of crude from 2017 at $50 would have ended up with almost 100% loss as the price crashed in April 2020. However, the actual trading is more complicated as the price itself is a benchmark, comprising a range of oil that was produced according to this specification. There is also a difference between spot and futures market in which the buy although may lose 100% in April 2020 due to oil glut and virus outbreak, the investor can also sell the oil in later months, for instance, June, July and so forth when the prices were still trading at a positive.

13.2 Oil prices and market

Together with these two distinctions, a barrel of crude can be referred to as light and sweet, such as the ones produced in the United States WTI or UK Brent produced in the North Sea. Typically crude oil that is sweet and light command a higher premium than their sour, heavy cousins. This is simply because light and sweet barrel will require less refinery processing in order to become usable product oil such as petrol or diesel. Transportation also affects the oil price enormously, depending on the location. A barrel of crude produced according to the specification of the WTI blend, i.e. with API gravity of 42.05 and sulphur content of 0.15% to be delivered at Cushing via pipeline, Texas with being more premium than South Texas sour crude such as Southern Green Canyon, API 29.9 and sulphur of 2.16%.[1] The overall trend is largely the same for both blend, but WTI tends to main a premium of at least $6 per barrel to South Texas sour crude.[2] This price differential was also maintained when the oil price dropped in May 2020, which saw the WTI blend crashing to $-41 per barrel and $-47 for South Texas Sour per barrel.

The mechanism of how crude oil traded is also important as it affects how the price moves. Typically crude oil is traded either at the spot or as futures. The barrels can also be delivered either physically or settled by cash alone. A typical trading scenario would run as follows:

> During the summer of 2017, a big refinery in the US that typically refines up to 300,000 barrels per day saw that the oil price was moving upwards due to economic growth and increased demand. Therefore, as a crude oil buyer, it is trying to purchase the crude as cheaply as possible since it makes a profit by refining it and then distributing the final products to customers. Seeing that the oil market was growing quickly and that a heightened demand happened during the summer as refineries across the states were preparing for the winter fuels, it saw a backwardated market in which the spot price for a barrel cost more than $55 while future deliveries at winter and early 2018 cost only $49 and $48,

---

[1] See Platts for contract specification - https://www.spglobal.com/platts/plattscontent/_assets/_files/en/our-methodology/methodology-specifications/americas-crude-methodology.pdf

[2] Different oil blends have quite a different price mechanisms and trends. See https://oilprice.com/oil-price-charts/50

Example 1 - Backtesting Strategy 195

respectively. This squeeze in the market concerned the refinery; therefore, it decided to enter the market in June for 4,200,000 barrels (2 weeks capacity) of WTI crude with a delivery date of September 2017 so that the final products would be ready for delivery at the start of the winter season in the US.

The time now is April 2020, and the same US refinery has been enduring the economic shutdown. Like other refineries across the states and other parts of the world, an enormous oil glut has seen the oil market plummeting despite the production cuts announced by OPEC. As a result of the low oil price, the refinery decided to shut down some of its operations as it can no longer sell the refined products with any profits. This saw a further decrease in spot oil price as the market has virtually stopped as refineries have no space to store new crude. By 20th April, the cut-off day for futures dated May 2020 delivery saw a negative price. This means that oil producers were effectively paying refineries to take away the barrels.

The above scenario has shown that the oil market can be very volatile, and the oil price is heavily linked to the local and world economy. As a commodity, it is also the most traded contracts on the New York Mercantile Exchange and the most liquid contracts available. Implicitly this implies that there would be no advantage in studying the oil price movement because of EMH. However, this is also not entirely true as there are long and short term trends that affect the price; therefore, it would be reasonable to think that a slow and fast combination of moving averages would reveal trends.

This forms the hypothesis that I am going to backtest: whether a long-short moving average cross over strategy would have been profitable for trading the oil market. The second hypothesis would then be whether the forecasts created from FAVAR and GVAR contribute to the profits?

13.3 Three cases: No forecast, FAVAR and GVAR forecasts

No forecast

The first case is for no forecast or perfect information. As explained in the last chapter, this is the best-case scenario in which the performance obtained here will be optimal for a single position trading. The success rates of the buy/sell and performance rely on the trading rule entirely. The tab under the "Single Position Backtest" shows that the oil price data has been populated on the table, starting from 03/01/2017 to 05/06/2020. It should be noted that the data is recorded on business day only. The data was compiled and published by NYMEX for the Crude Oil WTI price, which always uses the front-month futures for calculation. For example, if we are looking at the data on 15th May 2018, the data will show the WTI futures contract price deliverable for June 2018, then for one month in advance. As soon as the cut off for the June 2018 contract passed, i.e. on 20th May, the oil price will automatically collect the data of the July future contract since July is now the nearest yet unexpired month for a future contract. The data here, therefore, is showing a rolling front-month from the futures market price. The data is in daily format and also includes the open, high, low and close prices. Should the reader wish to calculate the intraday price volatility, this can be done from this existing dataset. The last column also shows an adjusted close price which is the same as the close price as the contract itself does not split nor accrue any dividend payments, which may distort the final price. The next two columns have been filled in with the daily close price forecasts generated from FAVAR and GVAR. As this case does not use the forecast, this part will be ignored until the next two cases.

In the next section, there are three boxes. The first is related to this case which is called Trading Rule - No Forecast. The first two columns calculate a moving average of 5 days and 25 days, respectively. The trade signal of buying or sell or do nothing is then generated in the next column, using the SMAs calculated. Per the explanation in the last chapter, the signals will be generated whenever it has met all conditions. The next column then records the transaction price: the closing price one day after the signal has been generated. This will automatically roll over to the next transaction price when the next transaction has triggered. The column for returns simply calculates the return generated from that transaction when the transaction has been cleared, i.e. a buy position has been sold resulting in zero position, or a sold position has been bought back, resulting in zero position. It is prudent to point out that the return calculation of covering for a sold position is the opposite of selling a long position. The example below shows how this is calculated.

On 07/03/2017, the trading rule has detected its first pattern that meets all conditions and triggered a Sell signal. From this, the trader will purchase on 08/03/2017 at the closing price of $50.28. Thus the trader now has a net position of -1 contract. The next signal was triggered on 04/04/2017, and it was for a buy. Thus the trader bought one contract back on 05/05/2017, which cost $51.15 per contract. Therefore, this trade's total return would be $50.28 - $51.15 = $-0.87, which meant the investor lost -1.73% from this trade. This is because the trader sold at a cheaper price but bought back higher at $51.15. Take another example; the trader has sold 1 share on 10/10/2017 at $50.92. Since the cost of buying it was only $47.48, the total return was 7.25%, making a profit.

Example 1 - Backtesting Strategy 197

Figure 13.2: No forecast rule performance

The above graph can be seen on the single position backtest tab. It pairs the cumulative return of holding an Oil WTI with the cumulative return of the trading strategy. The total returns were calculated in the second tab-performance comparison. It is simply an addition of all the positive and negative returns. From the graph above, we can then see that the total return for holding an oil contract has given the trader a considerable gain from 2017 to 2018. However, the long term decline from the end of 2018 has led to a downward trend that erased all gains by the end of 2018. Although the oil price picked up again throughout 2019, the massive crash, in the end, has again completely wiped out the profits. In the worst-case scenario, the contract would have been sold automatically to recoup some losses or per margin call that the broker issued. The point here though is that, a buy and hold strategy has failed quite dramatically. On the other hand, the strategy has proven to be quite versatile and accurate in its prediction. During much of the time, its performance has surpassed the buy and hold strategy. This is mostly due to the availability of shorting and the accurate calls of the buy/sell signals.

Figure 13.3: Performance

No Forecast	
Performance Metrics	
Positve Returns	153.87%
Negative returns	-67.17%
Positive Trades	19
Negative Trades	20
Hit Ratio	49%
Average Returns	2.22%
Highest Returns	50.5%
Lowest Returns	-12.3%
Sharpe Ratio	0.22

The total combined positive return for this strategy was over 150%, while the negative return equalled -67%. Out of 39 trades that were triggered, 39 of them were positive, while 20 were negative. The first trade was a sell order, whilst the last is a buy order. Since buying the last contract, the rule was not triggered again; therefore, the last net position is 0. Although the hit ratio is just under 50% because of the big returns made during the shorts, particularly in the 2018 year-end and 2020 April, this heavily skewed the total returns from positive trades. The Sharpe ratio was calculated at 0.22, taken using the mean of returns and divided by the returns' standard error. This Sharpe ratio will now be used as the benchmark comparing the other two forecasts.

Forecast with FAVAR

The next case is to test whether using forecasts produced from a FAVAR model can give any contribution. Given that there are always errors in forecasts and compared to the perfect information case, it is expected that the strategy performance using price forecasts will be less accurate. The forecasts generated here were using the same dataset as described in chapter 12. The aim is to input as much relevant data as possible, and the forecast of the oil prices would yield a satisfying performance, which should be as close to the perfect information as much as possible. As outlined in Part II, the independent variables are sorted into fast and slow groups. This sorting is similar to the trend lines of 5 and 25 days to differentiate near and long term trends.

Figure 13.4: With FAVAR forecasts

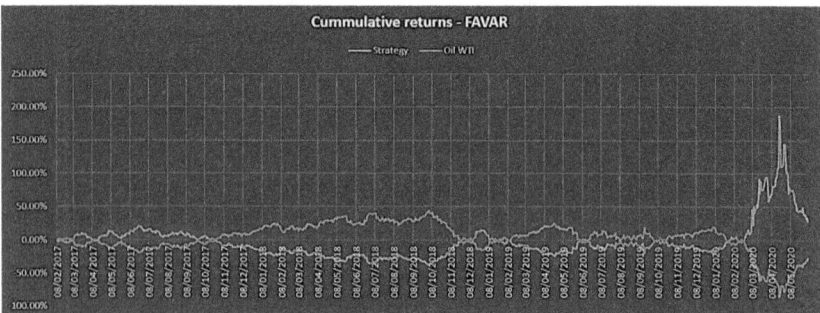

The trading rule now uses the forecast values from the FAVAR model. The trade signals are now triggered based on the SMA5 and SMA25 derived from the FAVAR forecasts. The FAVAR backtest was also run similarly to the one for the no forecast case. The metrics show surprisingly good performance with a positive return of 154% but a negative return of -82%. In general, the metrics are not too different from the no forecast scenario as it has the same hit ratio and similar returns pattern. However, when we look at the cumulative performance above, we can see that the strategy was only profitable for a short period in 2017 before losing ground to the buy and hold strategy. The year 2019

Example 1 - Backtesting Strategy 199

also saw a poor performance from the strategy where it triggered the buy and sell signals too early, thus making a loss. However, the reprieve came during early 2020 when the strategy entered into a sell that logged a 50% return and several other trades with the correct signals. This has heavily skewed the cumulative return to a peak of 180% before lowering to 50% in total. The overall Sharpe is similar to the no forecast case at 0.18.

Forecast with GVAR

The final case is to test whether using forecasts produced from a GVAR model can give any contribution. The forecasts generated here were using the same dataset as described in chapter 12. The aim is to input as much relevant data as possible, and the forecast of the oil prices would yield a satisfying performance, which should be as close to the perfect information as much as possible. The trading rule now uses the forecast values from the GVAR model. The trade signals are now triggered based on the SMA5 and SMA25 derived from the GVAR forecasts.

Figure 13.5: Performance

FAVAR	
Performance Metrics	
Positve Returns	154.60%
Negative returns	-81.96%
Positive Trades	19
Negative Trades	20
Hit Ratio	49%
Average Returns	1.86%
Highest Returns	43.6%
Lowest Returns	-12.2%
Sharpe Ratio	0.18

The GVAR backtest was also run similarly to the one for the no forecast case. The GVAR has so far fared worse when compared to both FAVAR and perfect scenario case. The strategy lost money most of the time during 2018 and 2019 but similarly gained a reprieve in 2020. The total negative return is the highest in all three tests at -90.22%, while the gain is the lowest at 148.88%. The Hit ratio is also at 44%, with 17 positive trades only and 22 negative. Therefore it is not surprising to see that the Sharpe ratio is also the lowest at 0.14.

Overall it has a similar pattern to the other two cases but delivered lower returns. We can see that some were triggered too early at the transaction times, thus making a loss. However, it has also performed very well during the last period in the crash.

13.4 Conclusion

As mentioned in the beginning, a priori belief is that no forecast / perfect information will perform the best. This was expected as it had the most information available and assumed that there is no forecast to be made from the investor at all. This, of course, is difficult to carry out in practice as most trades are not triggered at the end of the day due to liquidity reason. The main disadvantage of a moving average cross over is also observed during the live trading session. This is simply because it is essentially a backward-looking indicator and does not predict anything in itself unless, of course, if we put lines together so that hoping to find out the slower trend lines and the reverse point. As a result, regardless of the methods used in reality, the trader will always engage in some kind of forecasting, either implicitly with gut feeling or experience or with a macroeconometric model.

Figure 13.6: With GVAR forecasts

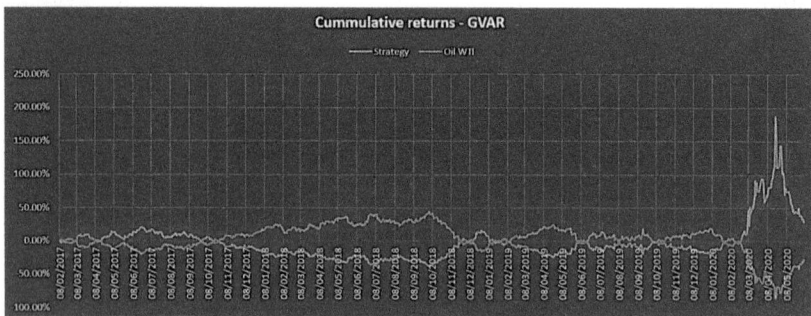

Figure 13.7: Performance

GVAR	
Performance Metrics	
Positve Returns	148.88%
Negative returns	-90.22%
Positive Trades	17
Negative Trades	22
Hit Ratio	44%
Average Returns	1.50%
Highest Returns	45.8%
Lowest Returns	-13.2%
Sharpe Ratio	0.14

The most surprising result from above is perhaps that the FAVAR model did quite an impressive job of matching the perfect information hit ratio. This backtest, of course, similar to others are based on a set of assumptions and by

Example 1 - Backtesting Strategy 201

changing those assumptions, the results would have appeared different. One of the biggest assumptions in this single position is that it does not require the trader to purchase/sell multiple positions. As a result, it ignores most portfolio management elements which are as important as the forecast itself.

Example 2 - Backtesting Strategy - Multiple Positions Long-Short

14.1 Introduction

The second trading scenario is a more complex one but more realistic. The main difference here compared to the single position backtest is the introduction of multiple positions and the risk and reward criteria. Now that we have introduced multiple positions, the investor can now purchase more than one contact at any given buy/sell triggered by the trading rule, depending on the investor's conviction of the forecasts and the trading rule. From this, I have calculated a buy/sell strength indicator. The higher the indicator, the bigger the investor is going to purchase or sell. This exact size of trade for transact entirely depends on the forecasts. As mentioned in an earlier chapter, the forecasts are also standardised by volatility before being translated into actual positions. This ensures that the trader adheres to the principles and volatility target set up in the beginning. Another assumption here, which was explained in the previous chapter, is that the price volatility has been assumed to be 5% here. By holding the volatility to a fixed level, we can determine whether other parts of the strategy can still be profitable. In practice, however, this assumption is likely to be invalidated and will need updating.

A very important implication here is that, when a forecast has been made correctly and that the forecast strength has also been calculated correctly, there is a much bigger room for profits and losses. This is due to the fact that the investor may no longer be restricted by one position only. Consider that the forecast from GVAR is asking the trader to purchase 10 contracts while the no forecast case is only asking for 3; whatever the profit and loss prompted by the forecast will be much bigger than that of the no forecast case.

Another important implication with holding multiple positions here is that the returns and risks are much smoother now. This is simply due to the diversification of positions. In the single position scenario, the trader will profit and lose solely on the trade's correct direction; therefore, if he wins, he wins big and vice versa. This, however, does not apply to the multiple holdings. This is because if the trader was prompted to sell, for example, 5 contracts on the first trade—which results in a net position of -5 contracts, but the forecast has prompted a buy signal of +12—, the investor would first buy back the first 5 contracts he had shorted at the new trade price and then buy a further of 7 contracts at the same price. Therefore by the end of this trading day, the investor now holds +7 in his net position. The mixing of clearing one's position from the previous trade plus adding new contracts according to the signal has resulted in smoothing the returns and risk. This is evidence by the highest, lowest returns in the excel example. The no forecast case in the single position strategy has the highest return of 50.5% and the lowest of -12.3% for a single trade. In contrast, the multiple positions of no forecast approach have the highest return of 16.8% and lowest of -2.2% only. This, of course, was also a result of setting the maximum annual volatility of 20%; therefore, the final return and risk would have also decreased as a result.

14.2 Portfolio management criteria

Data and period

The data used here is the same as the one used in the single position test for the exact period. There is, however, a difference in terms of the dates recorded in the multiple positions tab. This is because only trade dates are recorded for the calculation of profit and loss and other metrics. For example, when a sell signal was generated on 06/03/2017 and the trade was placed on 07/03/2017, the entry date of 07/03/2017 will be recorded. When the next signal for a buyback appeared on 03/04/2017, the trade will be executed on 04/04/2017 and the date recorded. Therefore all trades were recorded in the same method for the succession of all 40 trades.

Risk and reward preference/metrics

The assumption here is that the investor is willing to risk up to 20% of the capital in total on an annual basis. The initial capital is £50,000; therefore, the annual cash volatility target is £10,000. From this, the daily volatility target can be found by dividing by 16 as this is the equivalent of the annualised daily target. The initial daily volatility target is, therefore, £625.00. It will change according to the capital size. Therefore if the capital is now £49,236, then the daily volatility target is now £620.65. Of course, the change in the capital is linked to the profit and loss when trades occurred. For example, a sell signal was generated on 06/03/2017, and a transaction happened on 07/03/2017. The buyback happened on 04/04/2017 and resulted in a loss of £211.00; therefore, the capital will now be £49,789. Any new trade to take place, i.e. the additional positions that the trader needs to take in order to reach the recommended position, will be determined by the daily volatility target calculated from the previous trade date. For example, the daily volatility target for trade to be taken on 25/04/2017 will use the value from the last trade date, which is 04/04/2017.

Example 2 - Backtesting Strategy 205

This reflects the order of actions: 1) new trade date first clear the previous positions based on the new buy/sell strength. If additional trades need to be purchased or sold, the trader will either buy or sell new additional positions with the new trade date's price.

The profit and loss at the end period are then simply calculated by combining the daily returns. There are 40 trades; therefore, 39 daily returns are available. The first trade, regardless of whether it is a buy or sell, would not show a return unless it was cleared; therefore, there are 39 returns available. Similarly, the Sharpe ratio is calculated for each strategy for the whole period. Other metrics are also available to describe the details of the strategy and returns.

14.3 Three cases: No forecast, FAVAR and GVAR forecasts

No forecast

The first case here is for no forecast/perfect information. The assumption is similar to the ones in a single position. The biggest difference is how the forecasts were converted into buy/sell signal, translating into actual trading positions. Following the methods as set out in the method chapter and the assumptions described above, the graphs and tables below show the produced metrics.

Figure 14.1: Performance

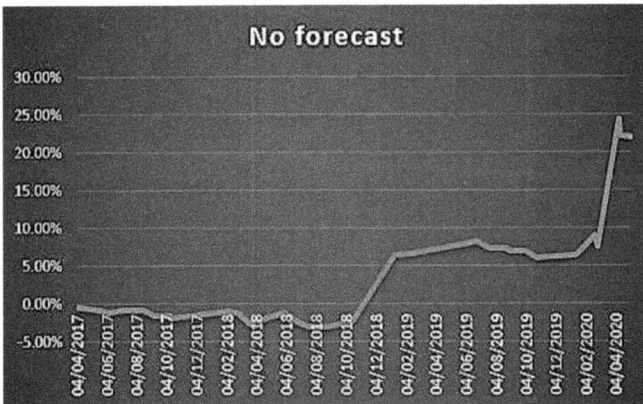

The graph shows that the cumulative return just over 3.5 years from the start of 2017 to June 2020. The strategy returned 21.94% or £11,171 in total. Similar to the single position backtest, there are also 40 trades here. This is because the trading rule is the same, therefore prompting the same trade dates. The only difference here is the magnitude of the buy/sell strength and thus the final positions. The end period's profit is much less than the single position strategy, as the overall return was over 80%. The Shape ratio is also marginally smaller at 0.18 compared to 0.22 for a single position. It would, therefore, be reasonable to ask when should we still keep this strategy neither the profit nor the Sharpe is better than the single position?

Figure 14.2: Performance

Capital	£50,000		
Annual percentage volatility target	20.0%		
Annual cash volatility target	£10,000	Average strength	0.05
P&L at end of period	£11,171	Average strength	0.05
Cummulative return %	21.94%	Higest Buy	2.82
Average return per trade%	0.6%	Lowest Sell	-1.10
Highest return %	16.8%	Total strength	2.05
Lowest return %	-2.2%	No. of Buy	20
Average position	0.05	No. of Sell	20
Maximum position	323.00	Sharpe ratio	0.18
Minimum position	-81.00		

The main reason to use multiple reasons over the single position is a matter of scale. For example, the maximum size allowed with one position is just one contract or the minimum requested by the broker. The obvious downside to this is the inability to upscale the strategy. It was only applicable to whatever the single contract worth. Higher capital would not be applicable as it cannot add more positions. However, other than this reason, there aren't many reasons why multiple positions should be taken as the primary. While the strategy is profitable, most profits were derived from trade 21 and 37, both of which were short.

Looking at the metrics, the average return per trade is 0.6%. The biggest advantage of multiple strategies is that the lowest return is much smaller, at only 2.2%. This is due to the volatility target that was set out in the beginning. The average buy and sell strength is near 0, which is expected as there are buys and sells at 50% each. The maximum position that the trader held is 323. The minimum size of a contract is assumed to the 5 barrels; therefore, 323 contracts would be equivalent to 1615 barrels. The biggest short position was -81 or -405 barrels.

Forecast with FAVAR

Using the same data from but that the trading rules are now generated from FAVAR forecasts. The cumulative return is now 19.3% or £10,300. This is marginally lower than the no forecast case. On the other hand, the highest return was just 4.3%, and the lowest was -5.2%. At any one point, the maximum long position is 546 contracts, while the minimum position is only -15. This result reflects that the strategy has a stronger preference for long position

Example 2 - Backtesting Strategy 207

compared to the no forecast case. This is shown in the total strength figure 3.6, much bigger than 2.05 in the no forecast case. Overall, FAVAR points to a stronger net-long than short position. Due to this overall long preference, there are more net long positions, and when the 2020 oil price collapse happened, this strategy meant a loss of 5% instead of gains like the in the no forecast scenario. The overall performance is still positive, similar to the no forecast scenario, as there are more lumps of positive gains scattered throughout the years than the two traders that happened with the no forecast case.

Figure 14.3: Performance

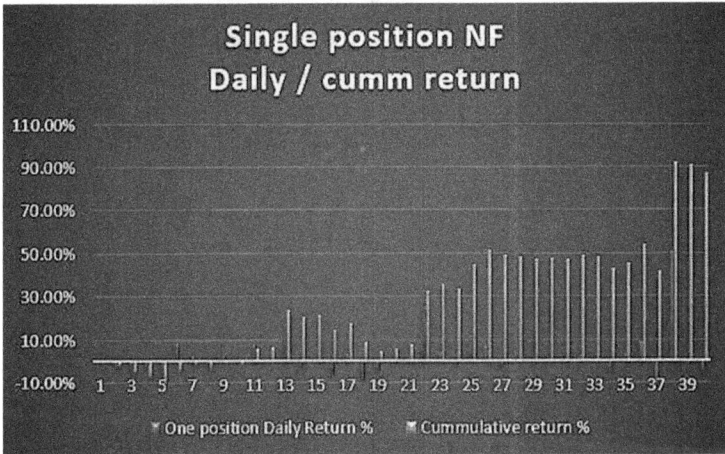

Figure 14.4: Performance

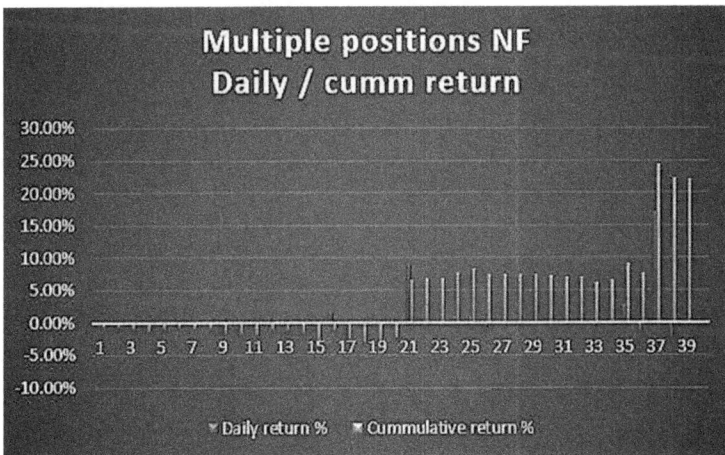

Figure 14.5: Performance

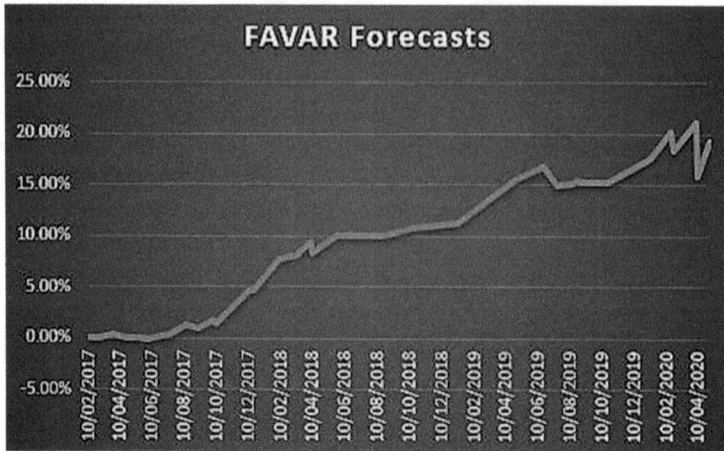

Figure 14.6: Performance

Capital	£50,000		
Annual percentage volatility target	20.0%		
Annual cash volatility target	£10,000		
P&L at end of period	£10,300	Average	0.09
Cummulative return %	19.30%	Higest Buy	2.93
Average return per trade%	0.5%	Lowest Sell	-1.44
Highest return %	4.3%	Total strength	3.60
Lowest return %	-5.2%	No. of Buy	20
Average position	0.09	No. of Sell	20
Maximum position	546.00	Sharpe ratio	0.30
Minimum position	-15.00		

Forecast with GVAR

The final case was made with GVAR forecasts. The GVAR performed the worse during the single position backtest. However, the performance here is much stronger than no forecast and FAVAR as the final return was a staggering 70.1% or £45,961 in just 3.5 years. While the forecast accuracy is on par with the other two cases, the main difference is in the calculated buy/sell strength. Early in the test period, the GVAR case already reached 25% for the cumulative return at trade 13 while no forecast was negative, and FAVAR had only 5%. This early profit has boosted the capital in the early period from the 13th trade, which saw the capital grew much bigger over time. This early increase in trading capital has enormously increased the daily volatility, which, in turn, magnified the position that it is allowed to take. This is reflected in the metrics where the biggest long position was over 580 contracts, and short was over -163 contracts—much bigger than the other two cases. This early profit-taking has

Example 2 - Backtesting Strategy 209

compounded the overall growth in the end. While the overall accuracy is on par with the other two but the increased trade size, the increased profit has led this case to be much bigger in the long-run. For example, it made the right calls and had very successful hit rates since 2018, calling all correct directions. The highest return was 25%, while the biggest loss was only -1.4%. As a result, the Sharpe ratio is a better figure of 0.35.

Figure 14.7: Performance

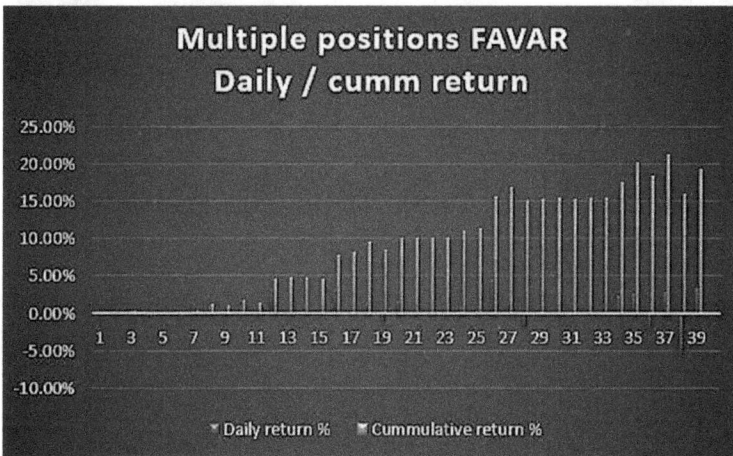

14.4 Performance Comparison

This exercise has shown that three different cases have been very different. The performance difference is staggering from a single position to backtest. We can see that the no forecast/perfect information has the worst performance from the comparison graph. While the FAVAR had a lower result, in the end, it was constantly above the no forecast case until the end, where it was the only case that made a loss. While forecast accuracy was the most important element in the single position backtest, its relevance is smaller. This shows that while it is important to have an accurate forecast model, it is also equally if not even more important to have set the risk and reward correctly in the beginning as it affects the outcome enormously.

While it may seem paradoxical to see that no forecast/perfect information would be the best outcome, it is actually not an unexpected outcome. Single position trading heavily depends on the forecast, but multiple positions trading is much closer to actual practice than art and science. The elements from portfolio management have also been proven to be crucial for the returns.

Figure 14.8: Performance

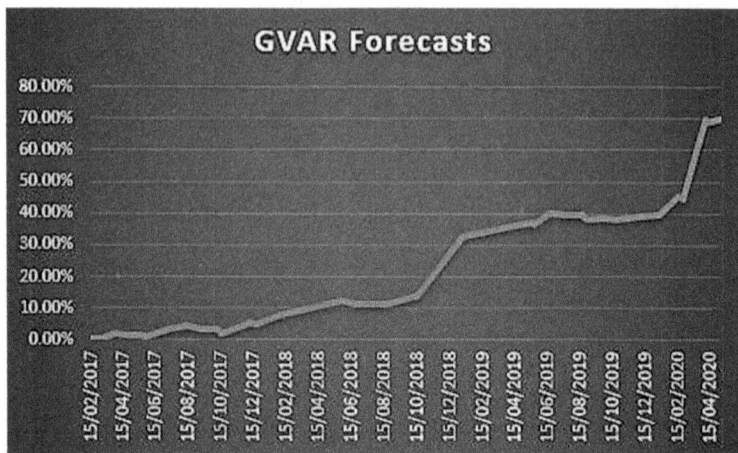

Figure 14.9: Performance

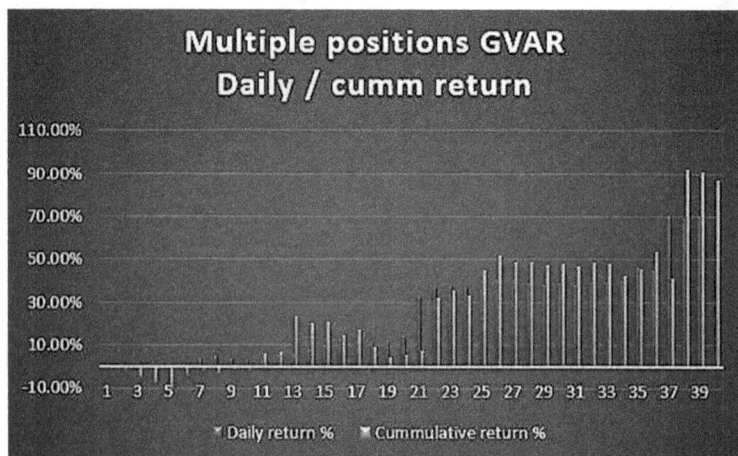

Figure 14.10: Performance

Capital	£50,000		
Annual percentage volatility target	20.0%		
Annual cash volatility target	£10,000		
P&L at end of period	£45,961	Average strength	0.01
Cummulative return %	70.10%	Higest Buy	2.66
Average return per trade%	1.8%	Lowest Sell	-1.26
Highest return %	25.4%	Total strength	0.47
Lowest return %	-1.4%	No. of Buy	20
Average position	0.01	No. of Sell	20
Maximum position	580.00	Sharpe ratio	0.35
Minimum position	-163.00		

Example 2 - Backtesting Strategy 211

Figure 14.11: Performance

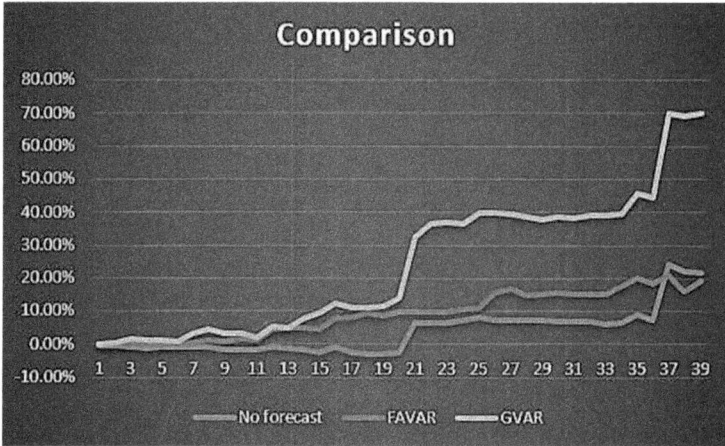

14.5 Conclusion

This chapter, along with all the other chapters in this part, has shown the mechanics of backtesting a strategy in two scenarios and with three different cases, therefore 6 different tests in the end. It has answered the questions that were asked at the beginning of how can we know whether a strategy works and the forecast usefulness. The single position test has been proven to be expected but not the case with the multiple positions as it is complicated by extra elements from portfolio management.

While this has shown how the backtest can be done, it should also be reminded that some elements could be added to further improve the backtest. For example, a dynamic way of including commissions would potentially decrease the profits somewhat. Diversification of assets is another way to ensure that not all eggs are put into the same basket. The correlation or the lack of it with diversification in a portfolio can almost always increase the return while lowering the volatility. This could be a factor to be investigated for further research.

Bibliography

Akerlof, G. A. & Shiller, R. J. (2010). *Animal Spirits: How Human Psychology Drives The Economy, And Why It Matters for Global Capitalism.* doi:10.1111/j.1475-4932.2009.00576.x

Kahneman, D. & Tversky, A. (1979). Prospect Theory: An Analysis of Decision under Risk. *Econometrica, 47* (2), 263–292. doi:10.2307/1914185

Acocella, N, Bartolomeo, G. D. & Hallett, A. (2016). *Macroeconomic Paradigms And Economic Policy: From The Great Depression to The Great Recession.* Cambridge University Press.

Adolfson, M., Lindé, J. & Villani, M. (2007). Forecasting performance of an open economy DSGE model. *Econometric Reviews, 26* (2-4), 289–328. doi:10.1080/07474930701220543

Al-Haschimi, A. & Dées, S. (2013). Macroprudential applications of the GVAR. In F. di Mauro & M. H. Pesaran (Eds.), *The GVAR Handbook: Structure and Applications of A Macro Model of The Global Economy for Policy Analysis* (pp. 151–165). doi:10.1093/acprof.arXiv:arXiv: 1011.1669v3

Amihud, Y. & Mendelson, H. (1986). Asset pricing and the bid-ask spread. *Journal of Financial Economics, 17* (2), 223–249. doi:10.1016/0304-405X(86)90065-6

Andersen, T. G., Bollerslev, T. & Meddahi, N. (2005). Correcting the errors: Volatility forecast evaluation using high-frequency data and realized volatilities. doi:10.1111/j.1468-0262.2005.00572.x

Ando, A, economic Review, F. M. T. A. & 1969, U. (1969). Econometric analysis of stabilization policies. *The American Economic Review, 59* (2), 296–314. Retrieved from http://www.jstor.org/stable/1823683

Andrews, D. & Ploberger, W. (1994). Optimal tests when a nuisance parameter is present only under the alternative. *Econometrica,* 1383–1414. Retrieved from http://www.jstor.org/stable/2951753

Angelidis, T., Benos, A. & Degiannakis, S. (2004). The use of GARCH models in VaR estimation. In *Statistical Methodology.* doi:10.1016/j.stamet.2004.08.004

Armstrong, J. (2001). *Principles of Forecasting: A Handbook for Researchers and Practitioners.* Springer.

Bachelier, L. (1900). Théorie de la spéculation. *Annales scientifiques de l'École normale supérieure.* doi:10.24033/asens.476

Backé, P, Feldkircher, M & Slačík, T. (2013). Economic spillovers from the euro area to the CESEE region via the financial channel: a GVAR approach. *Focus on European Economic Integration, 4,* 50–64. Retrieved from https://pdfs.semantic scholar.org/e6d1/bdf05ae47 29c25043a23d6c9b165e5195653.pdf

Bai, B. Y. J. & Ng, S. (2002). Determining the Number of Factors in Approximate Factor Models. *Econometrica, 70* (1), 191–221. http://www.jstor.org/stable/2692 167 Accessed: 08-07-2016.

Banz, R. W. (1981). The relationship between return and market value of common stocks. *Journal of Financial Economics.* doi:10.1016/0304-405X(81)90018-0

Barber, B. M., Lee, Y. T., Liu, Y. J. & Odean, T. (2009). Just how much do individual investors lose by trading. *Review of Financial Studies.* doi:10.1093/rfs/hhn046

Barclay, M. J., Kandel, E. & Marx, L. M. (1998). The effects of transaction costs on stock prices and trading volume. *Journal of Financial Intermediation.* doi:10.1006/jfin.1998.0238

Bekaert, G, Hoerova, M & Lo Duca, M. (2013). Risk, uncertainty and monetary policy. *Journal of Monetary Economics, 60* (7), 771–788. Retrieved from https://www.sciencedirect.com/science/article/pii/S0304393213000871

Bénassy-Quéré, A, Coeuré, B., Jacquet, P. & Ferry-Pisani, J. (2010). *Economic policy: Theory and practice.* New York: Oxford University Press.

Berger, D, Guerrieri, V & Lorenzoni, G. (2015). House prices and consumer spending. *The Review of Economic Studies.* Retrieved from https://academic.oup.com/restud/advance-article/doi/10.1093/restud/rdx060/4371413

Berkowitz, J. & O'Brien, J. (2002). How accurate are value-at-risk models at commercial banks? *Journal of Finance.* doi:10.1111/1540-6261.00455

Bernanke, B. S. (1986). Alternative explanations of the money-income correlation. In *Carnegie-Rochester conference series on public policy* (pp. 49–99). North-Holland.

Bernanke, B. S., Boivin, J. & Eliasz, P. (2005). Measuring the Effects of Monetary Policy: A Factor-Augmented Vector Autoregressive (FAVAR) Approach Author(s): Ben S. Bernanke, Jean Boivin and Piotr Eliasz Reviewed work (s): Published by Oxford University Press JSTOR is a not-for-profit serv. *The Quarterly Journal of Economics, 120* (1), 387–422.

Black, F. (1972). Capital Market Equilibrium with Restricted Borrowing. *The Journal of Business.* doi:10.1086/295472

Black, F., Jensen, M. C. & Scholes, M. (1972). The Capital Asset Pricing Model: Some Empirical Tests. *Studies in the Theory of Capital Markets.* doi:10.2139/ssrn.908569

Blanchard, O. & Quah, D. (1988). The dynamic effects of aggregate demand and supply disturbances. *The American Economic Review, 83* (5), 1387–1393. Retrieved from http://www.nber.org/papers/w2737

Blanchard, O. J. & Kahn, C. M. (1980). The Solution of Linear Difference Models under Rational Expectations Author (s): Olivier Jean Blanchard and Charles M. Kahn Published by The Econometric Society Stable URL: http://www.jstor.org/stable/1912186 REFERENCES Linked references are available. *Econometrica, 48* (5), 1305–1311.

Blanchard, O. J. & Watson, M. W. (1986). Are business cycles all alike? In E. Robert J. Gordon (Ed.), *The American Business Cycle: Continuity and Change* (pp. 123–180). University of Chicago Press. Retrieved from http://www.nber.org/books/gord86-1

Blume, M. E. & Friend, I. (1973). A NEW LOOK AT THE CAPITAL ASSET PRICING MODEL. *The Journal of Finance.* doi:10.1111/j.1540-6261.1973.tb01342.x

Boivin, J., Kiley, M. T. & Mishkin, F. S. (2010). *How has the monetary transmission mechanism evolved over time?* National Bureau of Economic Research. Retrieved from http://www.nber.org/papers/w158790ANATIONAL

Bollerslev, T. (1986). Generalized autoregressive conditional heteroskedasticity. *Journal of Comparative Economics, 31,* 307–327. Retrieved from http://linkinghub.elsevier.com/ retrieve/pii/0304393288901687

Bollerslev, T., Engle, R. F. & Wooldridge, J. M. (1988). A Capital Asset Pricing Model with Time-Varying Covariances. *Journal of Political Economy.* doi:10.1086/261527

Bonanno, G., Vandewalle, N. & Mantegna, R. N. (2000). Taxonomy of stock market indices. *Physical Review E - Statistical Physics, Plasmas, Fluids, and Related Interdisciplinary Topics.* doi:10.1103/PhysRevE.62.R7615.arXiv:0001268

Brayton, F. & Mauskopf, E. (1985). The Federal Reserve board MPS quarterly econometric model of the US economy. *Economic Modelling, 2* (3), 170–292. doi:10.1016/0264-9993(85)90022-7

Brayton, F., Levin, A., Tryon, R. & Williams, J. C. (1997). The Evolution of Macro Models at the Federal Reserve Board. *Carnegie-Rochester Conference Series on Public Policy, 47,* 43–81.doi:10.1016/S0167-2231(98)00004-9

Breusch, T. S. & Pagan, A. R. (1979). A Simple Test for Heteroscedasticity and Random Coefficient Variation. *Econometrica.* doi:10.2307/1911963

Bushman, R.M. and Smith, A.J., 2003. Transparency, financial accounting information, and corporate governance. *Financial accounting information, and corporate governance. Economic Policy Review, 9*(1).

Bussière, M, Chudik, A & Sestieri, G. (2009). Modelling Global Trade Flows: Results from A GVAR Model. Retrieved from https://papers.ssrn.com/sol3/papers.cfm?abstractid= 1456883

Cai, F. N. (2005). Does the Market Conspire Against the Weak? An Empirical Study of Front Running Behavior During the LTCM Crisis. *SSRN Electronic Journal.* doi:10. 2139/ssrn.292765

Campbell, J. Y. & Vuolteenaho, T. (2004). Bad beta, good beta. *American Economic Review.*doi:10.1257/0002828043052240

Campbell, J. Y., Lo, A. W. & MacKinlay, A. C. (2012). *The econometrics of financial markets.* doi:10.1515/9781400830213-004

Canova, F. (2007). *Methods for applied macroeconomic research.* Princeton University Press.

Carabenciov, I, Ermolaev, I, Freedman, C, Juillard, M, Kamenik, O, Korshunov, D & Laxton, D. (2013). A small quarterly projection model of the US economy. *IMF Working Paper 08/278.* Retrieved from https://papers.ssrn.com/sol3/papers.cfm?abstractid=1316746

Carnot, N, Koen, V & Tissot, B. (2011). *Economic forecasting and policy* (2nd). Palgrave Macmillan.

Cashin, P., Mohaddes, K. & Raissi, M. (2017a). China's slowdown and global financial market volatility: Is world growth losing out? *Emerging Markets Review, 31,* 164–175. doi:10.1016/J.EMEMAR.2017.05.001

Cashin, P., Mohaddes, K. & Raissi, M. (2017b). Fair Weather or Foul? The Macro-Economic Effects of El Niño. *Journal of International Economics, 106,* 37–54. doi:10.1016/J.JINTECO.2017.01.010

Cass, D. (1965). Optimum growth in an aggregative model of capital accumulation. *The Review of economic studies, 1* (32), 233–240. Retrieved from http://www.jstor.org/stable/ 2295827

Castrén, O., Dées, S. & Zaher, F. (2010). Stress-testing euro area corporate default probabilities using a global macroeconomic model. *Journal of Financial Stability, 6* (2), 64–78. doi:10.1016/J.JFS.2009.10.001

Cesa-Bianchi, A., Pesaran, M. H., Rebucci, A. & Xu, T. (2013). China's emergence in the world economy and business cycles in Latin America. In F. di Mauro & M. H. Pesaran (Eds.), *The GVAR Handbook: Structure and Applications of a Macro Model of the Global Economy for Policy Analysis* (pp. 195–211). doi:10.1093/acprof.arXiv: arXiv:1011.1669v3

Chacon, J. L. T. (2015). *Introduction to Dynamic Macroeconomic General Equilibrium Models*. Vernon Press. Retrieved from http://citeseerx.ist.psu. edu/viewdoc/ download?doi=10.1.1.829.4028rep=rep1type=pdf

Chen, Y., He, M. & Rudkin, S. (2017). Understanding Chinese provincial real estate investment: A Global VAR perspective. *Economic Modelling, 67*, 248–260. doi:10. 1016/J. ECONMOD.2016.12.019

Christiano, L. J., Eichenbaum, M. S. & Trabandt, M. (2017). On DSGE Models. *Journal of Economic Perspectives*, 1–29.

Chudik, A. & Fratzscher, M. (2011). Identifying the global transmission of the 2007–2009 financial crisis in a GVAR model. *European Economic Review, 55* (3), 325–339. doi:10.1016/J.EUROECOREV.2010.12.003

Chudik, A. & Pesaran, M. H. (2016). Theory and Practice of GVAR Modelling. *Journal of Economic Surveys, 30* (1), 165–197. doi:10.1111/joes.12095

Coase, R. & Wang, N. (2016). *How China became capitalist*. doi:10.1057/9781137019 370

Cooley, T. F. & Leroy, S. F. (1985). Atheoretical macroeconometrics: A critique. *Journal of Monetary Economics, 16* (3), 283–308. doi:10.1016/0304-3932(85)90038-8

Cowles, A. (1944). Stock Market Forecasting. *Econometrica*. doi:10.2307/1905433

Crowder, W. J., Hoffman, D. L. & Rasche, R. H. (1999). Identification, Long-Run Relations, and Fundamental Innovations in a Simple Cointegrated System. *Review of Economics and Statistics, 81* (1), 109–121. doi:10.1162/003465399767923863

De Jong, D. N. & Dave, C. (2011). Structural Macroeconometrics.pdf. Princeton University Press; 2nd edition.

Dees, S., di Mauro, F., Pesaran, M. H. & Smith, L. V. (2007). Exploring the international linkages of the euro area: a global VAR analysis. *Journal of Applied Econometrics, 22* (1), 1–38. doi:10.1002/jae.932

Dees, S., Hashem Pesaran, M., Vanessa Smith, L. & Smith, R. P. (2014). Constructing MultiCountry Rational Expectations Models. *Oxford Bulletin of Economics and Statistics, 76* (6), 812–840. doi:10.1111/obes.12046

Demsetz, H. (1968). The Cost of Transacting. *The Quarterly Journal of Economics*. doi:10.2307/1882244

di Mauro, F. & Pesaran, M. (2013b). *The GVAR Handbook: Structure and Applications of a Macro Model of the Global Economy for Policy Analysis*. OUP Oxford.

di Mauro, F. & Pesaran, M. H. (2013a). Introduction: An Overview of the GVAR Approach and the Handbook. In F. di Mauro & M. H. Pesaran (Eds.), *The GVAR Handbook: Structure and Applications of a Macro Model of the Global Economy for Policy Analysis* (Chap. 1, pp. 1–11). doi:10.1093/acprof. arXiv: arXiv:1011.1669v3

di Mauro, F. & Smith, L. V. (2013). The basic GVAR DdPS model. In F. di Mauro & M. H. Pesaran (Eds.), *The GVAR Handbook: Structure and Applications of a Macro Model of the Global Economy for Policy Analysis* (pp. 12–32). doi:10.1093/acprof. arXiv: arXiv:1011.1669v3

Doan, T., Litterman, R. & Sims, C. (1984). Forecasting and conditional projection using realistic prior distributions. *Econometric Reviews, 3* (1), 1–100. doi:10.1080/ 07474938408800053

Dragomirescu-Gaina, C. & Philippas, D. (2015). Strategic interactions of fiscal policies in Europe: A global VAR perspective. *Journal of International Money and Finance*, *59*, 49–76. doi:10.1016/J.JIMONFIN.2015.06.001

Dreger, C & Zhang, Y. (2014). Does the economic integration of China affect growth and inflation in industrial countries? *Economic Modelling*. Retrieved from https://www.sciencedirect.com/science/article/pii/S0264999313005671

Edge, R. M. & Gurkaynak, R. S. (2011). How Useful are Estimated DSGE Model Forecasts? *SSRN Electronic Journal*, (100). doi:10.2139/ssrn.1810075

Edge, R. M., Kiley, M. T. & Laforte, J. P. (2010). A comparison of forecast performance between Federal Reserve staff forecasts, simple reduced-form models, and a DSGE model. *Journal of Applied Econometrics*, *25* (4), 720–754. doi:10.1002/jae. 1175.arXiv:1099-1255

Eickmeier, S. & Ng, T. (2015). How do US credit supply shocks propagate internationally? A GVAR approach. *European Economic Review*, *74*, 128–145. doi:10.1016/J. EUROECOREV.2014.11.011

Elliott, G & Timmermann, A. (2013). *Handbook of economic forecasting*.

Engle, R. F. & Patton, A. J. (2001). What good is a volatility model? *Quantitative Finance*. doi:10.1088/1469-7688/1/2/305

Engle, R. F. (1982). Autoregressive Conditional Heteroscedasticity with Estimates of the Variance of United Kingdom Inflation. *Econometrica*, *50* (4), 987. doi:10.2307/ 1912773

Engle, R. F. (2000). The econometrics of ultra-high-frequency data. *Econometrica*. doi:10.1111/1468-0262.00091

Engle, R. F., Hendry, D. F. & Richard, J.-F. (1983). Exogeneity. *Econometrica*, *51* (2), 277–304.

Engle, R. F., Lilien, D. M. & Robins, R. P. (1987). Estimating Time-Varying Risk Premia in the Term Structure: The Arch-M Model. *Econometrica*. doi:10.2307/1913242

Fama, E. F. & French, K. R. (2004). The Capital Asset Pricing Model: Theory and evidence. In *Journal of economic perspectives*. doi:10.1257/0895330042162430

Fama, E. F. & French, K. R. (2007). Disagreement, tastes, and asset prices. *Journal of Financial Economics*. doi:10.1016/j.jfineco.2006.01.003

Fama, E. F. (1970). Efficient Capital Markets: A Review of Theory and Empirical Work. *The Journal of Finance*. doi:10.2307/2325486

Fama, E. F., Fisher, L., Jensen, M. C. & Roll, R. (1969). The Adjustment of Stock Prices to New Information. *International Economic Review*. doi:10.2307/2525569

Favero, C. A. (2001). *Applied Macroeconometrics*. doi:10.1017/S1365100502020084

Favero, C. A. (2013). Modelling sovereign bond spreads in the euro area: a nonlinear global VAR model. In F. di Mauro & M. H. Pesaran (Eds.), *The GVAR Handbook: Structure and Applications of a Macro Model of the Global Economy for Policy Analysis* (pp. 166–181). doi:10.1093/acprof.arXiv:arXiv:1011.1669v3

Favero, C., Giavazzi, F. & Perego, J. (2011). Country Heterogeneity and the International Evidence on the Effects of Fiscal Policy. *IMF Economic Review*, *59* (4), 652–682. doi:10.1057/imfer.2011.25

Feldkircher, M. & Huber, F. (2016). The international transmission of US shocks—Evidence from Bayesian global vector autoregressions. *European Economic Review*, *81*, 167–188. doi:10.1016/J.EUROECOREV.2015.01.009

Feldkircher, M. & Korhonen, I. (2012). The Rise of China and Its Implications for Emerging Markets- Evidence from a GVAR Model. *SSRN Electronic Journal.* doi:10.2139/ssrn.2151223

Feldkircher, M. (2015). A global macro model for emerging Europe. *Journal of Comparative Economics, 43* (3), 706–726. doi:10.1016/J.JCE.2014.09.002

Friedman, M. (1968). The Role of Monetary Policy. *The American Economic Review, 58* (1), 1–17.doi:10.1126/science.151.3712.867-a.arXiv:00368075

Galesi, A. & Lombardi, M. J. (2013). External shocks and international inflation linkages University. In F. di Mauro & M. H. Pesaran (Eds.), *The GVAR Handbook: Structure and Applications of a Macro Model of the Global Economy for Policy Analysis* (pp. 70–82). doi:10.1093/acprof.arXiv:arXiv:1011.1669v3

Galesi, A. & Sgherri, S. (2013). Regional financial spillovers across Europe. In F. di Mauro & M. H. Pesaran (Eds.), *The GVAR Handbook: Structure and Applications of a Macro Model of the Global Economy for Policy Analysis* (pp. 255–266). doi:10.1093/acprof.arXiv:arXiv:1011.1669v3

Gali, J. (1992). How well does the IS-LM model fit postwar US data? *The Quarterly Journal of Economics, 107* (2), 709–738. Retrieved from https://academic.oup.com/qje/article-abstract/107/2/709/1838344

Ganelli, G. & Tawk, N. (2017). Spillovers from Japan's Unconventional Monetary Policy: A global VAR Approach. *Economic Modelling.* doi:10.1016/J.ECONMOD. 2017.10.020

Garratt, A., Lee, K. & Shields, K. (2016). Forecasting global recessions in a GVAR model of actual and expected output. *International Journal of Forecasting, 32* (2), 374–390. doi:10.1016/J.IJFORECAST.2015.08.004

Garratt, A., Lee, K., Pesaran, M. H. & Shin, Y. (2006a). Introduction. In *Global and National Macroeconometric Modelling: A Long-Run Structural Approach* (June 2016, pp. 1–400). doi:10.1093/0199296855.001.0001

Garratt, A., Lee, K., Pesaran, M. H. & Shin, Y. (2006b). Macroeconometric modelling: Alternative approaches. *Global and National Macroeconometric Modelling: A Long-Run Structural Approach,* (June 2016), 1–400. doi:10.1093/0199296855.001.0001

Garratt, A., Lee, K., Pesaran, M. H. & Shin, Y. (2006c). *National and global structural macroeconometric modelling.* doi:10.1093/0199296855.001.0001

Georgiadis, G. (2015). Examining asymmetries in the transmission of monetary policy in the euro area: Evidence from a mixed cross-section global VAR model. *European Economic Review, 75,* 195–215. doi:10.1016/J.EUROECOREV.2014.12.007

Georgiadis, G. (2016). Determinants of global spillovers from US monetary policy. *Journal of International Money and Finance, 67,* 41–61. doi:10.1016/J.JIMONFIN. 2015.06.010

Giot, P. & Laurent, S. (2004). Modelling daily Value-at-Risk using realized volatility and ARCHtype models. *Journal of Empirical Finance.* doi:10.1016/j.jempfin.2003.04.003

Glosten, L. R., Jagannathan, R. & Runkle, D. E. (1993). On the Relation between the Expected Value and the Volatility of the Nominal Excess Return on Stocks. *The Journal of Finance, 48* (5), 1779–1801.

Graham, J. R. & Harvey, C. R. (2001). The theory and practice of corporate finance: Evidence from the field. *Journal of Financial Economics.* doi:10.1016/S0304-405X(01)00044-7

Granger, C. & Newbold, P. (2014). *Forecasting economic time series.* Academic Press.

Granger, C. (1999). *Empirical modeling in economics: Specification and evaluation.* Cambridge University Press.

Granger, C. W. & Jeon, Y. (2004). Thick modeling. *Economic Modelling, 21* (2), 323–343. doi:10.1016/S0264-9993(03)00017-8

Granger, C. W. & Jeon, Y. (2007). Evaluation of global models. *Economic Modelling, 24* (6), 980–989. doi:10.1016/J.ECONMOD.2007.03.008

Greenwood, R. & Shleifer, A. (2014). Expectations of returns and expected returns. *Review of Financial Studies.* doi:10.1093/rfs/hht082

Greenwood-Nimmo, M., Nguyen, V. H. & Shin, Y. (2013). Using global VAR models for scenario-based forecasting and policy analysis. In F. di Mauro & M. H. Pesaran (Eds.), *The GVAR Handbook: Structure and Applications of a Macro Model of the Global Economy for Policy Analysis* (pp. 97–113). doi:10.1093/acprof.arXiv:arXiv: 1011.1669v3

Gross, M. & Kok, C. (2013). Measuring Contagion Potential Among Sovereigns and Banks Using a Mixed-Cross-Section GVAR. *Working Paper Series,* (15), 1 –49.

Gross, M. & Kok, C. (2016). *Working Paper Series The impact of bank capital on economic activity - Evidence from a Mixed-Cross-Section GVAR model.*

Grossman, S. J. & Stiglitz, J. E. (1977). On Value Maximization and Alternative Objectives of the Firm. *The Journal of Finance.* doi:10.2307/2326771

Gürkaynak, R. S., Kısacıkoğlu, B. & Rossi, B. (2013). Do DSGE Models Forecast More Accurately Out-Of-Sample than VAR Models? *VAR Models in Macroeconomics– New Developments and Applications: Essays in Honor of Christopher A. Sims,* 27–79. doi:10.1108/S0731-9053(2013) 0000031002

Haavelmo, T. (1944). The Probability Approach in Econometrics. *Econometrica1, 12* (Supplement), 1–115.

Hájek, J. & Horváth, R. (2016). The Spillover Effect of Euro Area on Central and Southeastern European Economies: A Global VAR Approach. *Open Economies Review, 27* (2), 359–385 doi:10.1007/s11079-015-9378-4

Hamilton, J. D. (1989). A New Approach to the Economic Analysis of Nonstationary Time Series and the Business Cycle. *Econometrica, 57* (2), 357. doi:10.2307/1912559

Hamilton, J. D. (1994). *Time Series Analysis.* Princeton: Princeton University Press.

Han, L., Qi, M. & Yin, L. (2016). Macroeconomic policy uncertainty shocks on the Chinese economy: a GVAR analysis. *Applied Economics, 48* (51), 4907–4921. doi:10.1080/00036846.2016.1167828

Hansen, B. E. (1992). The likelihood ratio test under nonstandard conditions: Testing the Markov switching model of gnp. *Journal of Applied Econometrics, 7* (S1), S61–S82. doi:10.1002/jae.3950070506

Hansen, P. R. & Lunde, A. (2005). A forecast comparison of volatility models: Does anything beat a GARCH(1,1)? *Journal of Applied Econometrics.* doi:10.1002/jae.800

Harbo, I., Johansen, S., Nielsen, B. & Rahbek, A. (1998). Asymptotic inference on cointegrating rank in partial systems. *Journal of Business and Economic Statistics, 16* (4), 388–399. doi:10.1080/07350015.1998.10524779

Harris, L., 2003. *Trading and exchanges: Market microstructure for practitioners.* OUP USA.

Harvey, C. R. (1989). Time-varying conditional covariances in tests of asset pricing models. *Journal of Financial Economics.* doi:10.1016/0304-405X(89)90049-4

Herbst, E. & Schorfheide, F. (2015). *Bayesian estimation of DSGE models.*

Hill, R. C., Griffiths, W. E. & Lim, G. C. (2011). *Principles of Econometrics (Fourth Edition).*

Hoover, K. D., Johansen, S. & Juselius, K. (2008). Allowing the Data to Speak Freely: The Macroeconometrics of the Cointegrated Vector Autoregression. *American Economic Association, 98* (2), 251–255.

Hylleberg, S. & Paldam, M. (1991). New Approaches to Empirical Macroeconomics: Editors' Introduction. *The Scandinavian Journal of Economics, 93* (2), 121–128.

Iacoviello, M. & Neri, S. (2010). Housing Market Spillovers: Evidence from an Estimated DSGE Model. *American Economic Journal: Macroeconomics, 2* (2).

Iacoviello, M. (2005). House Prices, Borrowing Constraints, and Monetary Policy in the Business Cycle. *American Economic Review, 95* (3), 739–764. doi:10.1257/000 2828054 201477

Ireland, P. N. (2004). A method for taking models to the data. *Journal of Economic Dynamics and Control, 28* (6), 1205–1226. doi:10.1016/S0165-1889(03)00080-0

Issing, O. (2005). Communication, transparency, accountability: Monetary policy in the twenty-first century. *Federal Reserve Bank of St. Louis Review, 87* (2 I), 65–83. Retrieved from https://core.ac.uk/download/pdf/6958869.pdf

Jensen, M. C. (1968). The Performance of Mutual Funds in the Period 1945-1964. *The Journal of Finance.* doi:10.2307/2325404

Jensen, M. C. (1978). Some anomalous evidence regarding market efficiency. *Journal of Financial Economics.* doi:10.1016/0304-405X(78)90025-9

Johansen, S. (1988). Statistical analysis of cointegration vectors. *Journal of Economic Dynamics and Control, 12* (2-3), 231–254. doi:10.1016/0165-1889(88)90041-3

Johansen, S. (1991). Estimation and Hypothesis Testing of Cointegration Vectors in Gaussian Vector Autoregressive Models. *Econometrica, 59* (6), 1551. doi:10.2307/2938278

Katrin, A. (2013). Forecasting the Swiss economy with a small GVAR model. In F. di Mauro & M. H. Pesaran (Eds.), *The GVAR Handbook: Structure and Applications of a Macro Model of the Global Economy for Policy Analysis* (pp. 97–113). doi:10.1093/acprof.arXiv:arXiv:1011.1669v3

Kendall, M. G. & Hill, A. B. (1953). The Analysis of Economic Time-Series-Part I: Prices. *Journal of the Royal Statistical Society. Series A (General).* doi:10.2307/2980947

Khrapko, V. (2013). Testing The Weak-Form Efficiency Hypothesis in the Ukrainian Stock Market Versus Those of the USA, Russia, And Poland. *Ekonomika.* doi:10.15388/ekon.2013.0.1411

Kilian, L & Lütkepohl, H. (2017). *Structural vector autoregressive analysis.* Cambridge University Press.

Klein, L. R. (1947). The Use of Econometric Models as a Guide to Economic Policy Author (s): Lawrence R. Klein Published by The Econometric Society Stable URL: http://www.jstor.org/stable/1907067 Accessed: 09-06-2016 *Econometrica, 15* (2), 111–151.

Klein, L. R., Welfe, A. & Welfe, W. (1999). *Principles of macroeconometric modeling.* North Holland; Revised edition.

Klein, P. (2002). Using the generalized Schur form to solve a multivariate linear rational expectations model. *Journal of Economic Dynamics and Control, 24* (10), 1405–1423. doi:10.1016/s0165-1889(99)00045-7

Kocherlakota, N. (2010). Creating business cycles through credit constraints. *Quarterly Review-Federal Reserve Bank.* Retrieved from http://search.proquest. com/openview/1bb53d992fdd57a7bdc2836f3033284f/1?pqorigsite=gscholarcbl =47763

Koop, G., Pesaran, M. & Potter, S. M. (1996). Impulse response analysis in nonlinear multivariate models. *Journal of Econometrics, 74* (1), 119–147. doi:10.1016/0304-4076(95)01753-4

Koopmans, T. C. (1949). Identification Problems in Economic Model Construction. *Econometrica, 17* (2), 125–144.

Koopmans, T. C. (1950). When is an equation system complete for statistical purposes? In *Cowles commission monograph no. 10* (Chap. In Statist). New York: John Wiley. Retrieved from https://dialnet.unirioja.es/servlet/articulo?codigo= 4563201

Korinek, A. (2017). Thoughts on DSGE Macroeconomics: Matching the Moment, But Missing the Point? *2015 Conference "A Just Society",* (July), 1–13.

Kydland, F. & Prescott, E. (1991). Hours and employment variation in business-cycle theory. *Business Cycles,* 107–134. Retrieved from https://link.springer.com/chapter/10.1007/978-1-349-11570-95

Kydland, F. E. & Prescott, E. C. (1982). Time to build and aggregate fluctuations. *Econometrica, 50* (6), 1345–1370.

Levin, B. A., Wieland, V. & Williams, J. C. (2003). The Performance of Forecast-Based Monetary Policy Rules under Model Uncertainty. *American Economic Review, 93* (3), 622–645.

Levy, R. A. (1967). The Theory of Random Walks: A Survey of Findings. *The American Economist.* doi:10.1177/056943456701100205

Lintner, J. (1965). Security Prices, Risk, and Maximal Gains From Diversification. *The Journal of Finance.* doi:10.2307/2977249

Litterman, R. B. (1986). Forecasting With Bayesian Vector Autoregressions—Five Years of Experience. *Journal of Business & Economic Statistics, 4* (1), 25–38. doi:10.1080/07350015.1986.10509491

Litzenberger, R. H. & Ramaswamy, K. (1982). The Effects of Dividends on Common Stock Prices Tax Effects or Information Effects? *The Journal of Finance.* doi:10.2307/2327346

Liu, T.-C. (1960). Underidentification, Structural Estimation, and Forecasting. *Econometrica, 28* (4), 855–865.

Liu, Z., Wang, P. & Zha, T. (2013). Land-Price Dynamics and Macroeconomic Fluctuations. *Econometrica, 81* (3), 1147–1184. doi:10.3982/ECTA8994

Ljung, G. M. & Box, G. E. (1978). On a measure of lack of fit in time series models. *Biometrika.* doi:10.1093/biomet/65.2.297

Lo, A. W. & MacKinlay, A. C. (2014). 2. Stock Market Prices Do Not Follow Random Walks: Evidence from a Simple Specification Test. In *A non-random walk down wall street.* doi:10.1515/9781400829095.17

Long, J. B. & Plosser, C. I. (1983). Real Business Cycles. *Journal of Political Economy, 91* (1), 39–69. doi:10.1086/261128

Lubik, T. A. & Schorfheide, F. (2007). Do central banks respond to exchange rate movements? A structural investigation. *Journal of Monetary Economics, 54* (4), 1069–1087. doi:10.1016/j.jmoneco.2006.01.009

Lucas, R. (1976). Economic Policy Evaluation: A Critique. *Carnegie-Rochester Conference Series on Public Policy,* 19–46. doi:http://dx.doi.org /10.1016/S0167-2231(76) 80003-6.arXiv: 9809069v1

Lucas, R. E. (1978). Asset Prices in an Exchange Economy. *Econometrica.* doi:10.23 07/1913837

Ma, S., Zhou, X. & Feng, H. (2012). Exploring the Endogenous Links and Exogenous Shocks Based on Efficiency Improvement A Case Study of Zhejiang Province. *Journal of Zhejiang University Humanities and Social Sciences, 42* (6), 126–141. Retrieved from http://www.zjujournals.com/soc/CN/abstract/abstract10635. shtml

Malkiel, B. G. (2003). Passive Investment Strategies and Efficient Markets. *European Financial Management.* doi:10.1111/1468-036X.00205

Malkiel, B. G. (2005). Reflections on the efficient market hypothesis: 30 years later. *Financial Review.* doi:10.1111/j.0732-8516.2005.00090.x

Malkiel, B. G. (2013). *A random walk down Wall Street.* doi:10.1017/CBO97811074 15324.004.arXiv:arXiv:1011.1669v3

Mandelbrot, B. (1963). The Variation of Certain Speculative Prices. *The Journal of Business.* doi:10.1086/294632

Melecky, M. & Podpiera, A. M. (2012). Macroprudential Stress-Testing Practices of Central Banks in Central and Southeastern Europe: Comparison and Challenges Ahead.*Emerging Markets Finance and Trade, 48* (4), 118–134. doi:10.2753/REE15 40-496X480407

Mensi, W. (2017). Global Financial Crisis and Co-movements between Oil Prices and Sector Stock Markets in Saudi Arabia: A VaR based Wavelet. *Borsa Istanbul Review.* doi:10.1016/J.BIR.2017.11.005

Merton, R. C. (1973). An Intertemporal Capital Asset Pricing Model. *Econometrica.* doi:10.2307/1913811

Michailova, S. & Worm, V. (2003). Personal networking in Russia and China: Blat and guanxi. *European Management Journal.* doi:10.1016/S0263-2373(03)00077-X. Milgate & P. Newman, Eds.). WW Norton & Company.

Mobarek, A. & Keasey, K. (2000). Weak-form market efficiency of an Emerging Market: Evidence from Dhaka Stock Market of Bangladesh. *ENBS Conference held in Oslo.*

Morana, C. (2002). IGARCH effects: An interpretation. *Applied Economics Letters.* doi:10.1080/13504850210127254

Murphy, C. (1988). An Overview of the Murphy Model. *Australian Economic Papers, 27* (s1), 175–199. doi:10.1111/j.1467-8454.1988.tb00703.x

Musgrave, R., Musgrave, P. & Bird, R. (1989). *Public finance in theory and practice.* New York: McGraw-Hill.

Muth, J. F. (1961). Rational Expectations and the Theory of Price Movements. *Econometrica, 29* (3), 315–335.

Ng, T. & Eickmeier, S. (2013). International business cycles and the role of financial markets. In F. di Mauro & M. H. Pesaran (Eds.), *The GVAR Handbook: Structure and Applications of a Macro Model of the Global Economy for Policy Analysis* (pp. 83–96). doi:10.1093/acprof. arXiv:arXiv:1011.1669v3

Nyblom, J. (1989). Testing for the Constancy of Parameters over Time. *Journal of the American Statistical Association, 84* (405), 223–230. doi:10.1080/01621459.1989. 10478759

Oral, E. & Oral, E. (2012). Analyzing high frequency financial data and modeling volatility using GARCH models with normal and stable paretian distributions: An example from an emerging market. *International Research Journal of Finance and Economics.*

Ortiz-Molina, H. & Phillips, G. M. (2014). Real asset illiquidity and the cost of capital. *Journal of Financial and Quantitative Analysis.* doi:10.1017/S0022109014000210

Osborne, M. F. M. (1959). Brownian Motion in the Stock Market. *Operations Research.* doi:10.1287/opre.7.2.145

Osorio, C. & Unsal, D. F. (2013). Inflation dynamics in Asia: Causes, changes, and spillovers from China. *Journal of Asian Economics, 24,* 26–40. doi:10.1016/J.ASIE CO.2012.10.007

Oyelami, L. O. & Olomola, P. (2016). External shocks and macroeconomic responses in Nigeria: A global VAR approach. *Cogent Economics & Finance, 4* (1). doi:10.1080/23322039.2016.1239317

Pesaran, H. & Shin, Y. (1998). Generalized impulse response analysis in linear multivariate models. *Economics Letters, 58* (1), 17–29. doi:10.1016/S0165-1765(97)00214-0

Pesaran, M. & Timmermann, A. (2004). How costly is it to ignore breaks when forecasting the direction of a time series? *International Journal of Forecasting, 20* (3), 411–425. doi:10.1016/S0169-2070(03)00068-2

Pesaran, M. (1990). *Econometrics: The New Palgrave A Dictionary of Economics* (J. Eatwell, M. Pesaran, M. H. & Smith, R. (1995). The role of theory in econometrics. *Journal of Econometrics, 67* (1), 61–79. doi:10.1016/0304-4076(94)01627-C

Pesaran, M. H. (2015). Theory and Practice of GVAR Modelling. In *Time series and panel data econometrics* (Chap. 33, pp. 900–935). doi:10.1093/acprof.arXiv:arXiv: 1011.1669v3

Pesaran, M. H., Schuermann, T. & Smith, L. V. (2009). Forecasting economic and financial variables with global VARs. *International Journal of Forecasting, 25* (4), 642–675. doi:10.1016/J.IJFORECAST.2009.08.007

Pesaran, M. H., Schuermann, T. & Weiner, S. M. (2004). Modeling Regional Interdependencies Using a Global Error-Correcting Macroeconometric Model. *Journal of Business & Economic Statistics, 22* (2), 129–162. doi:10.1198/07350010 4000000019

Pesaran, M. H., Schuermann, T., Treutler, B.-J. & Weiner, S. M. (2006). Macroeconomic Dynamics and Credit Risk: A Global Perspective. doi:10.2307/3839005

Pesaran, M. H., Shin, Y. & Smith, R. J. (2001a). Bounds testing approaches to the analysis of level relationships. *Journal of Applied Econometrics, 16* (3), 289–326. doi:10.1002/jae.616

Pesaran, M. H., Shin, Y. & Smith, R. J. (2001b). Bounds testing approaches to the analysis of level relationships. *Journal of Applied Econometrics, 16* (3), 289–326. doi:10.1002/jae.616. arXiv: CAM.5093 [10.17863]

Ploberger, W & Krämer, W. (1992). The CUSUM test with OLS residuals. *Journal of Econometrics.* Retrieved from http://www.jstor.org/stable/2951597

Popper, K. (2005). *The logic of scientific discovery.* doi:10.4324/9780203994627

Qin, D. (2013). A History of Econometrics: The Reformation from the 1970s. doi:10. 1017/CBO9781107415324.004.arXiv:arXiv:1011.1669v3

Quandt, R. E. (1958). The Estimation of the Parameters of a Linear Regression System Obeying Two Separate Regimes. *Journal of the American Statistical Association, 53* (284), 873–880.doi:10.1080/01621459.1958.10501484

Quandt, R. E. (1960). Tests of the Hypothesis That a Linear Regression System Obeys Two Separate Regimes. *Journal of the American Statistical Association, 55* (290), 324–330. doi:10.1080/01621459.1960.10482067

Rabemananjara, R. & Zakoian, J. M. (1993). Threshold arch models and asymmetries in volatility. *Journal of Applied Econometrics.* doi:10.1002/jae.3950080104

Ramey, V. A. (2016). Macroeconomic shocks and their propagation. In J. B. Taylor & H. Uhlig (Eds.), *Handbook of macroeconomics* (V.2, pp. 71–162). Elsevier. Retrieved from https://www.sciencedirect.com/science/article/pii/S157400481 6000045

Ramsey, F. P. (1927). A Contribution to the Theory of Taxation. *The Economic Journal, 37* (145), 47–61. Retrieved from http://www.jstor.org/stable/2222721

Ramsey, F. P. (1928). A mathematical theory of saving. *The Economic Journal, 38* (152), 543–559. Retrieved from http://www.jstor.org/stable/2224098

Rey, H. (2015). Dilemma not trilemma: the global financial cycle and monetary policy independence. *National Bureau of Economic Research.* Retrieved from http://www.nber.org/papers/w21162

Roberts, H. V. (1959). Stock-Market "Patterns" and Financial Analysis: Methodological Suggestions. *The Journal of Finance.* doi:10.2307/2976094

Roll, R. (1977). A Critique of the Asset Pricing Theory's Tests. *Journal of Financial Economics.*

Rosenberg, A., 2011. *Philosophy of social science.* Routledge.

Ross, S. A. (1976). The arbitrage theory of capital asset pricing. *Journal of Economic Theory.*doi:10.1016/0022-0531(76)90046-6

Rotemberg, J. J. & Woodford, M. (1997). *An Optimization-Based Framework for the Evaluation.* Retrieved from http://www.nber.org/chapters/c11041

Sargent, T. & Sims, C. (1977). Business Cycle Modeling Without Pretending to Have Too Much a Priori Economic Theory. Federal Reserve Bank of Minneapolis. Retrieved from https://nyuscholars.nyu.edu/en/publications/business-cycle-modeling-without-pretending-to-have-too-much-a-pri

Sewell, M. (2011). History of the efficient market hypothesis. *RN.*

Sharpe, W. F. (1964). Capital Asset Prices: A Theory of Market Equilibrium under Conditions of Risk. *The Journal of Finance.* doi:10.2307/2977928

Sims, C. A. (1980). Macroeconomics and Reality. *Econometrica, 48* (1), 1–48.

Sims, C. A. (1986). Are forecasting models usable for policy analysis? *Federal Reserve Bank of Minneapolis Quarterly Review, 10* (1). Retrieved from https://ideas.repec. org/a/fip/ fedmqr/y1986iwinp2-16nv.10no.1.html

Sims, C. A. (1992). Interpreting the macroeconomic time series facts. The effects of monetary policy. *European Economic Review, 36* (5), 975–1000. doi:10.1016/0014-2921(92)90041-T

Sims, C. A. (2002). Solving Linear Rational Expectations Models. *Computational Economics, 20* (1-2), 1–20. doi:10.1023/A:1020517101123

Slutzky, E. (1937). The Summation of Random Causes as the Source of Cyclic Processes. *Econometrica*. doi:10.2307/1907241

Smets, F. & Wouters, R. (2007). Shocks and Frictions in US Business Cycles: A Bayesian DSGE Approach. *American Economic Review, 97* (3), 586–606. doi:10.1257/aer.97.3.586

Smith, R. P. (2013). The GVAR approach to structural modelling. In F. di Mauro & M. H. Pesaran (Eds.), *The GVAR Handbook: Structure and Applications of a Macro Model of the Global Economy for Policy Analysis* (pp. 56–69). doi:10.1093/acprof. arXiv:arXiv:1011.1669v3

Šonje, V., Alajbeg, D. and Bubaš, Z., 2011. Efficient market hypothesis: is the Croatian stock market as (in) efficient as the US market. Financial theory and practice, 35(3), pp.301-326.

Stiglitz, J. E. (2018). Where modern macroeconomics went wrong. *Oxford Review of Economic Policy, 34* (1), 70–106. Retrieved from https://academic.oup.com/oxrep/article-abstract/34/1-2/70/4781816

Stock, J. H. & Watson, M. W. (2002). Macroeconomic Forecasting Diffusion indexes. *Journal of Business & Economic Statistics, 20* (2), 147–162. doi: 10.1198/073500102 317351921

Stuart, A. & Markowitz, H. M. (1959). Portfolio Selection: Efficient Diversification of Investments. *OR*. doi:10.2307/3006625

Subrahmanyam, A. (2016). American Finance Association Investor Psychology and Security Market under- and Overreactions Author (s): Kent Daniel, David Hirshleifer and Avanidhar Subrahmanyam Source: The Journal of Finance, Vol. 53, No. 6 (Dec., 1998), pp .1839-1885 Publ. *The Journal of Finance, 53* (6), 1839–1885.

Tan, M. S.-L. (2016). Policy coordination among the ASEAN-5: A global VAR analysis. *Journal of Asian Economics, 44*, 20–40. doi:10.1016/J.ASIECO.2016.05.002

Taylor, J. (1993). *Macroeconomic policy in a world economy: from econometric design to practical operation*. New York: W.W. Norton. Retrieved from http://www.stanford.edu /johntayl/MacroPolicyWorld.htm

Tobin, J. (1958). Liquidity Preference as Behavior Towards Risk. *The Review of Economic Studies*. doi:10.2307/2296205

Tsay, R. S. (2002). *Analysis of Financial Time Series*. doi:10.1002/0471264105

Valadkhani, A. (2004). History of macroeconometric modelling: Lessons from past experience. *Journal of Policy Modeling, 26* (2), 265–281. doi:10.1016/j.jpolmod. 2004. 01.004

Vanessa Smith, L. & Galesi, A. (2017). *GVAR Toolbox 2.0 User Guide*.

Vayanos, D. (1998). Transaction costs and asset prices: A dynamic equilibrium model. *Review of Financial Studies*. doi:10.1093/rfs/11.1.1

Wald, A. & Wolfowitz, J. (1940). On a Test Whether Two Samples are from the Same Population. *The Annals of Mathematical Statistics*. doi:10.1214/aoms/1177731909

Wang, M., Keller, C. & Siegrist, M. (2011). The less you know, the more you are afraid of-A survey on risk perceptions of investment products. *Journal of Behavioral Finance*. doi:10.1080/15427560.2011.548760

Welfe, W. (2013). *Macroeconometric Models* (Advanced S). Springer-Verlag Berlin Heidelberg.

Wieland, V., Cwik, T., Müller, G. J., Schmidt, S. & Wolters, M. (2012). A new comparative approach to macroeconomic modeling and policy analysis. *Journal of Economic Behavior and Organization, 83* (3), 523–541. doi:10.1016/j.jebo.2012.01.006

Wilmott, Paul. (2006). *Paul Wilmott on Quantitative Finance.* doi:10.1002/1521-3773(20010316)40: 6<9823::AID-ANIE9823>3.3.CO;2-C.arXiv:arXiv:1011.1669v3

Working, H. (1949). The investigation of economic expectations. *The American Economic Review.*

Working, H. (1958). A Theory of Anticipatory Prices. *American Economic Review.* doi:10.2307/1816908.arXiv:00368075

Zakoian, J. M. (1994). Threshold heteroskedastic models. *Journal of Economic Dynamics and Control.* doi:10.1016/0165-1889(94)90039-6

Index

www.ingramcontent.com/pod-product-compliance
Lightning Source LLC
Chambersburg PA
CBHW060402220326
41598CB00023B/3001